L

for   rs

✿ vintage, inc. is a comprehensive geriatric service center where senior adults grow together. As a nonprofit corporation, Vintage is designed to meet multiple needs and to raise the quality of life for those 55 and over by using and developing their potential. Vintage acts as a catalyst in raising community consciousness among the elderly and among the agencies attempting to meet the needs of this age group. Vintage is located in Pittsburgh, Pennsylvania.

Vintage programs and services include regularly scheduled classes, daily recreational and social activities, annual events, a noontime lunch, in-home services, information and referral, counseling, outreach, adult day care, Vintage House personal care boarding home, and the Vintage Institute, dedicated to research, education, and training.

Vintage's health clinic is a designated satellite ambulatory care program of the Western Pennsylvania Hospital. The West Penn/Vintage program is a wellness center emphasizing health promotion, life-style changes, and early identification of disease processes.

Life-Enhancing Activities for Mentally Impaired Elders

A Practical Guide

Beverly Ann Beisgen

A project of  vintage, inc.

Springer Publishing Company
New York

Springer Publishing Company, Inc.
536 Broadway
New York, NY 10012
94 95 96 97 98 / 7 6 5 4 3

Library of Congress Cataloging-in-Publication Data

Beisgen, Beverly Ann.
   Life-enhancing activities for mentally impaired elders / Beverly
Ann Beisgen.
       p.   cm.
   Bibliography: p.
   Includes index.
   ISBN 0-8261-6790-X
   1. Mentally handicapped aged—Services for—United States.
2. Alzheimer's disease—Patients—Services for—United States.
3. Day care centers for the aged—United States—Activity programs.
4. Nursing homes—United States—Recreational activities.
I. Title.

HV3009.5.A35B44   1989
362.1'96831—dc20   89-1159
                                                                        CIP

Printed in the United States of America

Contents

Part I: ALZHEIMER'S DISEASE
AND RELATED DISORDERS

Foreword

The issue of elder care will be to the 1990s what child care was to the 1970s. In the forefront of aging issues will be the concern for and care of older adults with Alzheimer's disease. With this in mind, Vintage began exploring the needs of families who are caregivers. It was determined that the need to plan for day-to-day living after the diagnosis of Alzheimer's disease (or related disorders) was a burden left solely to the family. Professionals who work in new community-based care programs addressing the needs of the Alzheimer's older adult have a similar dilemma: What do we do with this older adult 24 (or 36) hours a day?

Beverly Beisgen began her authorship of *Life Enhancing Activities for Mentally Impaired Elders* with this question in mind. Ms. Beisgen has made an inestimable contribution to the geriatric field. Vintage is proud to share this text with dedicated families and workers in geriatrics. We believe it is more than just another book on Alzheimer's, it imparts part of the *science and art of enjoying life.*

ARLENE APFEL SNYDER
Executive Director
Vintage, Inc.

Preface

The ideas for this manual are based on the highly successful Vintage adult day care program. The Vintage program is designed to meet the multiple needs of the older adult who is physically and mentally impaired. Adult day care provides the participants with an opportunity to engage in constructive, enjoyable activities and social events. The individual with a dementing illness lacks the ability to plan and initiate activities independently. He relies on family, friends, and programs like Vintage adult day care to provide social and recreational activities. Confused persons can develop new friendships with peers and participate in activities when the activities are tailored to accommodate weaknesses and support strengths. *Life Enhancing Activities for Mentally Impaired Elders* is a resource guide for professionals, volunteers, and students who are caring for an older adult with a dementing illness at adult day care centers and extended care facilities. Many of the ideas and suggestions are also applicable for caregivers to use at home.

The manual focuses on the recreational needs of the older adult who is mentally impaired. Suggestions to promote optimal functioning, encourage independence, improve self-esteem, and enhance the quality of life are presented.

Life Enhancing Activities for Mentally Impaired Elders has two parts.

Part I, Alzheimer's Disease and Related Disorders, provides an introduction to dementing illnesses and suggestions for managing problems, improving communications, structuring the environment, and encouraging independence. Care for the caregiver, whether a family member or a professional working in a community setting, is addressed. Throughout this section, excerpts of a diary of a caregiver from the Vintage Adult Day Care program are included to promote a greater understanding of caring for a person with a dementing illness. Charlotte, the caregiver, cared for her sister Anne, who had Alzheimer's disease, until Anne's death.

Part II, Activities, discusses a variety of activities and projects that are relevant for a broad range of mentally impaired elders. *Life Enhancing Activities for Mentally Impaired Elders* offers step-by-step instructions for planning and implementing activities. Over 200 ideas for arts and crafts, exercise, games, sensory stimulation, reminiscence, music, horticulture, discussion groups, and activities with children and pets are included.

At the beginning of each section is a list of objectives to help the reader identify the key elements of that section.

Acknowledgments

A very special thank you to the West Penn Governing Board of Hospitality Shops of the West Penn Hospital for funding this project and to Mrs. James Say, President of the Governing Board, for her inspiration, encouragement, and leadership.

I am also deeply grateful to Michael Rose, Senior Vice President, Corporate Development, West Penn Hospital, Steven Caywood, President and Chief Executive Officer, West Penn Hospital, and Mrs. Frely Shea, President of the West Penn Hospital Foundation, for their support of Vintage and this project.

It would be impossible to list the contributions of all who helped, but I would like to acknowledge several people who offered their suggestions and ideas, for which I am very grateful: Maria Piantanida of the University of Pittsburgh Geriatric Education Center; Ginny Haring, Director of the Kane Adult Day Care Center at Ross; Lillian Paskovich, OTR, Community College of Allegheny County; and Bonnie Almsay and Abby Betz of Harmarville Rehabilitation Center Adult Day Program.

I would like to express my deep appreciation to the courageous caregivers of the Vintage adult day care center participants. The ideas and suggestions they shared with me were invaluable in putting this manual together. In particular, I would like to offer a very special thank you to Charlotte for working on the manuscript with me. For many years, Charlotte lovingly cared for her sister who had Alzheimer's disease. Charlotte is, and always will be, an inspiration to me.

For their encouragement, advice and assistance in reading and editing the manuscript, I wish to thank the wonderful members of the Vintage staff who worked with me on this project.

Above all, for her love, guidance and enthusiasm, I wish to thank Arlene Snyder, Executive Director of Vintage. Without her, this manual would never have been written.

Executive Director, Vintage Inc.	Arlene A. Snyder
Writer and Principal Developer	Beverly A. Beisgen
Produced by	Vintage, Inc.
Funded by	The West Penn Governing Board of Hospitality Shops West Penn Hospital Mrs. James Say, President
Illustrations	Fran Datalsky
Manuscript Typing	Mary Pat Campbell

Part I

Alzheimer's Disease and Related Disorders

OBJECTIVES

Upon completing Part I you should be able to:

1. Describe the incidence, pathology, symptoms, diagnosis, and treatment of Alzheimer's disease.
2. Identify areas of current research into the causes of Alzheimer's disease.
3. List and describe other types of irreversible dementia.
4. Identify the reversible causes of mental impairment in the elderly.
5. Identify ways to create a safe, supportive, and pleasant environment for the confused older adult.
6. Describe the steps that can be taken to reduce the stress of relocation and ease the transition to a new environment.
7. Identify ways to maximize the mentally impaired person's ability to function independently and perform the routine tasks of daily living.
8. Identify the measures that can be taken to prevent or manage incontinence.
9. Describe the problems the mentally impaired person experiences in trying to use and understand language.

1

10. Identify the steps that can be taken to enhance communication with a person who is memory impaired.
11. Describe how reality orientation and memory aids are used to improve communication and orientation to people, places, and objects.
12. Explain how touch, facial expressions, and body movements enhance the ability to communicate.
13. Identify techniques for working with the visually and/or hearing-impaired elderly.
14. Identify and describe strategies for managing problem behaviors.
15. Describe the effect a dementing illness has on the family and other caregivers.
16. Identify strategies for caregivers to use to care for themselves and to prevent burnout.
17. Identify the physical and sensory changes that occur as part of the aging process and how they can affect the person with a dementing illness.

1

It Used to Be Called Senility

Senility, hardening of the arteries, and dementia, have all been used to describe the symptoms of confusion, disorientation, and memory loss in the elderly.

Senility is not a normal sign of growing older; neither is it a disease. *Presenile, senile,* and *senility* are derived from a Latin root *(sen-)* that simply means "old." These words help to perpetuate the myth that aging necessarily includes mental decline. We have mistakenly come to assume that senility is a natural result of aging. Elderly persons who experience symptoms of confusion and forgetfulness are often labeled *senile,* an imprecise and a derogatory use of the word.

Benign senescent forgetfulness is normal as we age. It is characterized by the inability to recall relatively unimportant data and parts of an experience, but the forgotten event or person is eventually recalled. There is no progressive loss of mental ability and no interference with the individual's ability to function independently.

Dementia means loss or impairment of mental power that is occurring in clear consciousness. It is the preferred term to describe a group of symptoms, including confusion, disorientation, intellectual deterioration, and memory loss, that are sufficiently severe to interfere with a person's ability to function independently. Dementia can be caused by many underlying diseases.

ALZHEIMER'S DISEASE

Alzheimer's disease is the major cause of irreversible dementia. It is a progressive, organic brain disease named for Dr. Alois Alzheimer, a German neurologist who first described it in 1906 in a 51-year-old woman. Her symptoms included memory loss, disorientation, depression, hallucinations, and severe, terminal dementia. On autopsy her brain was found to be atrophied, with lesions in the area of the cerebral cortex and an unusual clumping and distortion of cortical neurons.

The disease Alzheimer described was originally called presenile dementia. It was thought to be rare and confined to the relatively young (under 65). Since then researchers have found the same pathology in elderly patients with dementia. Neurologists now agree that the dementia that occurs in the elderly is the same or similar to that occurring in those under 65 years and there is little reason to make a differentiation between the two. The etiology and pathology of Alzheimer's disease is the same no matter what the age of onset. It is evident that Alzheimer's disease, sometimes incorrectly called Oldtimer's disease, is neither presenile nor rare. Alzheimer's disease or dementia of the Alzheimer's type (DAT) is found in persons older and younger than 65.

Alzheimer's disease is characterized by a global deterioration of cognitive functions such as memory, attention, judgment, and intellect. The course of the disease is progressive and irreversible. The symptoms and rate of progress vary, but Alzheimer's disease usually leads to death in about 5 to 10 years. It can progress more slowly (as long as 15 to 20 years) or more quickly (3 to 4 years). Alzheimer's disease begins subtly with simple forgetfulness followed by noticeable, then severe, change in memory and intelligence. Eventually, affected individuals become unable to care for themselves. It is believed that Alzheimer's disease reduces overall life expectancy rates by as much as 50%.

Incidence

Approximately 5% to 7% of U.S. citizens 65 or older (25% of those 85 and older) are affected by a severe dementing illness. Another 10% of those 65 and older may be mildly to moderately mentally impaired.

It is generally believed that Alzheimer's disease accounts for at least half of all cases of dementia in the United States (an estimated 2.5 million). Alzheimer's disease is not related to sex, race, socioeconomic status, or occupation. As its prevalence increases with age, Alzheimer's disease primarily affects the elderly. Most of its victims are over 65, but it can strike adults in their 40s and 50s. United States citizens are living longer, and the number affected by Alzheimer's disease is expected to grow.

Pathology

On autopsy, examination of Alzheimer's disease brain tissue reveals changes in brain structure characteristic of the disease. These pathological hallmarks include abnormally large numbers of neuritic plaques and neurofibrillary tangles. These changes are found in most parts of the diseased brain but are concentrated in the cerebral cortex and the hippocampus, the centers of intellectual activity and memory.

Neurofibrillary tangles are large bundles of abnormal cell fibers that accumulate inside the nerve cell. The abnormal fibers that comprise the neurofibrillary tangle consist of pairs of filaments wrapped around each other to form a helix.

Neuritic (senile) plaques are filamentous and granular deposits representing degeneration of the neuronal processes. At the core of each plaque is a substance called amyloid, an abnormal protein not usually found in the brain. The amyloid core is surrounded by other brain cell pieces, most of which are degenerating or abnormal in some way.

Symptoms

The progression of Alzheimer's disease and other dementing illnesses is variable. The timing and sequence of lost function differ from person to person and are influenced by personality, life-style, health, and environment as well as type of dementia. Abilities may fluctuate from day to day or even hour to hour. Dementia primarily affects judgment, intelligence, and memory. The ability to perform routine tasks declines and the affected person eventually needs total care.

The onset of Alzheimer's disease is difficult to determine, even in retrospect. Early on, changes may be almost imperceptible. The subtle nature of these early changes do not usually interfere significantly with a person's ability to manage. The symptoms may be overlooked or written off as unimportant.

> In the beginning, the slips appeared to be preoccupation: failing to follow road directions, driving through stop signs, stopping when the traffic light was green. She did not take offense if redirected; she just shrugged and reversed her direction. She was forever leaving her glasses or anything else that she carried in her hands in airplanes, restaurants, or any place she was likely to visit. Keys, purses, and sunglasses she had mislaid all her life, so this behavior was exaggerated but was not all that unusual.[1]

Initially, affected individuals may be quite skillful in concealing their problem. Some may deny a problem exists, some adapt to their losses, and others become depressed.

> She never confided her concern about her memory loss to me, but she told an older sister that she cried a lot. On a trip to California, she seemed to have little to say to a friend whom we went out of our way to visit because she had been so fond of her. It was as though she hadn't really remembered her. On that trip she made comments about her poor memory. Later that year she kept bringing home signature cards for me to sign until she had everything she owned in both our names.

In a progressive dementing illness the affected person's memory gradually becomes worse. In the beginning the individual may appear absentminded. As the dementia progresses, deficits in memory retention and recall become increasingly obvious, particularly to those who know the individual well. There may be difficulty remembering names, dates, or recent events and managing finances. The individual may get lost in familiar places or while traveling. Learned, socially acceptable behavior is forgotten. Whole experiences may be forgotten—not just persons, places, or details. Difficulty with short-term memory is experienced, but events from the distant past may be remembered with great clarity. The person may experience difficulty learning new skills or information. He or she may become disoriented to person, place, or time. He may not know where he is, what time or day it is, or whom he is with.

Poor grooming and inappropriate habits may develop as normal daily routines are forgotten or left uncompleted. The telephone and other instruments of daily living become increasingly difficult to use. Motor abilities deteriorate and coordination and balance become impaired. The person may be unable to carry out purposeful movements such as dressing or walking (apraxia). Instructions are needed to perform multiple-step tasks.

Deficits in sensory perception may appear and the individual gradually loses the ability to recognize people or things (agnosia). The person may not recognize his spouse or other family members; he

[1]These excerpts, which run throughout the text, are taken from observations made by Charlotte, caregiver to an Alzheimer's patient.

may not recognize himself in a mirror or photograph. There may be less desire to meet new people or try new things. The individual may become increasingly self-absorbed and insensitive to the feelings of others. He may become less interested in his environment and personal affairs.

Aphasia develops as the dementia progresses. Aphasia is an impairment in the ability to use and understand language. The individual may experience difficulty finding the right words in conversation, lose the ability to name objects, or to comprehend what is read or heard. Loss of language skills makes communication very difficult and frustrating.

In the final stages of a progressive dementing illness, the individual may become physically as well as intellectually disabled. Susceptibility to injury, illness, and infection increases. There may be little or no response to stimuli, and family members may go unrecognized. Finally the victim becomes totally dependent, unable to chew, swallow, or move without assistance. Skilled nursing care may be required.

The following is meant to provide a comprehensive list of the symptoms that may be encountered. Remember: The course of a dementing illness varies with the specific disease and with each individual. No one should expect that all of these problems will develop.

- Memory loss, especially for recent events. Memory of the past is retained longer.
- Shortened attention span.
- Difficulty in expressing thoughts.
- Changing or unpredictable moods.
- Prefers the familiar, has less desire to meet new people.
- Difficulty learning new things and following directions.
- Misplaces items.
- Slowed reaction time.
- Difficulty concentrating.
- Impaired judgment.
- Increasingly preoccupied and inattentive in conversations.
- Immediately forgets what is read.
- Tends to get lost, even in familiar places; has difficulty traveling alone.
- Forgets appointments and to pay bills.
- Neglects basic social amenities, forgets learned, socially acceptable behavior.
- Withdraws from social situations.

- Lack of spontaneity.
- Less initiative.
- Impaired judgment.
- Difficulty making decisions.
- Inability to handle routine tasks such as marketing and finances.
- Difficulty dressing self and choosing appropriate clothing.
- Impaired ability to speak or write (expressive aphasia).
- Difficulty communicating; excessive pauses, interrupts the flow of speech.
- Difficulty finding the right word; loses less familiar words first.
- Cannot pair words correctly with people, objects.
- Inserts wrong word while speaking (paraphrasia).
- Inability to write (agraphia).
- Inability to understand spoken or written language (receptive aphasia).
- Inability to calculate simple arithmetic (acalculia).
- Inability to reason and perceive meaning in situations.
- Disoriented to person, place, and time.
- Becomes less and less aware of surroundings.
- Inability to think abstractly.
- Inability to perform skilled or purposeful movements (apraxia).
- Impaired sensory function.—Decreased pain perception and visual disturbances may occur.
- Fails to attach meaning to sensory impressions (agnosia); difficulty recognizing familiar objects by sight (alexia); sound (auditory agnosia); touch (asterognosia).
- Forgets mechanics of toileting.
- Fear of bathing.
- Needs more and more assistance with the activities of daily living.
- Restlessness, especially at night.
- Wandering.
- Sleep disturbances.
- Repetition of words, phrases, or gestures (perseveration).
- Attempts to touch every object in sight in a compulsive manner.
- Unable to recognize self in mirror (mirror sign).
- Personality changes.
- Abnormal increase in the sensation of hunger (bulimia).
- Loses short- and long-term memory.
- Inability to speak.
- Unsteady gait.
- Decreased emotional responsiveness (flattening affect).

- Apathetic.
- Tendency to touch and examine objects by mouth (hyperorality).
- Unable to recognize family.
- Irritability.
- Loss of psychomotor skills.
- Incontinence.
- Delusions, hallucinations.
- Seizures.
- Contractures of face, arms, and legs.
- Marked weight loss.
- Stupor, coma.
- Death.

Diagnosis

The hospital where she had volunteered as an escort suggested that she be examined by a geriatric specialist because of her forgetfulness. It was then that I realized we had a problem that could be serious. We consulted a physician who had been recommended to us. I think he knew what her problem was, but he did not tell us. He tried one or two prescriptions which were not effective. She agreed to spend three days in the hospital for tests. Following her release I phoned the doctor for the results. He said all the tests were negative. When I asked what her problem was he said she had Alzheimer's disease. I asked what it was, I'd never heard of it. He said it was a degeneration of the nerve cells of the brain, that it was progressive, the cause was unknown, therefore no treatment was possible. He said any drugs that might be taken for short-term agitation might be harmful for the long term. He said I might find some information about it in the encyclopedia and suggested that I keep her in familiar surroundings, continuing her life-style activities as long as possible.

There is no single clinical test to identify Alzheimer's disease. Before a diagnosis is made, all other conditions that might cause the symptoms of dementia must be excluded, including potentially reversible conditions. Once it is known what the diagnosis is *not*, there is one probable explanation left: Alzheimer's disease. The only sure way to make a diagnosis of Alzheimer's disease is to take a biopsy of brain tissue. Brain biopsies are not routinely done at present because the procedure is dangerous and invasive and no cure is available even if a diagnosis of Alzheimer's disease is made. An autopsy is the only way to confirm a diagnosis of Alzheimer's disease. An autopsy reveals the presence of the plaques and tangles that are essential for final diagnosis.

Minor forgetfulness and occasional lapses in attention and concentration are normal but are a cause for concern for many older adults. Changes in mental ability that are persistent, or unusual for a particular individual or occur in areas of previous strength are worthy of attention. A diagnosis should be sought if there are signs of frequent forgetfulness, difficulty in making routine decisions, confusion about the month or time of year, trouble in performing simple tasks, unpredictable mood changes, depression, denial of symptoms, and communication problems that interfere with daily functioning. Family, friends, and co-workers may delay recognition of the problem out of loyalty or denial. Early diagnosis is crucial because there are interventions available that can maximize the individual's functioning.

A diagnosis of senility is not a diagnosis at all. Families should insist on a differential diagnosis. If a physician is unable or unwilling to make such a diagnosis, another opinion must be obtained. If a diagnosis is made without a thorough investigation of symptoms and a complete medical evaluation, there may be a misdiagnosis. A thorough evaluation reassures the family that no treatable condition has been overlooked. An elderly person has as much right as any other patient to a comprehensive workup to discover the source of the problem. There is also a danger of overdiagnosis of Alzheimer's disease. To ensure an accurate diagnosis, an evaluation by an interdisciplinary team with specialized skills in geriatrics and assessing dementia is needed. Team membership can vary but should be drawn from the fields of medicine, neurology, psychiatry, nursing, social work, psychology, and rehabilitative services.

A good evaluation should include:

1. A complete *physical examination* to determine the presence of serious illness, poor nutrition, sensory losses, infections, and other conditions.
2. A detailed *personal and family history*, including how the person has changed and symptoms.
3. A *drug history* to determine medication usage, including over-the-counter medications and alcohol use.
4. A *mental status examination* to assess alertness, attention, orientation, memory, comprehension, calculation, and language.
5. *Laboratory tests*, in conjunction with the physical examination, to provide additional information to aid in making an accurate diagnosis.
6. A *neurological examination* to determine the presence of disease

in the nervous system or to evaluate changes in the functioning of nerve cells in the brain.

7. A *psychiatric examination* to determine mental status and evaluate if the patient has a major emotional disorder or is experiencing severe emotional stress.
8. *Psychological testing* to profile intellectual strengths and losses.
9. An *occupational* or *rehabilitation therapy evaluation* to determine how much the person can do independently and identify what can be done to compensate for limitations to help the person remain independent.
10. A *psychosocial evaluation* to assess the patient's social support system and help the family evaluate its emotional, physical, financial, and community resources.
11. The evaluation should be followed up by a *discussion* with the physician and other members of the assessment team. The evaluation can determine the exact nature of the person's illness, if the condition is treatable, and if other health problems exist. The extent of the problem, areas of loss, remaining abilities and strengths, and changes that can be expected or that may occur can be discussed. The family needs to be provided with information about Alzheimer's disease, assistance with locating resources, and the opportunity to ask questions. This information can be used by the family and the assessment team to develop a specific plan of care.

The individual's abilities need to be reassessed periodically to determine new problems, areas of loss, and strengths.

Treatment

While no treatment is available to cure, reverse, or stop the progression of Alzheimer's disease, much can be done to make life more enjoyable and fulfilling. Interventions are available that can help the affected individual adjust to the illness, improve conditions in the environment, and support the caregiver. Good planning and ongoing medical care can ease the caregiver's burden—caring for a person with a dementing illness is never easy.

It is very important that the person with a dementing illness be under the care of a physician. Proper medical care can reduce many of the symptoms. Patients and their families need guidance and emotional support to help them cope with the impact of the disease.

The physician must be willing to devote the time and interest required. Families need and want information and education about the disease. Support groups can help families vent their feelings and share caregiving tips. Legal assistance may be required to plan for the patient's future needs.

Appropriate medications can lessen agitation, anxiety, and unpredictable behavior, improve sleeping patterns, and treat depression. Techniques and environmental modifications can help individuals maximize their potential by supporting their strengths and minimizing frustrating situations.

Activities should be maintained at a normal level, if possible. Daily routines, physical activities, and social contacts should be continued. Meaningful activities can help keep a person with a dementing illness alert and involved.

Most older adults with a dementing illness are cared for by their family at home. Families may find it necessary to hire outside helpers to provide assistance with bathing, dressing, eating and toileting, companionship, and housework or to provide respite care. Adult day care programs can provide an opportunity to be involved in a variety of activities with other adults with similar impairments. As the condition becomes more severe, a special setting with a professional staff and full-time care may be required. If needed, such an arrangement can be in the best interest of both the individual and the family.

The Search for a Cause

The list of suspects implicated in Alzheimer's disease includes genetics, immunological or biochemical changes, infectious agents, and the environment. Alzheimer's disease may have several interlocking causes.

The cause of Alzheimer's disease remains unknown. Researchers are intensively investigating a number of possible causes of Alzheimer's disease. The following are the areas of the most intensive investigation.

Genetic Factors. Alzheimer's disease usually occurs sporadically, even though studies show a clustering of the disease in some families. The odds of an adult developing Alzheimer's disease increase slightly if a close relative is affected; the closer the relationship, the higher the risk. Because there is no clear-cut pattern of inheritance, geneticists suspect there is a genetic component in Alzheimer's disease.

A person's genetic legacy may be just one of several determining factors.

There are several interesting relationships between Alzheimer's disease and Down's syndrome. The conditions often show up in the same family. Down's syndrome is caused by a defect in the 21st chromosome. Researchers have found evidence that a gene that causes one form of Alzheimer's disease may be located on chromosome 21. Individuals with Down's syndrome who survive into middle age frequently develop a dementia and changes in the brain similar to those experienced by persons with Alzheimer's disease.

Neurochemical Changes. Certain chemical changes are associated with Alzheimer's disease. These include, but are not limited to, a decrease in an enzyme called acetylcholine. Acetylcholine is one of many neurotransmitters found in the brain. A neurotransmitter is an enzyme necessary for transmission of messages between nerve cells. Such transmissions are responsible for normal brain function. It is not known whether the decrease in acetylcholine is the cause (or one of the causes) of Alzheimer's disease or is a result of the disease process itself. This determination is being researched, as are suitable medical and surgical interventions to improve the level of this enzyme.

Trace Metals. Aluminum has been found in large amounts in the brains of some Alzheimer's disease patients—up to 30 times those of normal, age-matched controls. This has led some researchers to speculate that aluminum and other trace metals may play a role in the development of Alzheimer's disease. Contact with aluminum is unavoidable as it is the most common metal and is found throughout the food chain. It is not known if the higher concentration of aluminum in the abnormal brain cells of Alzheimer's disease patients is a cause or effect of the disease. How aluminum gains access to the brain is not known. Other metals are known to be associated with other forms of dementia. The role of environmental toxins in Alzheimer's disease remains unproven and controversial.

Viral Studies. Another possibility being explored is that Alzheimer's disease may be caused by a slow-acting transmissible virus. There are several known dementias that appear to be transmitted by a slow virus, such as Kuru and Creutzfeldt-Jakob disease in humans. Slow virus diseases may have incubation periods of 2 to 30 years. There is absolutely no evidence that Alzheimer's disease is contagious.

Other Factors. Many other factors are being studied. They include immunological alterations, chromosomal abnormalities, trauma, and intrinsic metabolic factors.

Many types of drugs are now being tested to improve cognitive functioning in Alzheimer's patients. These new drugs offer hope for the future for treating the symptoms of Alzheimer's disease. Research into the causes of Alzheimer's disease and other dementing illnesses offers the hope of finding a cure. The Department of Health and Human Services has established funding for Alzheimer's research centers throughout the country. The centers are conducting research on Alzheimer's disease and developing the assessment tools necessary for making an accurate diagnosis. Numerous projects on Alzheimer's disease are being supported by federal programs. The Alzheimer's Association (ADRDA) supports research into the causes, treatments, prevention and cure of Alzheimer's disease and encourages legislation that responds to the needs of Alzheimer's disease patients and family members.

OTHER CAUSES OF IRREVERSIBLE DEMENTIA

Multiinfarct Dementia. Multiinfarct dementia (MID) is characterized by cerebral softening and multiple small strokes or infarcts within the brain, causing widespread death of brain tissue. The obstruction of blood flow to the brain results in mental deterioration. Memory, coordination, and / or speech may be affected depending on what areas of the brain are damaged. Multiinfarct dementia is associated with strokes, or cerebral vascular accidents. Multiinfarct dementia accounts for approximately 20% of all cases of dementia. Another 15% to 20% of persons with a dementia may have both Alzheimer's disease and multiinfarct dementia.

Multiinfarct dementia generally has an abrupt onset and follows a stepwise course. Typically, the first episode may consist of short-term weakness in the extremities, slurred speech, or dizziness. The symptoms may be too slight to seek attention. Several episodes may occur before there is any noticeable intellectual decline. There may be numerous remissions and exacerbations. Multiinfarct dementias are variable in appearance and in their course.

Pick's Disease. Although its symptoms are very similar to Alzheimer's disease, Pick's disease is associated with different changes in the brain tissue. Pick's disease is much rarer and occurs more frequently in women. It is more common in Europe and is thought to result from intermarrying within families.

Creutzfeldt-Jakob Disease. Creutzfeldt-Jakob disease is a neurological disorder that is usually fatal and appears to be caused by an atypical infectious agent, sometimes referred to as a slow virus. The slow virus may lie dormant in the body for years. When activated, the virus produces a rapidly progressive dementia, involuntary jerks, and frequently an abnormal gait.

Parkinson's Disease. Parkinson's disease is a common disorder of the brain. It develops because of damage to the extrapyramidal area of the nervous system which controls movement, posture, balance, and walking. Symptoms of Parkinson's disease include stiffness, tremors, slowness and poverty of movement, poor balance, and difficulty in walking. Parkinson's disease leads to dementia in approximately one-third of those affected.

Huntingdon's Disease. Huntingdon's disease is a rare genetic disorder. The symptoms usually appear in late middle age and can include personality change, mental decline, psychotic symptoms, and a movement disturbance. Restlessness and facial tics may progress to severe, uncontrollable flailing of head, limbs, and trunk. Mental capacity can deteriorate to dementia.

Acquired Immune Deficiency Syndrome (AIDS). A large portion of those who develop AIDS also develop dementia due to brain infection by the virus that causes the disease.

CAUSES OF REVERSIBLE DEMENTIAS

A comprehensive evaluation should aid physicians in distinguishing between those disorders that can be successfully treated or reversed and the irreversible dementias. Approximately 10% to 30% of all cases of dementia are reversible. Reversible causes of mental impairment often have an acute onset and a changing level of consciousness.

Depression. Depression closely mimics a dementing illness. Depressed individuals may be passive, unresponsive, confused, slow, or forgetful. Depression can be very difficult to diagnose. Among the aged it often goes unrecognized and underdiagnosed. People affected by a dementing illness may also be depressed—either as part of the disease process itself or as a reaction to their loss of mental abilities.

Depression should be treated even if an irreversible dementing illness is also present.

Drugs. Adverse drug reactions are a major factor complicating the diagnosis of dementia. The elderly are a multimedicated group; they use both prescription and over-the-counter drugs. The physiological changes of aging often make the elderly more prone to adverse side effects and drug-to-drug interactions. Medications are sometimes taken improperly. Drug interactions or allergic reactions can cause delirium, dementia, lethargy, confusion, or mental decline. If identified early and treated, the problem can be corrected.

Heart and Lung Problems. Diseases of the heart and lung may also contribute to cognitive losses, depression, and other behavior changes. A decrease in performance of the heart and lungs may cause dementia through reduction of the brain's supply of oxygen and other vital nutrients. Many vascular problems, such as untreated high blood pressure, can affect memory and learning.

Deprivation. Sensory loss and social isolation may cause the older adult to become dull, forgetful, or confused. Vision and hearing loss can have a significant impact on the ability of a person to understand conversations and communicate and may cause withdrawal from social activities. Deprivation of meaningful human contact and interactions is experienced by many older adults who live alone or are institutionalized.

Structural Damage to the Brain. Brain tumors and subdural hematomas are expanding masses that compress and cause pressure on the brain and may result in subtle cognitive losses and changes in emotions or behavior. Subdural hematomas are usually a result of head trauma and cause pressure on the brain due to bleeding within the brain.

Normal Pressure Hydrocephalus. The cerebrospinal fluid surrounding the brain is absorbed too slowly, resulting in a buildup of pressure and compression of brain tissue. A slow progressive dementia, gait disturbances, and urinary incontinence may develop.

Chemical Imbalances. Many factors can disrupt metabolism and affect the brain: dehydration, thyroid dysfunction, uncontrolled diabetes, malnutrition, vitamin deficiencies, liver or kidney dysfunction, and metabolic or chemical imbalances in the blood. Mental symptoms may appear before physical ones. These problems may be worse in older people who are inactive, have poor appetites, or skimp on food. Tests can determine if any of these imbalances are present.

Delirium. Delirium may also be confused with dementia. It describes a group of symptoms that usually include mild to severe intellectual impairment, memory loss, confusion, and disorientation. The delirious person shows a reduced level of consciousness, fluctuating alertness, and diminished attention span and may alternate between drowsiness and restlessness. The symptoms often develop suddenly and are quite obvious and variable. Delirium can be caused by many different illnesses. A person with a dementing illness may also develop a delirium from some other illness or medication.

Other Causes of Reversible Dementias

- Chemical intoxication, including lead, mercury, arsenic, pesticides, pollutants, and carbon monoxide exposure
- Alcohol toxic reactions
- Meningitis
- Autoimmune diseases
- Accidental hypothermia
- Hospitalization, particularly after surgery, and while in intensive care
- Chronic pain

Once an adult has been diagnosed with an irreversible dementia, steps can be taken to help minimize the deficits caused by the disease. The chapters that follow describe what can be done, starting with a look at the importance of the older adults living environment.

2

Creating the Right Environment

The environment is extremely important to an individual with a dementing illness since it can make a great difference in the quality of his or her life. The environment needs to provide safety and security; it should be comfortable and pleasant, simple and consistent, stable and reliable. A warm, supportive environment accepts the person's behavior, removes stress, accommodates weaknesses, and emphasizes abilities.

Sensory deprivation, sensory overload, lack of privacy, noises, lighting, and shadows are all environmental factors that can contribute to confusion and disorientation. Each home or facility needs to be adapted to meet the special needs of the older adult with a memory impairment. Environmental modifications can help make routine activities easier to perform. Problems can be minimized with a little thought and imagination.

A SAFE ENVIRONMENT

Confused older adults become less able to take care of their safety needs as they lose their judgment skills and become less alert to the possibility of accidents. Accidents are a real problem, and care must be taken to develop an environment that takes safety into consideration. An emergency plan should be ready in case of fire, accidental injury, or illness. It is important to know the confused person's limits. Where safety is concerned, abilities shouldn't be overestimated. Physical changes diminish the older adult's ability to see, hear, smell, and feel. Limitations resulting from physical or mental impairment can make the older adult feel vulnerable and more prone to accidents and injury. The most common accidents involving the elderly are falls and burns. Most falls occur at night, in the home. Bathrooms, entryways, and stairways are the most frequent sites of accidents. The results of accidental injury are more likely to be serious in the older adult and can result in long-term disability or dependence. Most accidents can be prevented if simple safety rules are followed and safety hazards are eliminated.

Following are some suggestions to help make the environment of the confused older adult safe and pleasant. In the individual's own home, not every precaution will have to be taken. Families can modify the environment to suit their needs and the needs of the confused person. In settings like adult day care and nursing homes, where there are many different persons with mental impairments, every precaution needs to be taken.

Keep the environment simple and safe. Remove all tools and appliances. Put away glassware and other breakable items. Put away small items like pins and buttons—they may be mistaken for candy. Lock car and other household keys in a safe place. Never leave scissors, matches, medicines, or other sharp, dangerous, or poisonous items lying around. Store poisonous substances, toiletry items, and medications in locked cabinets. Lock up tools, lawn mowers, appliances and fire arms. Put a lock on thermostats.

The elderly's skin is less sensitive to changes in temperature and they can accidentally burn themselves. Water temperature should be kept at 120°F or lower. Paint faucet handles (red for hot) for easy identification. Radiators and hot water pipes should be blocked off. Spaceheaters should be avoided.

Never put any inedible substance in a food container. Have the poison control number and other emergency numbers posted at each phone.

• *Furnishings.* Use only sturdy furniture that won't tip over and chairs with armrests to prevent falls and encourage mobility. Low, deep, overstuffed, and soft furniture can be extremely difficult to get out of. Cushion sharp furniture edges. Use weighted lamps that can't be knocked over easily. Remove all unnecessary furniture.

• *Kitchen.* Disconnect all appliances that are potentially dangerous. Remove knobs from the stove. Check with an electrician, repair person, dealer, or the gas company for suggestions on how to make the stove safe. Look for hazardous items in the refrigerator. Even safe foods such as vinegar can cause illness if consumed in large quantities. A locksmith can put a lock on the refrigerator if necessary.

• *Bathroom.* Make sure towel racks are securely attached to the wall. Install grab bars in the bath, shower, and next to the toilet. These will help the older person keep his or her balance and prevent falls. Use only carpeting or nonskid mats on floors. Carpeting will help cushion a fall. Remove everything from the bathroom except such essentials as a washcloth, towel, bar of soap, toothpaste, and toothbrush. A raised toilet seat makes getting off the toilet easier. Remove glass doors from the shower since the confused person might fall into them. A bathtub or shower seat (instead of standing in a shower) can make bathing easier and helps the older adult feel more secure. A hand-held shower head may be less frightening to the confused person than the overhead kind. Unplug or remove all electrical appliances from the bathroom. The confused person should be supervised when using any electrical appliance, which may be accidentally left on or misused.

• *Stairs, Floors, and Hallways.* Handrails on stairs and in hallways can help the older adult retain mobility. They should extend past the top and bottom of stairs and contrast with the color of the wall. If stairs become difficult to climb, a sloping ramp or chair elevator will help. Stairs should be well lighted so that each step can be seen clearly when going up or down. Carpeting should be attached firmly to the steps. Avoid worn, deep pile, patterned, or dark color carpeting on steps; they make it difficult to see the edges of the steps. A contrasting color strip on the edge of each step can help make each step more visible. Gates can be installed at the top and bottom of stairs to prevent falls, especially at night. Gates can be used to block off entrances to the kitchen or basement if necessary. Avoid waxing floors. Rugs, mats, and linoleum should be secured. If scatter rugs must be used, they should have a nonskid backing. Baseboards should be painted a different color to help delineate the wall and the floor.

• *Bedroom.* Keep the bedroom simple and consistent. The rooms the confused person uses should contain as little as possible. Keep often-used items in the same place. That makes them easier to find. In a nursing home the residents' rooms should be easily distinguished from one another. The resident's name and picture and other identifying material can be placed on the door to help individuals find their way.

• *Windows and Doors.* Lock windows securely. A mentally impaired person may climb or fall out of a window. Secure doors, installing new locks if necessary. A lock can be placed at the top or bottom of the outside door, as the mentally impaired person usually will not think to look there. A double bolt lock that has to be turned with a key, two doorknobs that have to be turned simultaneously, a buzzer or bell attached to the door as a signal someone is coming or going, or an electronic warning device are other ideas to keep wanderers safe. The fire department can help you find the safest way to secure your windows and doors. Protective grillwork on doors and decals on sliding glass doors can help prevent a confused person from walking through or putting a hand through the glass. Mirrored walls may have to be replaced, as the affected individual might walk into them. Remove locks from interior doors or tape latches open to prevent the confused person from locking him- or herself in.

• *Outdoor Swimming Pools* must be securely fenced in and locked. Even if the person with a dementing illness was a good swimmer, the individual should never swim unsupervised since she or he may forget what to do in the water.

LIGHTING

Older adults may not be able to see obstacles, read signs, or recognize familiar people when lighting is poor. Adequate lighting is one way to help the older adult with vision loss remain self-reliant. The eyes of the elderly are less tolerant of bright lights, adapt more slowly to changes in light levels, and are more prone to night blindness. Reduced acuity makes objects appear fuzzy and unclear. A combination of glare and reduced visual acuity can "hide" objects from the older person. Glare may cause the older adult to feel anxious and unable to concentrate. Good lighting is essential for safety and comfort.

The average 60-year-old requires seven times more light and may need five times as long to adjust to glare as a young adult! The period of temporary blindness resulting from changes in light increases with age. It becomes increasingly difficult for the elderly to perceive cars and people on the periphery of vision.

Turning on the lights is one way to improve lighting, but older adults must first recognize and respect their loss of vision. Many older persons with visual impairments deny any loss of vision; others may be thrifty about turning on the lights. The older adult with a dementing illness may lack the skills needed to compensate for the loss of vision—you may have to turn the lights on for him. An orientation and mobility instructor can offer specialized advice on how to modify the environment to accommodate the older adult's vision loss. This can be done in the individual's home, personal care home, adult day care center, or nursing home. Most of us are not adequately trained to assess the impact of the environment on older adults with vision loss and we could use the expertise of someone who is. Some ways that we can improve the environment to accommodate the elderly's changing vision include:

- Use one 200-watt bulb, instead of four 60-watt bulbs, around the room. Eyes feel less tired and irritated when light is evenly distributed around a room. Use the maximum wattage bulb allowed by a fixture. Consistent lighting from room to room is important.
- Use dimmer switches to control the degree of light at various times of the day. Keep lights on during the day so that changes in lighting occur gradually. Focus light where it is needed.
- Allow adequate time to adjust to changes in light. Offer your arm and guide the older adult when entering a dark or very bright room. The individual may make slow, deliberate movements to help adjust to failing eyesight. Don't rush the person. Don't put furniture right inside the door or entryway; the older adult may bump into it if her or his eyes have not adjusted to the change in light.
- Fluorescent (blue) lights are very hard on older eyes and may cause tearing and headaches. Incandescent (yellow) light is preferable. Frosted bulbs and shades and globes on light fixtures reduce glare.
- Night lights help people find their way safely in the dark. At a minimum, they should be placed in the bedroom, bathroom, and the hallway leading to the bathroom.
- Shiny floors and furniture cause glare. Use nonglare floor and furniture finishes or carpeting. Arrange furniture to keep the sun from reflecting off a shiny surface. Low-gloss finishes and paints and textured fabrics help to reduce glare.
- Sheer curtains and venetian blinds are preferable to drapes; they reduce glare and still allow one to see outside.

THE STRESS OF RELOCATION

Moving is always a stressful event, whether from the individual's own home to the home of children, a personal care home, or a nursing home. Moving requires many psychological and social adjustments: giving up possessions, control, and independence; changing routines and social contacts; adjusting to living with other people under new rules and regulations.

The confused older adult, not having the mental capacity to prepare for a move and the adjustments it takes, is much more vulnerable to the stress of relocation. The mentally impaired elder relies on familiar surroundings to disguise failing memory. A strange new environment takes away security, contributes to confusion, and may engender fright and anxiety.

Both the elder and the caregiver need support and encouragement through the relocation process. Sometimes it may take a full year— through all four seasons—before the confused person successfully adjusts to a new environment. These are some suggestions to ease the transition to a new environment and life-style:

- *Prepare for the move in advance.* If able, let the mentally impaired person be involved in the decision-making process. Discuss the move ahead of time, if the person can remember.
- *Help the confused person to feel in control of the situation.* Listen and talk with the affected individual about concerns and feelings. Provide support for both the caregiver and the older adult.
- *Make sure that a new member or resident is well received and treated warmly.* People respond well to early gestures of warmth and kindness. Find out what name the individual likes and use the preferred name. Introduce staff, other residents, and family members by name. In a nursing home, adult day care center, or personal care home, staff should wear name tags.
- *Help the older adult to feel secure in the new environment.* Give a tour of the home or facility and point out landmarks. Describe the layout and location of important rooms or services. Maps of the building, directional signs, and visual points of reference can all be used to help individuals gain a sense of control over their environment.
- *Give the individual an opportunity to explore the new surroundings.* Don't mistake interest and curiosity in the environment as aimless wandering. People like to get a sense of where they are.
- *Help the individual know what is expected of him or her.* Let the elder know where rooms and services are and what the daily

routine is. Describe routines and procedures slowly. Repeat this information over several days or weeks until the individual feels more confident in the new surroundings.

- *Make the new environment feel cozy and familiar.* Favorite possessions such as pictures will bring a sense of familiarity to the new home. Use orienting cues like clocks, calendars, and newspapers in the individual's rooms as well as in lobbies and dining and recreational areas.

- *Keep the environment stable.* Don't move familiar services, furniture, or equipment unnecessarily. This can disrupt orientation and cause confusion.

CREATING A PLEASANT ENVIRONMENT

A pleasant, inviting atmosphere is so important. The environment should convey a sense of warmth, dignity, and friendship. Plants, flowers, birds, aquariums, and the like can give warmth to the institutional environment. Noninstitutional furniture can help the nursing home or adult day care center feel more like home. Objects from an individual's earlier life can be used to personalize individual rooms, provide a link with the past, and maintain orientation. The environment should encourage people to reach out, touch, and explore. The layout and decorations in each room should provide cues about what the room is used for. Conversation areas should be created to encourage people to interact with one another. Space should be provided for wandering. An outdoor patio or exercise area can help the person feel less confined. A skylit lounge or sunny plant room can provide a feeling of being outdoors when no outside area is available.

Colors help create a warm, pleasant atmosphere. Color can help stimulate the confused person's interest in the surroundings. The environment should be bright, colorful, and stimulating. Warm colors like pink and peach have a calming effect. Pale, pastel colors may all look alike, so it is better to use brighter shades. Too many bright colors and graphics can be overstimulating, so use bright colors for accent. Avoid busy prints and loud wallpaper patterns.

Contrasting colors are preferred; similar colors appear to blend together and become indistinguishable. White on white is particularly difficult to see. Serve dark food on a light-colored plate on a dark mat or tablecloth. Avoid glass cups and dishes, as they can be hard to see. Rugs should contrast with the color of the walls. Avoid contrast in flooring. A change in the color of the floor may appear to be a change in height, this is confusing and can cause falls.

Colors used for identification and location should be strongly contrasting. It might be helpful to paint the door to the confused person's room red or some other bright color. Bathroom doors can all be painted the same color for easier identification. Camouflage doors you do not want to call attention to by painting them the same color as the wall.

Bulletin boards and calendars help to give information about activities and events, but they are not very useful if they are hard to read. Signs should have contrasting backgrounds and large well-spaced letters. White letters on a dark red, dark green, or black background are easy to see. Extra-large objects such as large-print phone dials and calendars are easier to see and use. Signs or pictures can be used on doors or drawers to help with identification. Label the door of the confused person's room with her or his picture. Use a picture of the individual at a younger age, as he may not recognize himself in recent pictures.

Most people respond positively to carpeting. It is warmer and softens noises. Voices, footsteps, wheelchairs, and ringing phones are less irritating in carpeted units of institutions. The incidence of slips and falls decreases with carpeting, and falls on carpeted floors run less risk of injury. One thing to consider is that the confused person is prone to accidents, food spills, vomit, and urine on carpeting require prompt cleaning and deodorizing.

The impact of noise and activity must be considered, as this can be overstimulating and cause confusion and anxiety. Have at least one quiet area the confused person can retreat to when he or she is anxious or needs time alone. A soundproof room with carpeting and sound-absorbing furniture will help soften sounds and provide an area that facilitates conversation. The TV and radio should be shut off when not in use. The individual with a dementing illness generally does better in a calm, quiet environment, although soft classical music may be calming.

Every person needs space for privacy, solitude, and intimacy. Institutional residents may have the greatest need for privacy, as they live in shared quarters and are cared for by a variety of persons. Simple considerations like knocking on the individual's door and asking for permission to enter shows respect. Never move someone's personal possessions without the person's permission. Ask someone you are pushing in a wheelchair where she or he would like to be placed. Don't ever just move him abruptly without telling him what you are going to do. Individuals should be informed when you are going to change their clothes, feed them, give a bath, or take their blood pressure. Even if a person is very severely demented and no longer able to talk, the individual should be told when something is going to happen.

Consistent staffing is very important. Caregivers—family, adult day care center staff, nursing home staff, sitters, and personal care aides—should be fairly consistent. The confused person needs to feel safe and secure in familiar surroundings with familiar people. Individuals respond best to people they know well and trust. Caregivers who work with the confused person will learn what works best with that person.

3

Maintaining Independence: Daily Living Skills

One of the caregiver's most important roles is to provide simple, basic care for the mentally impaired older adult. This includes help with the daily living routine: eating, bathing, dressing, grooming, toileting, medication, exercise, recreation, and social activities. The challenge to the caregiver is to maximize the individual's ability to function as independently as possible.

An occupational therapy assessment can determine what skills the mentally impaired older adult still has and help the caregiver understand the person's limitations. The occupational therapist can teach the older person the skills necessary to continue the activities of daily living. Social and physical barriers in the home or institution that impede the individual's ability to do for himself and strategies to compensate for any losses can be identified.

- Always encourage the older adult to do as much as possible independently. It may take a lot longer, so be patient. Watch for signs of frustration.
- Simplify routines. Break down tasks into simple steps and ask the individual to complete one step at a time.
- Use a quiet voice, touch for reassurance, and praise for effort.
- Skills fluctuate from day to day. If the confused person claims he

or she cannot do it today, assume this is true and that you are not being manipulated.

- Sometimes all that is needed is for someone to start the motion. Put the washcloth into the affected person's hand, gently bring the hand up to the face, and start washing.
- The amount of time needed to help someone will vary with the individual and with the severity of the dementia.

BATHING

Bathing is a very private matter. Needing assistance with bathing is a very strong indication to the person that she or he is now dependent. Sensitivity and understanding is important. In a survey of geriatric long-term care facilities, the most frequent complaint of residents concerned bathing. Residents perceived a lack of respect and consideration from the caregiver during the bathing process.

Showers can be dangerous, as the older person may fall. If a shower is to be used, install grab bars and use a shower seat. A hand-held shower head is easier and less frightening than the overhead kind.

Bath time should be a regular routine. Do it at the same time of the day. It is probably not necessary for the person to bathe every day, especially when bathing becomes difficult. A sponge bath may be easier.

We reached a point that getting in and out of the bathtub became frightening for both of us, and we resorted to sponge bathing.

- Get everything ready ahead of time: soap, towels, clothing, and water in the tub. Talk to the individual to prepare her or him for the bath. Offer comfort and reassurance.
- Check the water temperature. Use only 2 to 3 inches of water in the bathtub. Avoid bubbles and oils, as they can make the tub slippery.
- Never leave the confused person unsupervised while bathing, shaving, or using electrical appliances.
- Try to follow old routines as much as possible. The confused person may be able to bathe himself if you remind him or get the motion started. Gently describe each step: "unbutton your shirt, pull down your pants, step into the tub." Make it seem easy. Never rush.

- Offer privacy. Close doors, shower curtain, or curtain around the bed.
- Look for changes in the skin's surface. There is an increase in skin cancers with age. The skin also becomes more vulnerable with age; it breaks easily, heals slowly, thins, dries, and loses its elasticity.
- Remind a resisting person why the bath is needed. Or try again later. One daughter told her father it was Saturday night to get him to bathe (he was used to bathing once a week—on Saturday night). Ask the confused person's physician to write a prescription: "Bath—every other day."
- Add tomato juice to bath water to remove persistent body odors.
- Be sure the genital area and area under the breasts is well washed. Check for signs of skin irritation and sores, especially if the person sits or lies down a lot. Apply dry skin lotion or oil. Use body powder or cornstarch under the breasts and in the creases of the skin.

Many caregivers find bathing to be a very difficult and tiring chore. Some individuals may cooperate better with someone from outside the family. Hiring a personal care aide to assist with bathing may be well worth the expense. It can provide caregivers with time for themselves while someone else is completing a difficult and time-consuming task. Some people respond well to aides wearing white or a uniform and seem less threatened by their assistance.

GROOMING AND PERSONAL CARE

Good grooming is very important to help the older adult maintain a positive self-image. Matted, unkempt hair, untrimmed and food-stained mustaches and beards, and food-stained clothing are inexcusable. They are easily corrected but often neglected in some institutions. We need to care for the whole person, not just physical needs.

- Apply light makeup if the individual is accustomed to wearing it. Makeup can be very important to mental attitude. A manicure, pedicure, painted nails, and facials are special treats. Check nails regularly and trim as needed.
- Many people can continue to go to the barber or hairdresser if it

is still enjoyable. Find a hairdresser who is patient and understanding and who can come to the home if necessary. A short,
simple cut is easiest to manage. Dry shampoos and wigs are
alternatives.

Many people commented on her appearance wherever she went. At least
she got that much attention from them and it was good for her.

Foot Care

The elderly tend to have more problems with their feet and foot care
is often neglected. The skin on the feet becomes more sensitive so that
care is needed to prevent sores and discomfort while walking. A
physician or foot specialist (podiatrist) should be consulted if pain,
itching, fungal infections, or other problems develop. Regular examination by a podiatrist is recommended. Toenails must be cut on a
regular basis to avoid ingrown toenails or other problems.

Oral Hygiene

Dental care is another basic need that is often neglected. Good oral
hygiene is needed to maintain and preserve teeth and gums and is
important to one's comfort and health. It should be part of the
regular daily routine. Rotting teeth and sore gums can make eating
difficult, unpleasant, and painful. Dentures also require good preventative care. Proper cleaning prevents odors and stain buildup and
removes debris. Dentures help the elderly to maintain adequate
nutrition and preserve their personal appearance. Ill-fitting dentures
may interfere with a proper diet. Dentures should be worn daily and
fixed if they don't fit properly. If dentures are not cleaned properly,
they can cause painful sores to develop on the gums.

- Make sure the confused person brushes his or her teeth regularly.
- If assistance is needed, tell what will be done at each step. Let the
  individual clean his dentures if he is able.
- If the person is completely helpless, wipe the tongue, gums, and
  inside of the mouth gently with soft gauze or cloth moistened
  with hydrogen peroxide or plain water.
- Toothettes, a disposable sponge and stick, can be used to promote
  good oral hygiene.
- Moisten cracked, dry lips with petroleum jelly to prevent infection.

DRESSING

The elderly want to look their best. They take pride in their appearance. Everyone feels better when well groomed with clothes that are clean and attractive and fit well.

Encourage the confused person to dress. Don't let her or him walk around in nightclothes all day. Choose clothing that is loose-fitting, lightweight, comfortable, easy to put on, and familiar. Clothes simple in design are best. Avoid busy patterns. Also keep in mind that an older person's body is less able to adjust to changes in temperature. There is an increased sensitivity to cold.

- Let the confused person dress himself as long as he is able. Lay out the clothes to be worn in the order they are to be put on. Help to put on one sock, then let the individual put on the other. Help by prompting at each step.
- If possible, offer a simple choice of two outfits. Choices give the older adult a sense of control over some aspects of life.
- Make clothing selection easier. Remove all unnecessary clothes from the confused person's drawers. Put away out-of-season clothes so the individual doesn't choose inappropriately.
- Hang belts or scarves that belong with an outfit on the same hanger. Eliminate unnecessary accessories.
- When buttons become difficult to manage, replace them with zippers or velcro. Choose clothing with buttons in the back if the individual likes to play with the buttons and unbuttons them. Choose clothing with the opening in the front if the person can dress unaided.
- Raglan sleeves, elasticized waistbands, tube socks, soft leather slip-on shoes, stretch fabrics, undefined waist, mittens, separates (two pieces versus one), cardigans, and jogging outfits are all easy to put on and wear. Leg warmers can be used in cool weather.
- Don't argue if the confused person doesn't want to change clothes. Try again later.
- Label clothing, hangers, and lockers for individuals who attend programs outside the home. This will help prevent someone from accidentally taking the wrong item.

TOILETING

The ability to use the toilet is usually impaired as the severity of the dementia increases. Not everyone with a dementing illness becomes incontinent and some simple preventative measures can be taken to help avoid toileting problems. Accidents can occur if the confused person is upset, sick, in a strange environment, or can't find the bathroom, when the normal routine is disrupted, or where there is lots of activity and excitement.

Incontinence

Urinary incontinence is not a normal part of aging. Incontinence must always be investigated to see if the cause is treatable. Urinary tract infections, prostate disease in men, constipation, dehydration, delirium, medication side effects, and dementia can all cause incontinence. Diarrhea and urinary incontinence may develop around a fecal impaction.

Incontinence has serious emotional and social effects. The confused person may feel angry, overwhelmed, ashamed, embarassed, helpless, or irritable over loss of control. The individual may become afraid of going out in public and may lose self-confidence. The attitude of the caregiver is extremely important in helping the individual cope with incontinence.

If incontinence cannot be prevented, it can be accepted and practically managed. Catheters should only be used as a last resort, as they can be a source of infection or cause stones to form in the bladder.

Families or health care staff may not try to take control, finding it easier to accept the incontinence. It takes time and effort to put the confused person on a schedule and use other preventative techniques. The effort is worth it because it really helps the older adult's self-esteem to remain in control. Acceptance without intervention can contribute to the individual's feeling of helplessness and dependence.

Preventative Measures

- Observe toileting habits over several days to see if there is a pattern. You can learn to anticipate when the individual has to go and get her or him on a schedule.
- Observe for cues. The person may become restless, pull at clothing, and unfasten buttons when having to go to the bathroom. He may not be able to communicate his needs in words or may use different words. Learn the words the individual uses when having to use the toilet.

- Make sure the bathroom is clearly visible and accessible. Accidents often occur when the confused person cannot find the bathroom. A sign on door or pictures of a toilet can help with identification. An individual who cannot find the bathroom may urinate in inappropriate places: flower pots, sinks, closets, water fountains, or wastebaskets.
- A portable commode in the bedroom or on the first floor can help prevent accidents if the bathroom is a long way off.
- Sometimes the confused person will not make it to the bathroom in time. Remind him to use the bathroom; don't just ask if he has to go. Show him where to go if necessary. Ask him to please come into the bathroom. Choose clothing that is easily removed.
- If the confused person cannot remember the sequence, point out what has to be done. Explain the procedure, using simple, step-by-step instructions: "Pull down your pants." "Sit down on the toilet."
- As the dementia becomes progressively more severe, the confused person may not be able to toilet alone, even with verbal instructions. Total assistance will be needed with undressing, getting on and off the toilet, wiping, and dressing.
- Be discreet. Respect the need for privacy. Recognize that the confused person may feel shame, discomfort, or embarassment at having others take care of his personal care needs. Be calm and reassuring.
- Develop a regular toileting schedule based on the individual's usual elimination pattern. In general, encourage the use of the bathroom every 2 hours, after waking, after meals, and before bedtime. If the person doesn't go at the 2-hour point, don't wait 2 more hours to try again. Try again in ½ to 1 hour. The time can be increased to every 2 ½ to 3 hours if this works well.
- To prevent accidents at night, restrict fluid intake in the evening (but be sure to give extra fluids in the daytime). Avoid diuretics such as tea, soda, coffee, and grapefruit juice. Drinking too little can cause constipation, which can bring on more incontinence.
- Encourage the individual to remain seated long enough to use the toilet. Give him something to hold. Try giving him a glass of water and a straw and asking him to blow bubbles. This seems to stimulate some people to go; others respond to running water.
- If the individual lives at home and attends adult day care or a similar program, the staff needs to work together with the family to provide a consistent toileting routine.

- When an accident does occur, comfort and reassure the individual. Never get upset or yell.
- Keep the skin clean and dry to prevent skin breakdown. Wash well after each accident and powder the skin to keep it dry.

She was never really incontinent. Getting her to the bathroom became a problem late in her illness. We used a panty liner off and on when we went out and I thought she might need it. When she needed more protection I used a 24-month-old infant disposable diaper in the same way, slipping it inside her underwear. I could not manage the adult diaper. I couldn't hold her and put the diaper on her at the same time.

Constipation/Impaction

Incontinence of the bowel is much less common. Adequate fluids, fiber in the diet, and regular exercise will help the older adult to maintain regular, comfortable bowel movements. Keep track of the individual's bowel movements. Lethargy, poor appetite, and abdominal distension are signs of constipation that should be watched for. Avoid using laxatives.

Products for Managing Incontinence

There are a variety of disposable absorbent products available to help manage incontinence. These items are available through drugstores and stores carrying hospital equipment and supplies. These include:

- pad and pants (undergarments with space for disposable pads)
- disposable adult diapers (from adult diaper services)
- incontinence pads
- protective bedding such as rubberized flannel sheets

Cost, comfort, how easy it is to use and carry, size, disposability, absorbency, bulkiness, and how the incontinent person accepts wearing or using it are factors to consider when choosing a product for incontinence.

COORDINATION AND WALKING

Posture, walking, and coordination may be affected as a dementing illness progresses. Apraxia, the inability to carry out purposeful

movements, may develop. The individual may know what he or she
wants to do, but the message doesn't get through from the mind to
the fingers or feet. Apraxia may progress gradually or change abruptly. Abilities fluctuate from day to day. Apraxia can cause unsteadi-
ness and difficulty walking. The individual can develop a slow, shuf-
fling gait, may trip, cross legs while walking, or get stuck as if glued
to the floor. The ability to use fingers and hands may be impaired,
making handwriting, managing buttons and zippers, and dialing the
telephone difficult to perform. An occupational or physical therapy
evaluation can be helpful to determine how the individual can be
assisted.

Changes associated with aging may also affect coordination and
walking. A decrease in circulation may cause coldness, numbness,
and a tingling sensation in the hands and feet. Eye-hand coordination
decreases with age. The bones of the elderly tend to become more
porous and brittle, particularly in women, increasing the likelihood
of fractures. The joints stiffen and may develop points and spurs.

Changes in walking, posture, stiffness, and coordination should be
discussed with the individual's physician to rule out any treatable
cause.

- Don't help too much. People do have a natural balance and
  pattern of walking. Helping or interfering too much can cause the
  individual to feel unbalanced.
- Let the older person grab your arm; don't grab hers or his. Hold
  your arm close to your body to help maintain your balance and
  place a firm hand under his arm.
- Try walking behind an unsteady person and hold his belt to keep
  him steady.
- If glued to the floor, suggest that the confused person walk
  toward an object or goal to help get him moving.
- Make sure the older adult's shoes are comfortable and well-
  fitting. A closed shoe with a nonskid sole is best.
- A cane or walker may be useful to help the individual walk
  unassisted. However, some confused people are unable to learn
  how to use walking aids, which may make getting around more
  complicated and confusing.
- The impaired person may need help getting in and out of chairs.
  He may have difficulty figuring out where his body is in relation
  to the chair. Help position his body and assure him it is safe to sit
  down. Use chairs that are not too low, are firm, and have
  armrests. Rocking back and forth in the chair can provide the

momentum to get out of the chair. Explain the sitting process one step at a time: "Put your hands on the armrests; bend forward; sit down slowly."

- Break down each task into its simplest parts. Think how the task can be done in a simple way. It is better that the activity be modified—not given up. Don't take away the impaired person's independence when some abilities remain.
- Keeping the impaired person active increases the risk of falls; however, the benefits of activity outweigh any risks. If the individual falls, stay calm. Check for injury or pain and signs of swelling, bruising, or agitation. When the individual is calm and appears okay, encourage him to get up.

SLEEP

Most people assume that the elderly need more sleep than younger people to stay healthy. Older people may tire faster, but this doesn't affect the amount of sleep needed. As we age, there are some natural changes in sleep patterns. These may cause anxiety if the older adult thinks something is wrong. The sleep of the aged is often lighter and more prone to frequent awakenings. Older people generally take longer to fall asleep. The ability to sleep seems to decrease over time. However, insomnia should be evaluated by a physician. Moderation in sleep, as in everything, is desirable. Here are some suggestions to help the older adult sleep better.

- Before bedtime, avoid caffeine, cigarettes, heavy meals, and strenuous exercise. Try offering a light snack, a glass of warm milk, or a massage to help the person relax. A warm bath is soothing and sedating to some. If the bath is a struggle, try it at another time of day.
- Make sure the bedroom is dark and quiet. As people get older, less noise is needed to awaken them. Use night darkening shades and a night light.
- Follow a consistent sleep-wake pattern. Following a regular schedule for sleeping and waking enhances sleep. Irregular sleep-wake patterns interfere with sleep.
- An active daily routine and regular exercise will help the older adult to sleep. Daytime naps should be discouraged if sleeping at night is a problem.
- A comfortable bed and bedding enhance sleep. Heavy blankets and quilts tangle less than sheets and light blankets.

- Bedrails may help some confused persons stay in bed. Others may try to climb over the rails and that could be dangerous.
- Remind the confused person who wakes up during the night that it is nighttime and ask him or her to go back to bed.
- Sleeping medications can be prescribed by a physician, but they should be taken only when all else fails. Avoid over-the-counter sleeping medications.

She required much less sleep than I and at times it was difficult to get her to bed. She would waken at 5 a.m. and walk in a circle around and around the apartment. I walked behind her lest she fall and hurt herself.

EATING

The older adult with a dementing illness may develop problems of overeating, poor nutrition, or loss of interest in food. Special diets may limit food choices. Physical problems and age-related changes, including decreased biting and chewing ability, decreased saliva production, difficulty swallowing, decreased eating pleasure, changing taste sensations, and decreased digestive enzyme flow, can affect the older person's desire and ability to eat. The sense of smell diminishes with age and can contribute to a lack of interest in food. A consultation with a dietician can be very beneficial in planning the person's meals. A physician should be consulted if a marked reduction in appetite occurs, as this can be a sign of illness.

Suggestions to Make Food More Appealing, Nutritious, and Easier to Eat

- Fortify foods with skim milk powder to increase protein content. Cereal, puddings, and cream soups are easily fortified.
- Enhance food flavors by using a variety of herbs and spices.
- Serve foods at their correct temperature. Flavor perception decreases at very hot or very cold temperatures. Check the temperature to make sure it is not too hot. Confused persons lack judgment and can burn themselves.
- Smaller, more frequent meals are better for improved digestion and absorption.
- Observe and record foods that are not tolerated well or cause gas.
- If drooling is a problem, avoid milk and citrus juice, as they produce more mucus and make the problem worse. Use other fruit juices and nectars instead.

- Offer poor eaters a liquid high-calorie substitute with or between meals.
- Learn the individual's food preferences. All caregivers, sitters, and staff who help feed the confused person should know the individual's likes and dislikes. It is important to recognize and respect ethnic, religious, and cultural preferences or food restrictions.
- Make mealtime part of the regular daily routine. Serve meals at approximately the same time of the day.
- Serve foods in pleasant surroundings. Use a variety of colors to make the food look more appealing. Set the table to make it look pretty. Avoid serving all white foods on white plates and vice versa. Make eating time pleasant and enjoyable—a time to socialize.
- Many mentally impaired persons enjoy eating out in restaurants. If necessary, alert the waiter or waitress that the person is confused. Explain what foods are available, as the individual may be able to read the menu but may not be able to make sense out of it. If the person becomes frustrated with too many choices, narrow the choices to two or order for both of you.
- Serve familiar foods; new foods may be confusing. The person with a dementing illness may develop rigid likes and dislikes. Learn by trial and error what foods are enjoyed.
- The confused person may have difficulty with the mechanics of eating due to memory loss and apraxia. Serve finger foods like fish sticks and french fries. Don't fill glasses to the top. You may have to start the motion; put the fork into the person's hand and guide the hand to the food and up to the mouth.
- Simplify mealtime by limiting choices. It may even be necessary to serve only one food at a time. Cut up the food to eliminate the need for a knife and offer a fork, spoon, or spork.
- Sometimes the mentally impaired person may be confused eating foods with different textures, such as soup and cereal. The individual may not know whether to chew or swallow the food.
- Include easy-to-chew foods on the menu, such as fish, eggs, and peanut butter. You may have to remind the confused person to chew. Puree, chop, or cube hard-to-chew foods such as beef, apples, and vegetables.
- Many aged persons experience dry mouth, which interferes with adequate moisture to wet food while chewing. Increase moisture in the diet by increasing fluid intake and serving moist foods and foods with broth, gravy, sauces, or dressings. Provide sips of

water with solids. Dipping breads and cookies in milk makes them easier to eat.

- Fluid intake is as important to total nutrition as solid food. Offer or give fluids hourly. Six to eight glasses of liquid daily is recommended. You may have to remind the confused person to drink. If fluid is restricted at bedtime, extra fluids must be given during the day. Dehydration can cause fatigue, apathy, constipation, and abdominal discomfort and increase confusion.
- When swallowing and choking become a problem, consult the individual's physician about the need for a special diet or modifications. Pureed and soft thick foods and liquids are less likely to cause choking (pudding, soft-boiled eggs, ice cream, yogurt, soft Jell-O). Pureed home-cooked foods are more appealing than baby foods. Avoid small hard candy, nuts, popcorn, and chewing gum.

When she could no longer feed herself, we took over the feeding. When swallowing became a problem—she was holding food in her mouth—I put her food in the blender. Sometimes it worked out well. If she didn't like it, I tried something else. There were a few canned soups that she liked. Stews went into the blender. Cantaloupe went into the blender after she choked on it one morning and scared me half to death. Cereals and bananas went into the blender, and when I learned about nutrients, Sustacal instead of milk was put in the blender with the cereal and banana. When even this was hard to swallow, we went to a liquid diet. At times, it took 1 ½ to 2 hours to get an 8-ounce can of Sustacal into her. When I had to start feeding her, I found that if I fed myself first I was much more relaxed and patient feeding her.

Feeding

When the impaired person can no longer feed her- or himself, you will have to feed the person.

- Make sure the individual being fed is sitting up straight with the head well up to prevent aspiration. Aspiration is a common cause of death or disability in Alzheimer's disease. Have the individual remain sitting up for at least 15 minutes after eating.
- Never rush. Allow sufficient time to accommodate the slow eating pace. Feeding can take an hour or more. Don't feed someone who is agitated or sleepy.
- Puree or cut up food into small pieces. Put only a small amount of food on the spoon at a time. If necessary, remind the individual to swallow. Offer each food separately and describe what it is.

- Gently wipe off the corners of the mouth throughout the meal.
- Gently touch the glass or cup to the lips.

Overeating

Sometimes confused persons will seem to forget that they have just eaten. They may look continuously for something to eat or accuse the caregiver of not feeding them. Avoid arguing.

- Serve smaller, more frequent meals.
- Serve low calorie snacks to nibble on: carrot and celery sticks, crackers, cheese cubes, and fresh fruit cubes.
- Hide or lock up foods that cannot be eaten.

Mealtime Aids

Mealtime aids are available to help physically or mentally impaired persons feed themselves and prevent accidents. Following is a list of ideas and utensils to help keep mealtime pleasant and enjoyable.

- An attachable plate guard provides a rim on one side of the plate. This makes it easier to scoop up the food. A bowl can be used instead of a plate.
- A rubber pad under the plate or a plate with suction cups attached to the bottom will keep the plate in position.
- Plates with a hot water container attached to the underside will keep foods hot when the individual takes a long time to eat.
- Silverware with built-up handles are easier to hold on to. Make your own by attaching a sponge to the fork and spoon.
- Sporks are a combination of a spoon and fork. Some people find a spork easier to eat with than a fork or spoon.
- Flexible plastic straws, spill-proof drinking cups, or lightweight mugs with large handles that are easy to grasp make drinking easier.

4

Enhancing Communication

The impact of age-related sensory changes may be even more profound for the person with a dementing illness—causing increased confusion, withdrawal, and isolation. Caregivers need to understand how dementia and age-related changes can affect the ability to communicate. Alternative techniques need to be developed when communication becomes a problem. The loss of ability to communicate is very distressing to both the individual and the family.

The individual with a dementing illness may lose the social skills that help maintain personal relationships: remembering names, being able to carry on an intelligent conversation, and good manners. Personality changes may further alienate friends and acquaintances. Withdrawal from social activities can result in loneliness and boredom. By enhancing the older adult's ability to communicate, feelings of isolation can be reduced.

The person with a dementing illness may also experience a progressive deterioration of the ability to use and understand language. Abilities can fluctuate from day to day. Language problems may be very slight at first and not interfere with the ability to communicate. Eventually the individual may be unable to speak and will have great difficulty understanding and communicating with others.

The individual with a dementing illness may have trouble expressing him- or herself because he:

- experiences difficulty finding the right word.
- has trouble remembering the names of familiar objects and people.
- cannot communicate a whole thought but can say a few words.
- can describe an object but cannot name it.
- substitutes similar sounding words or the wrong word (*car* for *cane*).

He may experience difficulty understanding others because he:

- quickly forgets what has been said.
- does not understand what has been said.
- may be able to read or hear the words but doesn't comprehend them.

Ask him to read and follow a simple instruction, such as "close your eyes." He may be able to read the instruction but may not be able to follow it.

TIPS FOR ENHANCING COMMUNICATION WITH THE MENTALLY IMPAIRED ELDERLY

She was always a little slow of speech, and with the loss of memory she often started off well but shortly lost her way in conversation. Perhaps it was the illness or that she wasn't given the opportunity to try to say what she wanted, but gradually she spoke less and less. She participated in prayers at church. I encouraged her to read out loud, which she did with no problem.

Remember that the confused person is an individual. Take every opportunity to communicate with the mentally impaired person as an adult. Talk with her or him about the same things you would with anyone else. Talk about his life experiences and interests. Respond to his remarks and recognize that he has something important to say.

- *Be pleasant and calm and try to develop a rapport.* Use a nurturing voice, eye contact, and close physical contact when conversing or providing physical care. Ask him what he would like to be called and identify who you are and what you are going to do.
- *Make sure you have the individual's attention.* Call him by name, touch him lightly, and establish eye contact.
- *Speak slowly and simplify your speech.* Communicate clearly in

nontechnical language. Use the same words the individual uses. Avoid using abstract words. Use the names of people and objects instead of *he, she,* and *it.* "Do you want an apple?" is better than "Do you want this?"

- *Ask simple yes or no questions.* Avoid questions that require decision making. Don't ask the confused person to make too many choices. "Would you like to go for a walk?" is better than "Would you like to go for a walk or eat dinner?"
- *Allow plenty of time for a response.* Wait for a response before asking another question. It may take a lot longer for the mentally impaired adult to answer. If there is no reply, get his attention, look him in the eye, and repeat the question, using the same words.
- *Supply the word if he is struggling,* but give him plenty of time to respond first. Don't supply the word if this upsets him.
- *Ask him to describe it or point out what he wants* if you don't know the word he is trying to say. Guess what he is trying to say and ask if you are guessing correctly. You can confuse the person more if you guess wrong. Don't guess if this upsets him.
- *Try to get at the underlying thought or feeling* if you don't understand what he is trying to way. Comment on the feeling behind the message: "I know you are worried." Listen for key words to provide clues to the conversation.
- *Use positive statements.* Tell the individual what you want him to do, not what you don't want him to do. "Stay on the porch" is better than "Don't leave the porch."
- *Present one idea, question, or statement at a time.* Don't shift from one topic to another.
- *Avoid correcting the confused person when he makes a mistake.* Avoid saying "You forgot" or "You don't remember." Don't argue.
- *Use nonverbal cues or signals to help get your message across.* Ask "Do you want an apple?" and show him the apple.
- *Give instructions one step at a time.* Avoid "We'll have lunch after exercise" because it means something has to be remembered. It is better to say "It is time for exercise." Demonstrate how you want something done.
- *Always assume the individual can understand more than he can express himself.* Never talk about him in front of him. Use a respectful tone of voice; don't be condescending. Converse with him even if you get no response or the response doesn't make sense. This is important to the individual's self-esteem.
- *Do not communicate information that is likely to cause anxiety*

until it is time to do so. For example, don't tell the individual it is time to go to the doctor's until it is actually time to go.
* *Write down reassuring information* for the confused person to read when he becomes anxious and asks repeated questions (if he is able to read).

She participated little in conversations, but it was obvious that she was absorbing and enjoying all of it: Her responses when they came were all too appropriate to believe that she was unaware of what was happening around her. Her occasional comments indicated that she was listening and took some pleasure in the exchange.

REALITY ORIENTATION

The confused person needs help to understand the world around him or her. With the loss of memory and the sense of time, he becomes confused about with where he is and whom he is with. He may have been living in the same home for 20 years, but he'll want to go home. Being confused and disoriented is frightening and frustrating. Reality orientation can help the confused person function more successfully and helps him feel less anxious about what is going on around him.

Twenty-Four Hour Reality Orientation

Twenty-four hour reality orientation is a technique designed to be used by everyone who has contact with mentally impaired adults. It is a consistent approach of continual awareness to help confused persons sort out and remember necessary information. Repetitive orienting activities help make affected elders more alert and aware of themselves and their surroundings. It is a simple way of communicating to enhance understanding of the environment.

A statement can include information such as your name and who you are, what day it is, the weather or season, what you are going to do, and a description of what you are doing. Statements such as these provide a lot of information in a meaningful, friendly way.

"Good morning, John. Today is Monday. I am Jane, your wife. We are going to eat breakfast. Here is your orange juice."

"Hello, John. My name is Jane. I am a nurse. I am going to take your blood pressure. I am going to roll up your sleeve" (rolls up sleeve).

"John, you are at the Adult Day Care Center. It is 3:00—time to go home. Your cab is here. Here is your coat."

Basic information such as this is gently repeated in the conversation as needed to help orient the person to her or his surroundings. In this way the confused person is reassured that he is worth something and that other people care about him. Clear directions help to guide his actions.

Memory Aids

Providing clues and reminders of tasks or events can help the confused person understand what to expect next and thus lessen his or her anxiety. Some memory aids that have been found to be helpful include:

- Large-print calendars or appointment books to record special events
- Large, easy-to-read clocks
- Timers
- Checklists
- Labels or pictures on drawers, doors, and cupboards
- Notes placed in appropriate places as reminders
- A photo album, diary, journal, or scrapbook to collect and record events the confused person wants to remember
- Schedule of activities
- Reality orientation board

The individual's needs and preferences must be taken into account when using memory aids. While one person may find signs and labels helpful, another may find them upsetting. Lists may be helpful to someone who has always used them and was always well organized; a person who was never a list maker won't become one now. What may work at one time may not work at another. Success may depend on the degree of dementia. Avoid overlabeling, as it may be too confusing to the person and too much work for the caregiver. Try to use aids where the confused person has the most trouble remembering and where they have the best chance of success. A mildly confused person may devise reminders for him- or herself. A severely demented person may only become increasingly confused and frustrated because he cannot use the aid.

A reality orientation board can include the following kinds of information:

- Day and date
- Name of place
- Address and location
- Weather
- Season
- Daily activities

A simple daily activity schedule can be used in the individual's residence or in an activity center. The schedule can include basic information such as this:

Home	Activity Center
8:00 Wake up	8:30 Arrive
9:00 Breakfast	9:00 Social Hour
10:30 Exercise	10:00 Current Events
12:00 Lunch	11:00 Exercise
2:00 Walk	12:00 Lunch
5:00 Dinner	1:00 Arts and Crafts
8:00 Snack	2:00 Games
9:00 Bath	3:00 Snack
10:00 Bed	3:30 Return home

NONVERBAL COMMUNICATION

I conversed with her or was silent in the normal way we always had. If I moved out of character in the slightest I got a look of disdain. We giggled a lot over nothing, as was our pattern. At each point that we reached that I had to take over more and more care of her and her person she accepted it without protest. I was more affectionate as time went on and this, too, was accepted and returned. We understood each other to the end.

As the dementia progresses, nonverbal communication becomes increasingly important. Facial expressions communicate a great deal about our reactions and feelings. Posture and body position indicate interest and attention. Gestures emphasize the verbal message and provide clues to our interest and feelings. The voice can convey excitement, fear, love, and many other feelings.

- Observe behavior and body cues for signs of pain or discomfort: posture, guarding, grimacing, changes in behavior, and increased restlessness.
- Listening is very important. Take the time to listen to what the

individual has to say. Listening attentively using verbal and nonverbal responses conveys a feeling of acceptance so that the individual feels free to express her- or himself.
- Moving slowly, be calm, relaxed, and reassuring, and the confused person will respond similarly.

Touch

Touch is a powerful component of close and meaningful communication, yet so simple that its effectiveness is often overlooked. A loving touch communicates acceptance, care, and concern. Touch can calm, reassure, comfort, and stimulate feelings of love. Any expressions of affection should be accepted and returned.

The need for touch increases during periods of stress, illness, loneliness, and depression. Touch is very important when communicating with blind, deaf, and mentally impaired individuals. Holding or squeezing a hand or a gentle pat lets the individual know where you are and that you are listening.

Some guidelines for using touch are:

- Touch only if you are comfortable doing it.
- Know what types of touch each individual responds to.
- Use touch to the degree the person is comfortable with it.
- Don't give people a pat on the head or touch them in a condescending way.
- Try a deep massage to create a sense of comfort and well-being.
- Use touch to accentuate verbal communication.

TECHNIQUES FOR WORKING WITH ELDERS WHO ARE ALSO VISUALLY AND HEARING IMPAIRED

Every effort must be made to determine the presence of specific hearing, speech, and language disorders and to treat them. A hearing and vision evaluation should be conducted early in the progress of the dementing disease before testing becomes difficult or impossible. The caregiver can help identify any problems that the confused person may be unaware of. Sensory impairments can make a dementing illness seem worse, as they add to the individual's confusion, frustration, and isolation.

A normal part of the aging process is sensory change. Most people in their late 70s and early 80s discover that their vision, hearing, and senses of taste, touch, and smell are not what they used to be. We rely on our sensory organs to communicate with others and to relate to the environment. Sensory changes that occur with age can influence an individual's functioning, activities, and perception. They also influence perception of the individual by others. Understanding these changes can help us to provide assistance when it is needed.

Hearing Impaired Persons

Hearing loss is very common in the aged but is frequently overlooked. Hearing loss interferes with the individual's ability to participate in conversations and social situations.

- For many older adults, the progressive loss of hearing begins after age 50 and declines gradually thereafter. By the age of 80, as many as 50% of the elderly may be hearing impaired. Hearing loss should be evaluated.
- Background noises interfere with the person's ability to hear. With age there is a general reduced ability to hear sounds and difficulty in locating their origin. The intensity of sound decreases and may be distorted.
- Men experience greater loss of hearing than women do.
- Hearing loss, more than any other sensory loss, tends to isolate a person. It becomes very difficult to understand one's environment, and hearing decline is very hard for most people to adjust to.

Some of the warning signs of hearing loss may seem like memory impairment. These include:

- Avoiding social situations and withdrawal
- Less small talk
- Shorter attention span
- Appearing to daydream
- Blank looks
- Asking others to repeat a question or statement
- Misunderstanding what is said
- Making inappropriate responses
- Arguing and blaming others, paranoia

Just knowing that the individual has a hearing loss is not sufficient. Testing must be done to determine the nature of the loss, how much it interferes with communication, whether it is treatable, and if a hearing aid would be useful. An audiologist who has experience working with the mentally impaired may be able to suggest other amplification devices that can be used. There are a number of suggestions we can follow to improve listening condition and make hearing easier.

- *Get the hearing-impaired person's attention before speaking.* Don't talk to the individual from behind or from another room. Face the person directly and talk toward (but not in) the best ear.
- *Eliminate background noise.* The hearing impaired are especially susceptible to noise. Background noise makes it difficult to select out desired sounds and may be irritating or cause anxiety. Turn off the TV and radio when not in use.
- *Speak slowly and clearly.* Don't shout, overarticulate words, or exaggerate sounds, as this distorts the message and makes it hard to read facial expressions.
- *Keep your hands away from your face and don't chew or eat while talking.* Be sure your face is visible to the hearing-impaired person so that your lip movements, facial expressions, and gestures are easy to see.
- *Allow adequate time for a response.* Rephrase the statement in short, simple sentences if misunderstood. Use visual cues and hand gestures to get the message across.
- *Don't talk as if the hearing impaired person weren't there.* Tell the individual what is being discussed so that he or she doesn't feel left out or talked about. Describe things that are happening—or about to happen—around him.
- *Provide opportunities to participate in activities that require little conversation,* such as playing cards, walking, or cooking. Encourage participation in group activities.
- *Use a hearing aid if the person will wear it.* If the individual refuses to wear it, removes it, or has difficulty operating it, you'll have to try other techniques. Don't force wearing it. Make sure the hearing aid is in proper operating condition. Know how it works, how to clean it, and how to operate the batteries.

Remember: Hearing takes work. Hearing-impaired people are often accused of listening or hearing when they want to. What appears to be selective hearing may be due to factors such as fatigue, background noises, distractions, and the speaker's voice. Hard-of-hearing people hear and understand less well when they are ill or tired.

Visually Impaired Persons

Changes in vision do occur with age, but vision loss is not inevitable in old age. Early detection of visual impairment is the most effective method of avoiding vision loss. Visual impairment is more likely to be disabling when a person must cope with the effects of other impairments such as a dementing illness. Without proper assistance and training, the visually impaired become vulnerable to further disabilities from falls or injuries and are often isolated and lack socialization. Low-vision aids and rehabilitative services can help the visually impaired enhance their vision and minimize functional limitations. An individual's adjustment to vision loss relates closely to her or his own attitudes and the attitudes and behaviors of significant others.

- Some normal changes can cause a gradual loss of vision, but most older people maintain near normal eyesight. The key to maintaining one's vision is regular eye examinations. Because changes are gradual, many eye conditions may go undetected. Early detection and treatment of visual impairment are extremely important.
- Visual acuity (the smallest object that can be discriminated) declines with age.
- As the lens of the eye ages, it becomes opaque and yellow. This results in the fading of colors and an inaccurate perception of certain color intensities. The cool colors—blue, violet, and green—become especially hard to distinguish. The warmer colors—red, yellow, and orange—are seen more easily. Bright colors may be preferred.
- Visual efficiency decreases with age. The lens of the eye becomes less able to adjust its focus to objects at varying distances.
- The pupil is slower to react to changes in light. This causes increased difficulty in going from bright lights to darkness and vice versa.
- Focusing ability gradually declines. There is a tendency toward farsightedness, and vision at the usual reading distance starts to become blurry and difficult.
- Glare decreases the older adult's ability to see. It takes longer to recover from the effects of glare.
- Older people need more light for general vision. Night vision decreases, necessitating the use of a night light.
- Depth perception may be impaired.

- The ability to respond to rapid movement or blinking lights decreases with age.

Helping the confused older adult to enhance and maintain vision will go a long way toward improving the quality of life. Following are some suggestions for communicating with the visually impaired:

- *Address the visually impaired person before you touch him or her,* so you don't startle him. Identify yourself. Touch him to help him place where you are. Let him know when you are leaving so that he is aware of your departure. Speak normally—don't shout.
- *Speak descriptively of the surroundings to help orient and familiarize the individual to his environment.* Tell the visually impaired person when you move the furniture or his belongings. Describe the location of items in relation to a clock's position (the door is at 3:00).
- *Introduce yourself and others every time you come in contact with the individual.* Tell him what you are going to do, as there are no nonverbal cues to help.
- *Increase the identifiability of people.* Have staff wear name tags or brightly colored jackets.
- *Help the individual explore the environment and stimulate the other senses* (hearing, touch, smell, and taste) since visual stimulation is absent.
- *Clean eyeglasses often.*
- *Avoid glare and provide adequate lighting.* See Chapter 2, "Creating the Right Environment."

WHAT SHOULD YOU TELL THE MENTALLY IMPAIRED PERSON ABOUT HIS/HER ILLNESS?

Many families ask if they should tell the person affected by Alzheimer's disease or another dementing illnesses about the diagnosis. Families are afraid the individual will become depressed if she or he realizes the hopelessness of the situation. This is a very individual decision that each family must make. Families should be encouraged to communicate openly with one another.

Most persons with mild to moderate dementia recognize that something is wrong. They may be aware of problems with their memory and declining intellectual abilities. Withholding information from those who are aware of their own developing problems can make them feel even more anxious, frustrated, and depressed.

If the dementia is more severe, the individual may have little awareness of mental loss and may or may not be told about the diagnosis. The diagnosis may be quickly forgotten or its significance not understood.

- *Tell the individual only what he or she wants to know.* Answer questions directly.
- *Be honest.* Explain what will happen. Let him know the disease will make it harder to remember and he will eventually need help from others.
- *Let the affected person participate in managing the problem and planning for the future.*
- *Talk with the individual and share your concerns.* Reassure him that you love him and understand his feelings. Let him know that you will be there to help him whenever he needs it.
- *Never make promises that you might not be able to keep.* Some families promise the impaired person that they will never put him away in a nursing home. This kind of promise can interfere with the family's planning and decision making at a later date.

Telling Family and Friends

Explain to family, friends, and neighbors that the person has a neurological illness. Help them to understand that the impaired person can not control her or his behavior. Let them know that he needs their love, understanding, and support. The person with a dementing illness often does not look sick, and others may not understand the seriousness of the situation.

5

Managing Problems and Disturbing Behaviors

I know her sometimes bizarre behavior was entirely contrary to her life pattern. My concern became making her as comfortable as I could, reiterating my affection for her, reassuring her when she seemed troubled and presenting her in as positive a way as I could to others.

Persons with a dementing illness and their families may find it difficult to understand the changes that are taking place in thinking and behavior. Because problems and behaviors are caused by damage to the brain, caregivers may conclude that there is nothing that can be done. Much can be done to improve the situation and the individual's quality of life. The individual is responsive to care. The care of a person with a dementing illness is difficult and time consuming, but patience, understanding, and management skills will result in a more satisfying and humane life. What we say and do can help the confused person function better or worse.

Solutions to problems are idiosyncratic. What may work for one caregiver may not work for another, and what works one day may not work the next. Each individual will cope differently. Functioning may be quite variable, depending on such factors as fatigue, mood, or illness. Be flexible and take advantage of good periods by interacting more. Sometimes the most important thing you can do is to be there to listen.

GENERAL GUIDELINES

Establish a simple, predictable routine. The need for structure, consistency, and direction increases as the disease progresses. Structure and routine, based on the individual's lifelong pattern of living, provide a sense of comfort and security about what will happen next. Do things the same way at the same time each day. Plan difficult activities during the time of day the individual is the most cooperative. Limit unnecessary choices to reduce confusion. Use memory aids to help facilitate orientation.

Avoid changes and surprises. When you must change the daily routine, prepare and reassure the person but avoid lengthy explanations. Don't surprise the individual by suddenly doing something such as moving his or her chair. Use a light touch to get the person's attention and gently explain what you are going to do.

Be patient and maintain a calm atmosphere. Don't rush. Wait until the individual understands what you are saying and wait for a reply. Keep your voice calm and reassuring as the confused person will respond to your tone of voice. If you are tense and hurried, the person will become tense and resistant. A slower pace is necessary for all activities. Even a small amount of excitement can cause agitation. Allow time to adjust to a new situation.

Be realistic but positive in your expectations. Learn what the confused person is capable of doing. Realistic expectations will reduce frustrations. Psychological testing and rehabilitation therapy evaluations can help caregivers understand the individual's capabilities. Treat the person as an adult. We tend to treat the elderly as children instead of as mature adults suffering from an illness. Avoid talking down or babying. Be positive in your approach: Treat the individual with dignity and respect, and assume she or he is intelligent and capable of understanding.

Err in the direction of assuming greater mental awareness than may be present. Always assume the older adult can understand what you are saying or doing. The person may be much more aware of what is being said than he or she indicates. Include him in conversations taking place; never talk about him as if he weren't there.

Accent Capabilities. Focus on the individual's strengths—what she or he can do. Never assume because he cannot meet some of his needs he is incapable of meeting any. Remind him of what he can do. Don't undermine his abilities and make him more dependent by doing for him. When assistance is needed, it is better to say "let's do this together" than "let me help you." Assist him to do it for himself. If you take over a task he can still do, he will forget how to do it. Help the individual maintain his self-esteem by involving him in the activities of daily living. Don't forget to consider what he can do for you.

Simplify Tasks. Break down complex tasks into simple steps. Give the mentally impaired person step-by-step instructions to help him or her complete an activity. For example, asking the confused person to "make a salad" might be too overwhelming a task. It is better to ask him to do one step at a time: tear the lettuce, rinse the lettuce off, and so forth. Tasks that were once easy may become increasingly difficult to perform. If the person becomes frustrated by a task or refuses to cooperate, reevaluate his abilities. Demonstrating each step or starting the motion may help. The individual with a dementing illness may have difficulty learning new things. Try to get old familiar items fixed, not replaced. The affected person might be able to operate the old washing machine but would be confused by a new one. Use repetition to help confusion.

Encourage Recognition. It is easier for the confused person to recognize objects and people than to recall them. It is better to say, "I am Jane, your wife," than to ask, "Who am I?" Affected elders will often forget the name and relationship of their caregiver but will recognize that person as the one who cares for them. Limit the demands for recalling facts, names, dates, and other information.

Build Self-Esteem. Self-esteem is an inner assurance of personal worth based on feelings of being valued, useful, and competent. Aging and dementia can threaten an individual's self-esteem. Help the confused person feel successful. Look for activities and situations that lift the spirit and help improve feelings of self-worth. Provide praise for *efforts* made and tasks accomplished. Express thanks for cooperation and patience.

- Ask for the affected elder's opinion and help to solve a problem. Ask the individual to teach you something she or he knows about.
- Look for face-saving ways out of embarassing situations.
- Don't point out mistakes. Don't confront the individual and make him acknowledge his memory loss.
- Allow opportunities for choice as much as possible. When this is not possible, create the illusion of choice. Ask permission for the smallest of things and wait for a response. Knock and wait to be invited in before entering a room.

SUGGESTED APPROACHES

Identify Precipitants. Prevention is the most effective approach for reducing problems. Look for precipitants to problem behaviors and find ways to avoid them. Try keeping a record to identify precipitants and observe the time of day the problem occurs. Some possible precipitants are:

- Changes in routine, the environment, or medications
- Illness
- Fatigue
- Boredom, restlessness
- Overstimulation, noise, activity
- Rushed or tense caregiver

Reassess. When new problems arise, reassess the person's physical and mental status. Often changes in behavior may signal a change in physical health. To correct even minor medical problems is important because this can improve the person's functioning.

Reconsider. Is this behavior dangerous to the individual or to others? Is it really a problem or appropriate under the circumstances? If not, it might be easier to let it continue. This might require the caregiver to examine his or her feelings and change attitudes.

Rechannel. Find a way for the behavior to continue in a less disruptive way. Instead of confining a confused person to a geri-chair to prevent wandering, provide a safe area for wandering. Channel the person's restlessness into a constructive or repetitive physical activity.

Divert. Most memory-impaired persons are easily distracted. Distract the individual from whatever is upsetting him or her. Focus on something new, suggest a walk, something to eat or go look at something new to help him forget. Use his memory loss to your advantage. After awhile, the confused person will forget what was upsetting him. Physically stick to the person, either by holding or walking beside him to gently redirect him.

Ignore. It is more effective to ignore a behavior you want stopped than to react to it. Don't argue or respond in any way. Everyone has to ignore the behavior for this to be effective. Select one specific behavior you would like to change and work on it.

Reassure. Frequently and gently remind the individual that you know what is happening and you understand how he feels. Reassure him that you will be there to help him if he needs it. Help him to deal with his fears and anxieties. It is a terrible feeling to feel out of control.

Try Again Later. If the person is resistant, temporarily give up. Allow time to pass and try again or go back to the beginning of a familiar sequence. Remember: What works well one time may not work the next but may work later.

MANAGEMENT TECHNIQUES FOR SPECIFIC PROBLEMS

Aggression

The memory-impaired person who feels out of control may strike out at others.

- Be calm and reassuring. Speak softly.
- Avoid sudden moves.
- Don't try to reason with the person.
- Try to express some understanding; for example, "I know how angry you must feel."
- Get out of the way or stay out of striking distance. Step back and allow the individual personal space.
- Never strike the person back. Caregivers who strike back need professional help immediately.
- Get professional help if there is danger of physical violence or if aggressive incidents increase. You need to protect yourself.
- If a loved one does not recognize you and attacks you repeatedly, placement should be considered.

Anxiety

A person who feels insecure and is forgetful may become anxious or upset. Try to identify what is making the confused person anxious: loud noises, too much activity, being asked to do something the individual is afraid he or she can't do, or perceptual difficulties.

- Try to calm him. Stay calm and try to inspire confidence.
- Take him to a quiet area.
- Help him regain a sense of control. Assure him you are in control and will be there to help him.

- Reassure him that you understand how he feels.
- Divert his attention with a calming activity: read poetry, talk quietly, or read a magazine together.

Catastrophic Reactions

I took her to our older sister's apartment while I was otherwise occupied. Not long afterward, I had a call from my sister to come and get her because she was tearing up the place trying to get out. She seemed more disturbed that day than at any other time during her illness . . . I think she was frightened, but of what and why I had no way of knowing. This eventually happened with both our other sisters, so that leaving her other than in our own apartment was no longer an option.

A confused person may become excessively upset and experience rapidly changing moods over what appears to be a minor incident or request. She or he may cry, become angry, combative, tense, restless or agitated, and generally overreact to a situation. Accept that these are responses the individual cannot help.

- Learn what precipitates a catastrophic reaction and prevent the circumstances that lead to it. Strange situations; feeling lost; small accidents; crowds; being rushed, scolded, or argued with or asked several questions at once; illness; or feelings of frustration can all precipitate a catastrophic reaction.
- Recognize that a catastrophic reaction is caused by the disease. The individual is not behaving in this way to get back at you or attack you.
- Respond in a calm, reassuring voice.
- Don't argue or try to reason with the person. Try not to show your anger.
- Limit decision making if this causes frustration.
- Use a gentle touch but don't restrain, as this can cause panic.
- Remove the person to a quiet place in a calm, unhurried way.
- To calm, rock, hold hands, or pat. Reassure the person that you understand how he feels.
- Gradually distract the person with something new. The incident will be forgotten.
- Simplify a task, a request, and the environment.
- Ignore the behavior and leave the person alone if there is no risk of injury.
- Leave or call for help if your safety is in jeopardy.
- Seek professional help to reduce the occurrence of future episodes.

Clinging

Caregivers are often angered and frustrated by a person who clings to their every move. Every time they turn around, the person is there. Even in familiar places, the confused person feels lost and insecure. This causes the desire to stay close. He or she forgets where you are, when you'll be back, and how long you've been gone.

- Touch him and provide affection to assure him that he is loved and wanted.
- Give him a simple task such as sorting objects or winding a ball of yarn to keep him occupied.
- If he becomes too anxious, bring in a companion or neighbor to stay with him so that you can get away.
- When you leave, say goodbye and remind him that you will return. Put your coat on elsewhere. Write a note telling him when you will be back. Call him while you are gone to reassure him.

False Ideas, Suspiciousness, Insults, and Complaints

Persons who are insecure and are trying to cover up memory loss may blame others for their mistakes or accuse them of stealing when an item is mislaid. They may have little insight into their own problems. Because the ability to reason is impaired, they lack the ability to make sense out of the environment and may become suspicious of other people.

The confused individual may insist a spouse or child is not that person. She or he may not recognize people or things. He may forget that someone he once knew is dead; the memory is stronger than the death. He may not realize he is in his own home. Help him to focus in on one familiar detail: "This is your house. Here is your chair."

The individual with a dementing illness may lose the ability to be tactful and may make inappropriate and insulting remarks. He may not be upset with you but with a situation that he can't control. Understand that it is the dementia that is affecting his behavior and that he is responding to overwhelming feelings of loss and confusion.

- Avoid contradicting or arguing with the individual. Don't play along. Attempts to reason with him or her will not succeed.
- Reassure the person. Respond sympathetically to the feeling being expressed.
- Don't tell him he is hurting your feelings. Don't start a fight.

- Ignore insulting or accusing remarks. They may stop if you don't pay attention to them.
- Explain the problem to others so that they understand and are not insulted by the person's remarks.

Hallucinations and Delusions

Persons with a dementing illness may see, hear, taste, or smell things that are not there (hallucination). They are very real to the person. They may be worse if the person has visual or hearing impairments and they may occur more often at night.

A confused person may also hold fixed or persistent untrue beliefs (delusion). He might believe that someone is going to hurt him or that his wife is an imposter. These can be disturbing and cause fear and anxiety.

- Respond calmly to what the person is feeling. These experiences or beliefs are real to her or him.
- Determine if the delusions or hallucinations bother the person. If they don't upset him, let him be.
- Don't contradict, deny, confront, argue, or try to reason with the person, but don't agree with what he says either. Hallucinations and delusions can't be stopped because they are unreal to you.
- Don't play along or agree with the hallucination. Respond to the feeling: "I can't see the man, but I know he must be scaring you."
- Reassure him and stay with him until he calms down.
- Make sure there is no basis for the hallucination. He may be misinterpreting something he has seen. Glare, shadows, and lights may look like something else to him. One person thought the cemetery headstones outside his window were ghosts when the moon shone on them.
- Consult a physician if the hallucinations or delusions persist.

Inappropriate Sexual Behavior

Inappropriate sexual behavior in people with a dementing illness is *uncommon*. The mentally impaired person may become less modest or engage in inappropriate behavior that appears to be sexual but is actually unrelated to sex. Accidental exposure and masturbation do occasionally occur.

- Handle the problem quietly. Don't overreact. Don't yell at the person or try to reason with him or her.

- Confused persons may fidget with their clothes suggestively: unbuttoning a blouse, unzipping a zipper, loosening a belt, or pulling up a dress. This may be an indication the individual has to go to the bathroom. Change the type of clothes worn; for example, avoid shirts and blouses with buttons if the confused person likes to play with the buttons. Give him something else to occupy his hands. Pin or secure the top to the pants to prevent the individual from disrobing when in public.
- If the individual is masturbating, lead him to a private area. He may have forgotten this behavior is inappropriate in public.
- Discuss upsetting sexual behavior and changing sexual habits with the doctor.
- A confused person may not know how to respond to the sexual advances of another person. The caregiver will have to intercede to protect the individual.

Losing and Hiding Things

It is very common for the confused person to hide and lose things. This is very frustrating to her or him. He won't remember where he put it, so it doesn't help to ask.

- Keep valuables locked up or out of sight.
- Establish a place where things are kept. Organize belongings so that everything is in one place. Label items.
- Learn hiding places. Limit the number of hiding places.
- Check wastebaskets before they are emptied.
- Reassure the individual that you will help him find what is lost. Help him look for misplaced items.
- Don't expect the person to return things to their usual place.
- If the individual takes the mail and hides or throws it away, get a post office box or have mail delivered to another address.

Loss of Sense of Time

A dementing illness may affect the internal clock that regulates daily routines and keeps one on a regular schedule. The person with a memory impairment loses the ability to judge the passage of time. He or she has no way to measure how much time has passed. The confused person may lose the ability to read and understand a clock. He may be able to read the time but the information is meaningless to him. This may cause a general feeling of anxiety.

- Use a timer or hourglass to help the memory-impaired person judge the passage of time.
- Use memory aids such as a large-print clock, activity schedule, or calendars.
- Orient the individual to time during the daily routine: "It's noon. Time for lunch."
- Make sure the physical surroundings help reflect the time of day. Closed blinds and dark, heavy curtains make rooms darker and give the illusion that it is night.
- Use reassurance. Let the person know you'll help him get where he has to go on time or take his medication on schedule.

Perseveration

A person with a dementing illness may engage in perseverative behavior: continuously repeating a word, phrase, or movement.

Repetitive Questions. A confused person may ask the same question over and over again. This can be very irritating, but she or he cannot remember asking the question. The repetition may be a way of expressing generalized concern or of indicating that something is bothering the person. Someone who can no longer make sense out of his environment feels anxious and insecure. Try different approaches to see what works best.

- Look for clues as to what the concern really is and try to reassure the individual. A person who keeps asking what time he goes home may need to be reassured that you will make sure that he gets home.
- Write down the answer to the repeated question and then ask the questioner to answer it.
- Ignore the question to try to get the person to stop asking it.

Repetitive Actions. The memory-impaired person may also get stuck in an activity such as pacing, packing and unpacking, or constantly rearranging cupboards.

- Suggest a new task but don't pressure him or her to stop. Use touch and nonverbal communication to get the message across.
- Use distraction: Give him something else to do. Give him something to fiddle with or provide another outlet for the repetitive behavior. Provide a drawer to rummage through and lock the other ones. If he likes to take things apart, give him something he

can work on that is similar to past interests or work (give a plumber piping).

- Learn to accept the behavior and ignore it if it is harmless.

Sundowner's Syndrome

Individuals with a dementing illness may become more confused, restless, and disoriented late in the day and after dark. This condition, called sundowner's syndrome, may worsen after a move or change in routine. No one is sure of its etiology.

- Look for reasons for the behavior. If it occurs after a trip or event, that activity will have to be stopped or slowed down. The individual may no longer be able to cope with that activity.
- Make the evening easier. Plan activities the person resists or finds difficult to perform earlier in the day.
- Plan an early afternoon nap if the individual becomes too tired in the evening and becomes agitated or wants to go to bed early.
- Reduce noise, distractions, and the number of people and activities around her or him later in the day.
- Keep him active during the day so that he is too tired to be active during the night.
- Distract him and give him something to do if he becomes agitated. Don't try to restrain him.
- Keep the house well lit. Changes in the environment as darkness approaches are confusing to the mentally impaired person.

Wandering and Restlessness

Her behavior was unpredictable. It seemed every time my back turned on her she disappeared. Becoming accustomed to this need for watchfulness doesn't come easy or all at once. We drove to mass every morning, but several times before I was ready she took off and I would find her walking down the middle of the road . . . five minutes was about as long as she could wait anywhere.

A confused person may wander because he or she is bored, feels lost, is looking for something, is trying to go somewhere or do something, is tense, restless, or hungry, has to use the bathroom, or is in a strange environment.

- Look for reasons for the wandering behavior. Is there a pattern to it? Reduce the stressors that contribute to the need to wander.

- Provide a safe and appropriate environment for wandering. Create an environment that calms the person.
- Provide alternative activities to reduce boredom. Exercise, walking, and other physical activities will decrease the need to wander.
- Ask if he needs to use the bathroom and show him where it is. He may have forgotten where the bathroom is.
- Avoid crowded situations where the person gets confused or upset.
- In a new setting, reassure the individual about where he is and why and repeat the information as needed. Help him feel comfortable.

Driving with her was sometimes hazardous. She would open the car door while we were moving. It was a two-door, and I tried putting her in the back seat, but she tried to climb over the seat while the car was in motion. She played with the rear view mirror. A few times I was able to run into a shop, try to keep my eyes on her and make a quick purchase. I tried it once too often and found the car empty when I returned in a few minutes. After searching the neighborhood I went to the police station. Shortly afterward a drugstore across the street from where I had left her called the police concerning the odd behavior of a woman who was in the store.

- Never leave a confused person alone in a parked car. He may wander away or accidentally start up or move the car. Use seat belts and lock doors to prevent the person from opening the door of a moving car. Special locks may have to be installed to prevent him from opening the car door.
- Look for environmental cues. The presence of coats and shoes may give the mentally impaired the idea to leave. Hide shoes and coats. In an adult day care setting, a separate exit area is desirable so the remaining participants don't get departure anxiety when the others leave.
- Offer comfort and reassurance. Respond to the general feeling being expressed. Don't argue or try to reason with the individual. Provide one-on-one attention and supervision.
- Provide an immediate distraction: Serve a snack, look at pictures, ask the person to hold or do something. Direct him to an enjoyed activity.

We drove to town one day for lunch. I turned my back to pay the parking fee and she was gone. A friend who was with us and I searched the area, called the police and went home. I alerted friends in our old neighborhood to be on the lookout for her. Each time she was lost I had a horrible thought we would never find her again. I prayed. About six in the evening a friend called that she was at their house. She had alerted the paper boy, and when a car drove up the street with her in it he accompanied the driver to her home. The driver said he found her wandering around and when he offered to help her she gave him our old address.

- Make sure the confused person wears an identification bracelet with name, address, telephone number, and memory impairment on it. Have a current photo of the person available to give to the police in case he gets lost. Alert neighbors to the problem, tell them how to approach the person, and ask them to call you if they see him.
- To stop a wanderer, approach him slowly and calmly. Follow him and watch where he goes. Fall into step with him and walk with him a short distance. Reassure him. Gradually guide him back with you. Don't grab, physically force, or otherwise restrain him. Don't touch him if he becomes agitated.

Restraints. Restraints, chemical or physical, should only be used as a last resort and only with the doctor's permission. The physician can recommend the best type of restraint to use. If a restraint is absolutely necessary, it should be used for only short periods of time.

Families considering long-term care placement need to consider how the home or institution deals with restraints. Special Alzheimer units may provide increased supervision and optimum freedom and security to decrease or eliminate the need for restraints. Prolonged periods of physical restraint to chairs or beds have been found to cause mental changes, mental anguish, withdrawal, depression, physical disorders, and exacerbation of dementing behavior.

Driving

Giving up driving is very difficult for many people because it represents a loss of freedom, independence, and mobility. Caregivers have a responsibility to act when the confused person is no longer able to drive safely. Impaired judgment, the stress of dealing with the rules of the road, and lowered reaction time make the memory-impaired person a danger on the road. Motor vehicle insurance companies may not defend or pay a claim if the company was not informed of the dementing illness at the time of issuance or renewal of a policy.

- Involve the affected person in the decision, if possible.
- If necessary, take the car keys away and hide them.
- Get rid of the car.

- Make the car inoperable when not in use by removing the distributor cap. A service station attendant can show you how to do this.
- Assure the person that she or he will still be able to get around without the car. Let him know that you will make transportation arrangements.
- Ask the doctor to advise the State Department of Motor Vehicles why the person can no longer drive. The doctor can write out an order stating "no driving." This takes the burden off the family and puts it on the doctor.

Smoking/Drinking and Medications

If the confused person continues to smoke, he or she must be supervised because of the danger of fires. Cigarettes, lighters, and matches should be stored in a safe place. A memory-impaired person will eventually forget about smoking after a few difficult weeks of being without a cigarette. Use the memory impairment to your advantage to stop him from smoking. Try giving him an unlit cigarette.

An occasional drink is okay. Some older adults enjoy a glass of wine, or beer, or a cocktail as a way to relax. Check with the doctor, especially if the person is on medications. The caregiver should fix the drink, as the confused person may not be able to judge how much alcohol to add. Alcohol should be locked up, as it can be poisonous if excessively consumed.

The person with a dementing illness should be supervised when taking medications to prevent misuse. If the individual refuses to take the medications, try again later. Don't force him to take medicine against his will; this will only agitate him. Don't try to reason with him. Try crushing the medicine and putting it in soft food like applesauce or ice cream or in juice (unless medically contraindicated).

6

Care for the Caregiver

It troubled me when people would comment, "I don't know how you can stand it." All I could think of was how can she stand it?

Dementing illnesses affect the family as well as the patient. Families are often unprepared for the burden, stress, strain, and changes they experience. They often have a poor understanding of dementia. The caregiver may feel ill equipped to handle the responsibilities. Families become frustrated when the person continues to deteriorate despite their best efforts.

I was forever castigating myself for my own inadequacy. I had never had to provide personal care for anyone in my lifetime. She loved cooking and grocery shopping. I had no interest in either. I was pretty patient with her, but a real klutz at bathing, dressing and cooking, and there she was more than patient with me.

Most caregivers are spouses or adult children, supplemented by other family members. Adult-child caregivers are likely to have competing demands on their time: jobs, children, and spouse. They may feel guilty about ignoring their own family to care for their elderly parent and vice versa. The way the adult child interacts with his parent changes as the adult child takes on more of a caring role. Many adult children find this role reversal difficult to accept.

The round-the-clock care that is needed is one of the most signifi-cant strains on the family. Families often become isolated and feel abandoned by their friends and relatives. They may not get the support and understanding they need as it may be difficult for others to realize the extent of the problem or even its existence. Mental impairment is not obvious like a broken leg.

The caretaking role does not end when the elder is placed in a nursing home or other living arrangement. The elder continues to need the family's love and support. The caregiver still must spend time visiting at the new residence and managing the elder's financial and medical affairs. The feelings of relief from the burden of care may be mixed with feelings of doubt and guilt. Many caregivers find it difficult to relinquish the daily responsibility of caring for a loved one. It is painful to watch someone you love die slowly. The family's pain continues even after death.

THE EMOTIONS OF CAREGIVING

Caregivers experience many conflicting emotions that are normal and natural reactions to the responsibilities of caregiving. Following are some of the most common feelings expressed by caregivers:

Anger. Caregivers often feel angry at the constant demands, at the limitations put on their life-style, at friends and relatives who could do more, at God for what has happened, at people who give advice but don't help out, and at themselves for being out of con-trol. They may feel angry and resentful that someone else is depend-ing on them.

> There is a period when you become disappointed in friends. You are not certain just what you want from them or how you can use their help when they offer. Then you remember that you were not always so helpful with others in similar situations, not so much from not wanting to, but from a feeling of ineptness and inadequacy. She was good at stepping in and taking over, I was not. This is your problem and you have to work it out in the best way you can in the interest of both of you. Anger and resentment are self-destructive, and you need that least of all.

Guilt. Feelings of guilt are common among caregivers. Caregivers may feel guilty because of their wish to be relieved of the caregiving role, for their desire to return to their jobs, for placing or considering nursing home placement, for neglecting their family, for wishing the elder would die, for feeling ashamed of their loved one's behavior, for allowing themselves time off, and for having all these thoughts and feelings. Guilt can interfere with the caregiver's ability to make decisions that are in the elder's best interests.

Fear. Caregivers may fear that they will lose control and not be able to handle the situation. They may fear their own aging and loss of health and that they may be next in line. The caregiver may worry about the future and all of its uncertainties. The caregiver may worry about the cost of caring: of the nursing home, respite, and in-home care, of medications and medical care. The caregiver may be concerned about lost wages.

Frustration. Caregivers may experience frustration at the elder's refusal to help him- or herself, at irrational behavior, at the lack of assistance from others, and the feeling that no matter what is done, the elder will not get better.

Grief. Grief is experienced not just following the loss of a loved one. Caregivers may experience grief over the elder's declining physical and mental abilities, over the loss of companion or confidant, or over the way the elder and life used to be.

Loss. Caregivers may experience a sense of loss: of personal and living space, of freedom, of independence, of income or standard of living, and of privacy. The caregiver may feel pulled in different directions.

Pride and Satisfaction. Caregiving is hard work, but it can be rewarding, too. The most valuable care that an elderly person can receive is the love and support of the family. Many families enjoy caring for their loved one. It can be a very satisfying experience. Caregiving can help to strengthen family ties. Caregivers need to feel proud of what they are doing: It is very special.

SUGGESTIONS FOR FAMILY CAREGIVERS

Take Care of Yourself. The only way to be there for your relative is to be there for yourself. One of the best things you can do is take time off from your caregiving role. Accept the fact that you need or deserve time for yourself. Do things to lift your spirit and maintain your perspective on life. Keep up your personal appearance. Schedule time for yourself, and regularly find ways to get away from your caregiving responsibilities.

A healthy body helps you to cope with stress and the demands of caregiving. See your physician for regular checkups. Eat a well-balanced diet in a relaxed atmosphere. Exercise regularly to control weight and maintain a healthy body. Participate with your elder in an exercise or walking program. Make sure you get the rest and sleep that you need. A certain amount of uninterrupted sleep is needed to maintain physical and mental equilibrium.

Make relaxation part of your daily routine. Use relaxation techniques such as massage, meditation, deep breathing, or soaking in a tub. Try to maintain a sense of humor. Humor works well to alleviate stress. Tell jokes or watch a comedy. Laugh at the funny aspects of caregiving. Laugh at yourself and laugh together.

Maintain social contacts and meaningful relationships. Do something you enjoy with a friend. Continue to participate in hobbies and organizations. Stay in touch with family and friends: call, write, or visit. Plan an occasional night or weekend away. Leisure time helps to improve morale.

Get Help When It Is Needed. Set limits on what you can do. Don't let feelings of guilt cause you to rearrange your entire life around your elder. It is not possible to do everything alone.

Accept help when it is offered. Let others know when you need help; don't expect them to know this. Tell them what kind of help you need. People will help if you tell them what to do. Realize that some people will help more than others. Show your appreciation for the help they give and stress its importance to you.

Take advantage of the many available sources of assistance. Know where to go for help in your community. Join a support group or seek advice from a counselor. Contact the Alzheimer's Association (ADRDA) for sources of help and information. Hire someone to help you if necessary.

Find someone to listen: a confidante. A confidante can help you put your situation into perspective and explore new solutions to problems. Many caregivers find comfort in talking with their clergy.

Pace Yourself. Set reasonable expectations for yourself. Let go of what you can. Unrealistic expectations compound problems by increasing anxiety and agitation in the care receiver and the caregiver. Talk to the person you care for about what you can and cannot do. Think about your priorities. Ask yourself, "Does it have to be done?" What can you do to simplify your life? Decide what activities are the most important and say no to the others.

Focus on one problem at a time or on small parts of a larger problem. Determine what is bothering you and do something constructive about it. Don't try and solve all your big problems. Take one day at a time, tackling each problem as it arises.

> It was at this time that I had to come to grips with my own anger and my faith. I had leaned on my faith all my life, and it had worked out well for me. This cruel thing that had happened to her was beyond my comprehension and belief and my faith was shaken. The situation was hopeless, it could only grow worse. The idea of suicide and murder that would appear to be an accident crossed my mind. Such a choice was unacceptable to me. There had to be a reason for all the suffering in the world which she and I were sharing. I did not understand it, but could accept it based on faith. As I examined it, our problem seemed relatively minor in comparison with the enormous problems throughout the world. We could handle it on a day by day basis with whatever resources we could make available.

Discuss Your Feelings. Don't keep everything inside: Talk about your feelings and concerns with others. Most caregivers will sometimes feel angry, tired, helpless, resentful, guilty, embarassed, or frustrated. Understand and accept the feelings you have as normal, natural responses. Feelings are not deeds.

Learn whether your actions come out of a sincere desire to help or are motivated by feelings of obligation. Don't be a martyr. Not every caregiver loves or likes the person they are caring for. Professional help may be needed to help resolve negative feelings and family conflicts. Caregiving is more difficult if the caregiver is forced to care for the personal care needs of someone he or she doesn't like.

Try keeping a journal. Listen or participate in radio or TV call-in programs. Write a letter to the person you are caring for with the intention of tearing it up. Get your feelings out in the open.

Communicate Openly. Be honest and direct. Poor communication is the root of a lot of stress in families. Listen and show your care and concern.

Involve everyone concerned in your decision making. Plan a family conference and let everyone have an opportunity to give opinions. Seek professional guidance if a rational discussion is not possible. Young children have been found to be very supportive and resourceful when allowed to be part of the problem solving. They need to be involved in what is happening to someone they love. Unrelated caregivers should also be given an opportunity to express their opinions and concerns. If possible, involve the elder in any decisions that are made. Ask for his opinion. Shared decisions produce the best results.

Don't make promises. Never promise the person you care for that you won't put her or him in a nursing home. Promises can prevent you from making realistic plans for the future.

Don't be Embarassed. Alzheimer's disease and other dementing illnesses are just that: medical conditions. It is disease that causes your elder to behave the way he or she does, not because he wants to. Explain this to others. People need to know; it will help them understand the confused person's behavior and the stress you are under.

Understand Your Responsibilities. Know what to expect and be aware of what is involved. Education about dementia and aging will help you and your family understand and accept the older adult and set realistic expectations. This will result in the elder receiving better care and help you to maintain patience and understanding.

> I regretted that I did not know what was happening to her in the early days of her illness. I might have been more patient and understanding of her behavior. I was always too fond of her and too protective of her feelings to ever be more than momentarily angry with her, but I might have been able to ease the anguish and fears that most surely had overwhelmed her at times.

Plan for the Future. Hope for the best but plan for the worst. Early planning is important. Begin making legal and financial plans early when the elder can still participate in the decision making. Know what the implications are of each decision you make. Don't wait too long to institute services such as home health care, respite care, or adult day care. The confused person will accept such services more readily if they are started early in the illness.

Avoid making decisions in a crisis. Planning and working with your doctor, elder, friends, and others will help you make well-informed decisions. Consider under what conditions nursing home placement would be necessary. Look into long-term care facilities, even if the elder doesn't need them now. There may come a time when institutionalization is necessary, when it is more harmful to maintain the elder at home than it is beneficial.

WORKING WITH THE MENTALLY IMPAIRED: HOW TO PREVENT BURNOUT

What You Can Do to Help Your Staff

- Let prospective employees know about the emotional demands of the job so that their expectations are in line with reality. A realistic job preview will help prevent the new employee from being frustrated and disillusioned with the job.

- Provide adequate information, education, training, and access to resources. Lack of knowledge contributes to staff tension and inferior quality of care. Provide information on burnout and coping strategies.
- Provide support groups for staff. Plan regular staff meetings to explore feelings but not as gripe sessions. Encourage communication among the staff. Provide the staff with an opportunity to get things off their chest. Humor helps to reduce stress; laugh together.
- Provide a system of rewards and recognition to boost morale. Provide positive feedback to each other.

What You Can Do to Help Yourself

- Arrange to take intermittent breaks or rest periods. Rest, take a short walk, or practice relaxation techniques. Know what to do to relax yourself. Create your own breaks and diversions to make the work pleasant. Find a quiet hideout when you need to "take five." Let someone else take over your responsibility while you do some less stressful work.
- Get help from others. Have one person you can talk to about your experiences. Get together with your co-workers and colleagues for support and encouragement. Others can give you a new perspective on the problem by helping you look at it in new ways.
- Do the same things differently. Vary your work routine to get out of a rut and feel in control. Change your home routine if your work routine is dull. The person with a dementing illness likes a predictable environment; you may not.
- Ask for help when you feel stressed. When the person you are caring for gets to you, hand him off to someone else. Give each other relief. Share the more difficult tasks and take turns doing the most unpleasant work.
- Be sensitive to your feelings. Know what you are feeling and why. Pay attention to your own needs. Identify what gives you the most stress. Keep a log of the time of day, source, and cause of stress.
- Don't take things personally. Don't take your work home and relive it. Leave your work at work.
- Accentuate the positive. Find something to feel good about. Focus

on one good thing that happens in the day. Identify the positive aspects of your work: what is good, pleasant, and satisfying.

- Ask for feedback from the confused person. The individual may not remember to thank you or show appreciation for what you have done. Actively seek out feedback rather than waiting for it and feeling bad when you don't get it. Ask the person, "Did you enjoy this activity?" "Do you feel better now?" or something similar.

SUPPORT GROUPS

Support groups help bring people together who share a common problem. Support groups can decrease the sense of loneliness and isolation many caregivers experience. They no longer have to feel so alone. Support groups can help the caregiver better understand and manage his or her life situation so that the relationship between the elder and the caregiver can be improved.

A support group can be educational, providing the caregivers with practical information and assistance to help them better understand the needs and problems of the older adult with a dementing illness. Accurate information about dementia and aging can help the caregivers plan and prepare for the future. Support group members have access to literature and speakers on a variety of topics related to caregiving and dementia. Caregivers can learn what community resources are available.

Support groups provide fellowship and a supportive, caring network for caregivers. Support groups help the caregivers identify and understand their feelings and accept the limits of responsibility of caring for another person. Caregivers can obtain peer support for their caregiving roles from others who share similar experiences. Support groups provide caregivers with a forum to deal with a strongly felt need or problem. When problems are shared with others, they can be viewed more objectively and managed more effectively.

Support groups provide its members with an opportunity to share information, ideas, and the frustrations and fears of caring for a loved one with a dementing illness. Caregivers can share practical caregiving techniques that have proved successful. Group members can provide one another with first-hand consumer information about the quality of community services. Caregivers may gain a sense of satisfaction and strength when they are given the opportunity to help others solve their problems.

WHAT FAMILY AND FRIENDS CAN DO TO HELP THE CAREGIVER

- Listen. This may be the single most important thing you can do for the caregiver. Give the caregiver an opportunity to ventilate concerns.
- Don't tell families that it is all right when their world is falling apart; it invalidates their feelings.
- Provide support, encouragement, and reassurance. Tell the caregiver that she or he is doing a good job.
- Continue to call and visit the family and invite them out. Help the family to stay active and involved.
- Offer your help. Ask what you can do. Be specific about what you will do.

The chapters in Part I have given a framework for care of mentally impaired elders. It is within that framework that the activities presented in Part II are best utilized and most life enhancing.

Part II
Activities

OBJECTIVES

Upon completing Part II you should be able to:

1. Identify the desirable components of an activity program for the elderly.
2. Identify strategies to implement activities.
3. Describe ways to assess an individual's interests and abilities.
4. Explain the benefits of a group activity.
5. Describe how a group activity should be planned and implemented.
6. Describe the leader's role in group activities.
7. Define remotivation and describe its five basic steps.
8. Explain the benefits of reminiscence for the elderly.
9. Explain the importance of sensory stimulation and describe the materials and activities that can be used to stimulate the senses.
10. Describe the benefits of music to an activity program for the mentally impaired elderly.
11. Explain the benefits of exercise and physical activity for the mentally impaired elderly.

12. Identify the precautions that should be taken when developing an exercise program.
13. Describe how to introduce and modify games so that a confused person can participate in them.
14. Identify and describe the strategies and precautions to be taken when implementing an arts and crafts activity.
15. Describe the benefits of a horticulture program.
16. Describe the benefits of an intergenerational program and identify how it should be implemented.
17. Describe the benefits of pet therapy and identify how pets can be incorporated into an activity program.
18. Explain the importance of religion as a component of an activity program.
19. Describe an ideal schedule for a daily activity program for the mentally impaired elder at home and in a community setting.

7

How to Stimulate the "I Can" Response

Losing interest in life is not a part of growing old. Recreational and social activities are an essential part of an individual's physical, social, and mental well-being. Meaningful activities can help enrich the individual's quality of life.

Older adults with a dementing illness lack the ability to initiate activities on their own. They need help to make creative and satisfying use of their leisure time—something they have a lot of. Confused persons are capable of enjoying life, laughter, and developing new friendships. An important part of living with a dementing illness is keeping active, having fun, and socializing with others. Confused persons can be helped to feel their lives are of value when they have the desire and the opportunity to use their remaining skills.

An activity program designed for the older adult with a dementing illness has many benefits. Studies have indicated that when individuals participate in a regular program of activities, their self-esteem increases and depression decreases. Involvement in a program of activities helps to promote a sense of productivity and independence and provides meaning to life. An activity program provides an outlet for releasing tension and reducing boredom. It can help to maintain or stimulate interests and provide an opportunity for self-expression and creativity. It can help the individual to retain or develop new skills or abilities.

A group program provides the individual with the opportunity to socialize with others. Persons with a dementing illness can still make friends, most likely among those with similar impairments. They need the opportunity to do so.

DESIRABLE ACTIVITIES

- Activities that help *restore old roles*—that are familiar and meaningful.
- Activities that are *adult*—that are appealing, interesting, and similar to those the individual has done as an adult.
- Activities that give people pleasure, make them happy, and are *enjoyable.*
- Activities that promote *dignity.*
- Activities that *take advantage of retained skills* will help build the confused person's confidence. The best activities for the confused older adult are those that do not require fine motor skills, verbal or math skills, or extensive use of reasoning and memory. Physical activities are preferable to mental.
- Activities that are *meaningful*—that have a purpose, or provide a way to be helpful (care for plants, set the table).
- Activities that help promote the older adult's *independence.*
- Activities that incorporate the confused person's need for *structure and repetition.*
- Activities that promote the development and maintenance of *self-esteem* and provide recognition from others.
- Activities that *stimulate interest and awareness* in the environment.
- Activities that provide an opportunity for older adults to *share their knowledge and experiences.*
- Activities that provide an opportunity to *socialize* with peers.
- Activities that meet a *variety* of needs and interests. An activity program should include the following kinds of activities:

Physical	Competitive
Mental/intellectually stimulating	Spiritual
Individual	Social
Small group	Personal care/beautification
Service to others	Health maintenance
Cultural	Sensory
Creative	Intergenerational
Entertaining	Activities with pets

SUGGESTIONS FOR IMPLEMENTING ACTIVITIES

• *Keep the activity relatively easy and failure free.* Plan activities that will result in success. Less complicated activities that build on old skills and provide immediate gratification are the most successful. Be patient. Activities take time to complete. The confused person works at a slower pace.

• *Take a break between activities.* Encourage conversation during these times. Take the opportunity to serve water or other fluids to help prevent dehydration.

• *Simplify each activity—break it down into its simplest parts.* Give instructions one step at a time. Bring out only the items needed for each step—don't put everything out at once. Keep the activity short. Don't expect anyone to sit for long periods of time. Stop before interest lags.

• *Demonstrate what is to be done.* Show what the completed project will look like.

• *Repeat successful activities often.* Repetition offers reassurance to confused persons and helps them learn.

• *Be consistent.* Do the activities the same way at the same time each day.

• *Match the activity to the individual's abilities.* As the severity of the dementia increases, use more sensory stimulation, music, and physical activities. Shorten the activities and increase the attention given to each participant to accommodate shortened attention spans. One-step, very repetitive activities are best for very confused persons. Sometimes all you can realistically expect is for the very confused individual to actively watch what you are doing.

• *Adapt the activity to the individual's or the group's needs.* Stay away from rigid rules and regulations. Adjust the activity to accommodate the participants' moods and abilities and different situations. Develop new techniques so that everyone can participate. Substitute slower movements for faster ones (walking instead of running). Substitute different body positions (sitting instead of standing). Substitute lighter equipment (nerf balls, bean bags) or modify equipment to increase the impaired person's ability to participate. Learn to "go with" the individual or group—follow their lead. Schedule difficult activities requiring more concentration earlier in the day.

• *Offer a minimum of help.* Let the individual do the activity him- or herself. Help make it possible for the affected elder to complete the project independently by providing support, guidance, and assistance where needed. Activities are best when done in small groups.

• *Be positive in your expectations.* Acknowledge the individual's abilities by asking for help. Recognize that each individual has a lot to give and make it possible for her or him to do so.

• *Provide a lot of praise and compliment efforts made.* Reassure the confused person often. Use touch to convey your support, encouragement, and pleasure. When an activity sparks a memory, an interest, or an effort, provide a lot of praise and encouragement. Success can create a generally positive mood. The activity may be quickly forgotten, but the good feeling remains.

• *Plan the daily activities around a specific theme.* All of the activities can incorporate the theme. For example, if apples are the theme, apple pies can be baked, apple stencils can be made, and a poem about apples can be read.

• *Provide a calm, supportive environment.* Limit the other things in a room that the confused person can get distracted by. Noise, crowds, and lots of confusion can be upsetting.

• *Anticipate areas of resistance or difficulty.* Don't force participation if the person is resistant or upset. Provide the opportunity, encouragement, and incentives. *Be prepared* for the activity in advance. Provide individual assistance where needed to avoid the participants' becoming confused or frustrated.

• *Provide nonthreatening activities.* Don't ask people to do activities that are beyond their abilities. Never ask a person who once excelled in a specific craft or area to do it or a simplified version of the same thing. Many recognize their loss of skills and this can be very threatening to them. Find a related activity. The concert violinist may not be able to play the violin but may enjoy listening to classical music.

• *Ask for the individual's or group's advice and input when planning activities.* Offer them the opportunity to make some choices about the activities. Let them know that their opinion matters to you.

• *Be flexible and creative in devising activities.* Sometimes a person will enjoy an activity one day and be disinterested or unable to do it the next. Abilities can fluctuate from day to day and hour to hour. Offer a choice of activities.

HOW TO ASSESS INTERESTS AND ABILITIES

Current and past interests of the mentally-impaired adult must be taken into consideration when planning activities. It is important to have a clear understanding of the person's strengths and weaknesses and to identify needs and problems. Each individual is unique and a successful activity program must respond to individual differences. It is important to select activities that the individual enjoys doing and is able to do successfully. Boredom is a major concern to families caring for an elder with a dementing illness. Caregivers often describe the confused person as being incapable of and uninterested in doing anything. They need help to find activities of interest and ways to motivate and enable the confused person to stay active. A good physical and mental evaluation, an occupational or physical therapy evaluation, time, and trial and error can all help assess individual abilities and interests.

Each individual assessment should look at:

1. *What the individual does now:* habits, life-style, cultural and religious preferences, activities of daily living—obtained from the individual, caregivers, and observation.
2. *Past interests, hobbies, jobs, and roles.* While past interests may not be indicative of current interests, they do provide clues about the individual's past and likes and dislikes.
3. *What the individual thinks he or she can do now.*
4. *What the individual wants to do:* current interests.
5. *What the individual can do:* the ability to perform tasks. Performance testing can provide an appraisal of abilities and limitations.
6. *Factors that help or hinder performance:* health problems, vision and hearing impairments, mobility, the environment, social skills, the ability to communicate, motivation, and mental status.

Attitudes

Our attitudes—the attitudes of those working with the elderly—will have a strong influence on the older persons's own attitudes and their ability to adjust to change and loss. If we convey an attitude of expectancy, the elderly will come to expect more of themselves. There is evidence that the attitudes of professionals working with the elderly—nurses, social workers, clinicians, therapists, and others— are often negative. Pessimistic attitudes, lack of knowledge, lack of sensitivity, and fears of aging can cause neglect and inferior quantity and quality of care. If we are pessimistic about what we can do for the elderly person with a dementing illness, then we will be less likely to involve that person in activities and health, social, and rehabilitative services that would enhance functional capacities. Our attitudes toward aging can negatively affect how we treat older people in general. When persons are both old and confused, they are even more likely to be victims of discrimination, neglected and possibly treated as invalids.

A positive view of aging contributes to the maintenance of good health. Dementia is not a reason to discontinue interest and enjoyment in life. A positive outlook fosters increased efforts to maintain independence, activity, and good physical health during the later years of life, even in the presence of a dementing illness.

As caregivers we need to develop a positive attitude toward the elderly in our care. Our challenge is to create a warm, supportive environment that emphasizes strengths and minimizes weaknesses. We must examine our own feelings and attitudes toward aging and dementia and understand how we convey these to the elderly persons we care for.

The very fact that a person lives to an old age illustrates that he has many physical and emotional strengths. We can become so preoccupied with an impaired person's illnesses and problems that we fail to see the strengths. By focusing on strengths and conveying a positive image of aging, we can help the individual successfully adjust to loss of memory. With some thought and imagination, we can enhance the affected person's quality of life by helping the individual to be an active, contributing member of the family or group.

8

Fun With Groups: Discussion Groups and Other Group Activities

The older adult with a dementing illness is capable of developing new friendships and just needs the opportunity. A group activity program is the ideal place to meet new friends and enjoy the companionship of other older adults. Group activities can counteract feelings of boredom and loneliness by providing meaningful adult interaction.

A group provides the older adult with a feeling of belonging. Acceptance by one's peers contributes to increased self-esteem. A group program that provides successful experiences can motivate, increase socialization, preserve sensory capacities, and enhance the individual's quality of life. Belonging to a group increases the self-confidence of its members. Group members can provide encouragement and support to one another and recognition to individuals.

GROUP GUIDELINES

• A group activity can become an anticipated event if held on the same day and at the same time and place. Even the seating arrangements should be consistent. Sit in a circle or around a table. The leader should sit beside the most confused, hard of hearing, or anxious members. The placement of participants should be determined by their ability to hear and see well.

• The meeting should be relatively short in duration, approximately 30 minutes. Groups should be planned at a time of day when the participants are the most cooperative. The meeting should end before the group gets tired or runs out of things to say.

• The group members should have some verbal skills, the ability to concentrate for at least 20 minutes, and the ability to function appropriately in a group. A variety of personalities and a balance of talkative and quiet members will make the group work easier. Very disturbed, agitated, and restless persons should be excluded. Small groups of six to eight participants seem to work best. Whenever possible, it is important to have a balance of males and females. A coed group helps to affirm the importance of sexuality in our interactions throughout life. Individuals should be invited to join the group and be given a choice as to whether they want to be included in the group; however, they may need encouragement to participate.

• The leader and the participants should wear large, easy-to-read name tags. Use the member's names profusely to help keep the group oriented. Each member should be welcomed on arrival and thanked for coming.

• The physical environment is important. A supportive, accepting, relaxed atmosphere is necessary for the group to work well together. The setting should be pleasant, comfortable, well lit, and free of distractions. There should be no forced adherence to routines.

• Use props to facilitate discussions, create interest, and stimulate the senses. Props can be used as a trigger device to guide the group to the topic. Posters, pictures, souvenirs, a collection, displays, demonstrations, music, and food can all be used to maintain the members' attention. Some light exercises prior to the beginning of the group session can increase verbal responsiveness and attention span.

• Serve refreshments. Food and beverages provide an element of surprise and nourishment and help keep the older adult hydrated. Refreshments can be the theme or part of it.

The Leader

The leader helps the group to stay on track and guides the group to an understanding of the topic. Two leaders may be needed for a larger group.

• Learn something about the topic, give basic information, be prepared to ask intelligent questions, and have everything ready in
advance. Choose topics, activities, and conversations that will evoke
memories. Be flexible. It is helpful to have several ideas in reserve in
case the topic doesn't work out.

• Use simple, concrete, and familiar words, short sentences, and
props to get the point across. A slow pace is necessary. Maintain the
conversation flow by making conversational transitions, reflecting
and amplifying what the participants say and summarizing what has
been discussed. Be sensitive to each person's verbal and nonverbal
responses, reactions, and needs. Respond to the feelings being expressed. The participant's comments should not be judged or evaluated. Ask open-ended questions to avoid yes-no responses.

• Help each member feel a part of the group by facilitating interactions and giving each member an opportunity to participate.
The members should be introduced to each other. Participation
should be encouraged, praised, and rewarded. No one should ever be
put on the spot. Change the subject or divert attention to someone
else.

• If a participant becomes restless, try to involve the individual by
calling his or her name or asking a question. Try distracting him or
asking for his help. Reassure him.

• The participants should be given every opportunity to make
decisions or give suggestions. Giving the group members a role to
play can enhance self-esteem. Group roles can include hostess, server,
clean-up person, or leader's assistant.

• Use touch and eye contact to show interest and affection. Keep a
low profile, but share things about yourself with the group.

• If a group member begins to ramble on, help to refocus thoughts.
Pick out the essence of what the participant is trying to say. Rephrase
a confusing statement or talk about the feeling being expressed, such
as, "John seems to be feeling sad." This will help support the person
and keep the others from becoming confused or losing interest.

DISCUSSION GROUPS

Almost anything can be the focus of a discussion group. Have the
members of the group suggest a topic for the next meeting. The leader
and the group can prepare for the topic in advance. Research the
history of the topic or person. Select pictures, smells, music, movies,
books, stories, poems, and food related to the topic. Plan a perfor-

mance and make decorations around the chosen theme. After each reading or display, encourage the participants to share their experiences and reminisce. Let the participants touch the objects and look at pictures. Choose objects that are familiar.

Plan a discussion around another planned activity. For example, if you are planning a field trip to the circus, plan a discussion and program around a circus theme. Mount circus posters on the walls and show a film on the circus. Cut out pictures or borrow books and brochures on the circus. Play calliope music and invite a clown to attend. Read a poem or short story about the circus. Serve peanuts, popcorn, hot dogs, cotton candy, lemonade, or other circus foods. Talk about the history of the circus. Ask the participants to share their experiences at the circus. Ask questions about their favorite acts and circus performers.

Discussion Topics

Aging	Holidays
Amusement parks	Hometown
Animals	Moving pictures
Babies	Pets
Cars	Picnics
Celebrations	Radio
Churches	Schools
Circus	Seasons
Country fairs	Slogans
Current events	Sports
Farm life	Superstitions
Fashions/fashion quiz	Traditions
Food	TV
Friends	Vacations
Good old days	Work
Hobbies	Zoos

A number of books are available that have developed some of the topics listed above. They provide resources and suggestions for books, music, films, and discussion questions related to the topic. The following are brief descriptions of specific themes around which discussion groups can be focused.

CURRENT EVENTS

Current events discussion groups can increase interest and awareness of community, national, and international affairs. Props such as a map of the world or globe can be used to enhance the discussion. The newspaper headlines can be cut out, blown up, and mounted for all to see. The leader can read the feature stories and articles of interest. The participants can be asked to give their opinion and suggestions for solutions for the story being discussed.

Current Event Topics

- Politics: issues and ideas
- Religion: role of minister and the churches, power of pope and other leaders, what the church does to help/hurt society
- Economy: employment/unemployment
- Weather/natural disasters: how they affect us
- Foreign affairs: how they relate to our lives—wars, immigration policy, foreign aid
- Sex: changing values, prostitution, homosexuality, love and affection among people of all ages

Questions to Stimulate Discussion During Current Events

Do you think:
  It is a good idea to . . .?
  We should, will, can, might . . .?
  This is good/bad for everyone because . . .?
  You would like to . . .?
What were/are the causes of this?
Has this . . . ever happened to you?
What would you do if . . . ever happened to you?
Did you ever feel like this?
How would it feel?
How did it feel when . . . happened?
Did anyone you know ever . . .?
What can/should be done?
How can we solve this problem?
What can we do to make things better?
How would it feel to be hurt by this decision?
Why do things like this happen?
What other factors affect this?

Desert Island

This discussion can help you learn something about each individual. Discuss what each person would take if she or he knew he was about to be stranded on a desert island. The items can be limited to one, what can be carried in the hands or taken in a pocket. Ask what three foods the participants would like to take with them and whom they would like to be stranded with.

Dear Abby

This is a good way to show you value everyone's opinions. Relevant letters to Dear Abby, Emily Post, and other advice columnists can be read aloud. The participants can be asked what advice they would give before the magazine solution is read.

Travel Talks

Travel talks can bring up memories of places lived in and visited. A travel film or slide show can serve as a catalyst for this discussion group. Travel posters, pictures, maps, postcards, and souveneirs from the area being discussed can be shown. Participants can be asked to talk about their favorite vacation or place. Films and posters can be obtained through travel agencies, government offices, and local libraries.

My Favorite . . .

There are no incorrect answers in this discussion. Everyone can participate. Ask the group to name their favorite things. Use a flip chart or a blackboard to record their responses. Start with this list of "My Favorite . . .". Have the participants talk about why it is their favorite. My Favorite . . .

color	pet
food	animal
drink	person
car	movie star
place	U.S. president
city	holiday
vacation spot	season

How Would You Feel If . . .?

This is a discussion about feelings. Here're a few questions to start everyone talking. Add some of your own. How would you feel if . . .

- everyone forgot your birthday?
- your husband or wife forgot your anniversary?
- you were celebrating your 100th birthday?
- you won a million dollars on the lottery?
- you were in a foreign country and didn't know the language?

- you lost your wedding ring?
- you found out you (or your wife) were expecting triplets?
- you were asked to give a speech to a large crowd?
- you were asked to appear on your favorite television show?
- you were invited to dinner with the President of the United States?
- you met your favorite movie star?
- you were in a restaurant and the waiter spilled a drink on you?
- your marriage license was invalid?
- you were told there would be no more Christmas?
- you had a flat tire in the middle of the night?
- you ran out of gas in the desert?
- you were lost in the woods?
- you were asked to travel to the moon with the astronauts?

Ask if any of the participants ever experienced a similar event: "Did you ever travel to a foreign country? Did you know the language? Did you have any trouble communicating with the residents?" You can also begin the discussion around a question such as: "Do you have a favorite possession? How would you feel if it was lost or stolen?"

POETRY

Discussions centered on poetry can be lively and stimulating. The leader doesn't have to be an expert on poetry, and neither do the participants. Poetry deals with thoughts, feelings, and sensations. It is a way the older person can express feelings and relive experiences of earlier years.

A poem should be enjoyed for its rhythm, sound, and images. Read the poem aloud several times to give a sense of the way it sounds. Focus on the descriptions, images, and metaphors created in the poem. An interesting line can be repeated for emphasis or discussion. After reading the poem, the leader asks how the group liked the poem and how they feel about it. It should be stressed that there are no right and wrong answers.

Choose poems about familiar topics. Ask the participants to recite or bring in a favorite poem for the group to enjoy. Poetry can be read alone or used to enhance another activity.

After the participants feel comfortable reading the poetry, try writing a group poem. Choose a subject and ask everyone to contribute a thought. The leader records the thoughts and puts them together. The participants can suggest a title after all the thoughts are collected. The poems can be written down and distributed to the group or printed in a newsletter or book. This is a group poem put together by the Vintage adult day care center participants.

WHAT VINTAGE MEANS TO ME

My place, your place, our place, a place where I can feel comfortable and give these poor legs a rest.

I've been coming here for a long time and I've heard a whole lot and one thing I know people here are love—that's it LOVE.

I need to be around people and I 'shore nuff might as well be around happy ones. That's what we have here— HAPPY PEOPLE. I need it!

Who wants to stay home alone? I like to get out, see people, go places. I can't work anymore but as long as I get these bones movin' I'll be right here. I like to be with people. I like ACTIVITY. I like Vintage.

Friends—we need 'em. Here are my friends and my family. It's the children now who have to care for us. But that's alright. That's how it's got to be. But friends is it. Here I have my FRIENDS.

An old chair papa used to sit in, he would never let anyone else sit there. Not even mama. Now that's home and comfort. Vintage is like that—a big old chair. SAFE and COMFORTABLE. Mama would give us the babies and say "Now you hang on tight and don't you let that bugger fall." Thats how I feel about it. We'll just hang on tight and we won't fall if the good Lord is willin'.

VALIDATION

Validation is a novel approach to working with very confused older adults. Naomi Feil developed the Validation technique from her work with the residents of the Montefiore Home for the Aged in Cleveland, Ohio. She found that disoriented old-old residents withdrew and sometimes became hostile and abusive when she tried to orient them to reality. She felt another approach was needed. Feil believes that the disoriented old-old have many unfinished issues they are struggling to resolve. They return to the past to restimulate old memories in order to resolve them and find peace.

Validation means accepting the old-old person where he or she is now, without argument or judgment. The Validation leader listens to the older person and empathizes with him. The leader tunes in with the person's movements, mood, voice, and sounds and tries to understand his behavior. The leader communicates verbally and nonverbally to let the confused person know she or he understands and accepts his feelings. The confused person's behavior and feelings are validated.

The Validation leader doesn't tell the confused person what to do, how to act, or try to change the behavior. Reality is not forced on the individual. If the confused older adult is asking for his mother, who is deceased, the reality of her death doesn't become the issue. The Validation leader focuses on how the individual feels about his mother—how he misses her, loves her, and is concerned for her. The goal of Valication is to help the disoriented old person feel happy, reduce his stress, and restore his self-respect and dignity.

A Validation group combines discussion with movement, music, and food in a clearly defined ritual. Feil believes that in a group, when feelings are validated, the disoriented old-old will share with each other in a desire to help one another. The Validation group helps to meet the need to belong and feel useful. After 5 years of Validation, the residents Feil followed showed improvements in their speech, continence, awareness, and ability to communicate and appeared more contented.

In Chapter 9 another group therapy technique for working with confused older adults is presented: *Remotivation*.

9

Sharing, Exploring, and Appreciating Life: Remotivation

Remotivation is a simple group therapy technique used to reach out and stimulate individuals who are confused, withdrawn, and unmotivated to bring them back to reality. Remotivation is a structured program of discussion based on reality. Objective materials and topics are presented to which participants are encouraged to respond. The goal of remotivation is to help restore the individual's ability to perceive people, things, and relations as they really are.

Remotivation was devised in 1949 by Dorothy Hoskins Smith. She developed the technique with a small group of mentally ill male hospital patients. As a teacher, she used readings of strong, rhythmic poems to focus the attention of restless children. She adopted this technique to work with a group of seriously regressed, withdrawn, and difficult-to-motivate patients.

Remotivation is designed to stimulate communication among group members by providing the opportunity to share opinions, ideas, and life experiences. Remotivation helps participants to take a renewed interest in their surroundings by focusing attention on exploring and appreciating the simple, objective features of everyday life. Even the most confused person is given an opportunity for personal expression.

Remotivation is a simple inexpensive technique that does not require a leader with extensive training or experience. Almost anyone can be trained in the remotivation technique, including nurses, aides, volunteers, recreation leaders, and students. Remotivation has worked well as a student assignment at the Vintage Adult Day Care program. Students are trained in the remotivation technique by the Director or Program Coordinator. The students choose the topics for discussion. They like the structure of the remotivation group process and the opportunity to be creative in developing the topic and choosing props.

In an effective remotivation program participants should seem interested and attentive. They should be able to participate in the discussion and respond to the materials presented. Participants should be able to initiate conversation and interact with the other members of the group. Above all, remotivation should be fun!

HOW TO CONDUCT REMOTIVATION THERAPY

A remotivation group usually consists of 5 to 15 participants. A mixture of males and females is desirable. It is helpful to include both alert and talkative participants and individuals that are more confused. Participation should be voluntary.

The remotivation group usually meets once or twice a week, but it can meet more often. There are usually 10 to 12 sessions, lasting 30 min to 1 hr, depending on the attention span of the participants. The participants sit in a circle facing each other. A table can also be used, especially if materials are going to be used and passed around.

The discussion is stimulated through the leader's questions, which center around and explore one specific topic. Reminiscence should be encouraged as a part of sharing with the group. Visual aids are used to maintain interest and attention and to encourage reaction.

It is the leader's responsibility to make the remotivation group fun, interesting, and enjoyable for everyone. The leader should always respond to every comment. Everyone's contribution—no matter how small—should be acknowledged. Participation must be recognized and rewarded.

The leader must encourage interaction and sharing within the group and try to include everyone in the discussion. Quiet members should be asked specific, explicit questions. The leader throws out questions back to the group for them to answer. The leader helps the group to refocus on the topic if the group shifts to an unrelated topic. If someone's statement is confusing, the leader should restate the portion of the comment that was relevant to refocus the group. The leader helps those with a limited attention span maintain their focus on the topic by periodically restating and repeating what has been said.

THE REMOTIVATION TECHNIQUE

The Remotivation technique consists of five basic steps.

Step 1: Creating a Climate of Acceptance
(3 to 5 minutes)

> A warm, friendly ambience should be established. Each participant is greeted by name and welcomed to the group. The leader introduces himself and all the members of the group to one another. Name tags should be used to help the members remember each other's name. The leader should tell the members that it is good to be with them and help them feel special for being part of the group.

Step 2: Creating a Bridge to Reality
(5 to 10 minutes)

> The leader uses prepared, interest-getting questions to lead into the topic. A limerick, verse, quotation or poem pertaining to the topic is read to the group. The reading should be short and objective, with a regular rhythm and rhyme.

Step 3: Sharing the World We Live In
(15 to 20 minutes)

> The leader continues to explore the topic by asking questions and encouraging the members to participate. To help keep the conversation going and to add interest, props can be used. The leader can demonstrate how the prop is used, talk about its origin, and pass it around for everyone to see and hold. The participants can be asked to describe it and speculate on ways it might be used.

Step 4: Appreciating the World of Work
(15 to 20 minutes)

> The leader asks questions to investigate the work involved in the topic chosen. The questions should stimulate the participants to think about work in relation to themselves and the work they've done. They can be asked what job they would like to do pertaining to the subject. The value of work, tools involved, transportation required, people and training involved and how the job is done are typical questions. The participants should be encouraged to share their opinions and experiences. The leader should be flexible. If the topic is not applicable to work, it can be discussed in other terms.

Step 5: Creating a Climate of Appreciation
3 to 5 minutes)

> Enjoyment at being together is expressed. The leader should summarize what has been said, learned and shared, and invite any closing comments. The participants should be thanked for coming and shown appreciation for their

contributions. The leader should invite them back and ask the participants what they would like to discuss at the next meeting. The participants can be invited to bring objects relating to the topic chosen to the next session.

TOPICS FOR DISCUSSION

In remotivation therapy almost anything can be used as a topic. Topics that are subjective and emotionally laden should be avoided. Sex, religion, politics, death, family relationships, love, and individual problems are not appropriate topics for a remotivation group.

The topics chosen should be based on the group's past history and background and should appeal to individuals from a variety of backgrounds. Suggested topics include:

Seasons
Spring, fall, winter, summer
Holidays
Christmas, Easter, Mother's Day, Father's Day, Thanksgiving, Fourth of July, Halloween, Valentine's Day
Weather
Snow, storms, hurricanes, floods
Nature
Fruits and vegetables, animals, insects, flowers, trees, oceans, seashore
Geography
Places lived, cities, rivers, countries
Trips/Vacations
Camping, seashore, cruises, tours, foreign countries
Recreation
Picnics, circus, swimming, parades, amusement parks
Celebrations
Birthdays, anniversaries, graduations, weddings, parties
Hobbies/Interests
Gardening, stamp collecting, painting, doll collecting, coin collecting, music, arts, antiques, dancing, singing, poetry
Sports
Baseball, football, hockey, fishing, golfing, horseback riding
Industry/Occupations
Farming, homemaking, nursing, armed services, musicians, mining, police work, presidents, architecture, writing
Pets
Dogs, cats, fish, snakes, ponies, goats, unusual pets
Homemaking
Quilting, dressmaking, cooking, shopping, decorating, baking, washing, canning, cleaning
Food/Drink
Seasonings, breads, pastry, beer, wine, whiskey, popcorn, ice cream

Clothing and Fashions
Hats, shoes, purses, undergarments, jewelry, ties, costumes
Transportation
Ships, boats, buses, trolleys, inclines, cars, airplanes, trains, trucks, buggies, fire engines, subways
Communication
Telephones, newspapers, magazines, books, television, radio, greeting cards

EXAMPLES

Birthdays

1. *Creating a Climate of Acceptance*
2. *Creating a Bridge to Reality*

   - Once a year each of us celebrates a special day. Can anyone tell me what it is?
   - Can you tell me when your birthday is?
   - Poem: "A Birthday Is"

3. *Sharing the World We Live In*

   - Can you tell me your flower, birthstone, and zodiac sign?
   - What did having a birthday mean to you when you were young?
   - How did you celebrate your birthday when you were young?
   - What do you think of birthdays now?
   - What do you think birthdays mean to kids nowadays?
   - What are some of the disadvantages of birthdays?
   - What do you like best about birthdays?
   - What are some of the symbols of birthdays? (Birthday cakes, birthday cards, presents, candles)
   - If you could have anything you wanted for a birthday gift, what would you ask for?
   - What was the best present you ever received?
   - Did you ever have a surprise birthday party?
   - Props: birthday cards, birthday cake, candles

4. *Appreciating the World of Work*

   - What are some of the jobs that we have to do for a birthday party? (Make or buy a cake, buy a present, wrap a present, write and send invitations, make decorations, decorate)
   - What are some of the jobs that we have to do during a birthday party? (Make sure all the guests are happy, light the candles, open presents, serve the cake)

- What do we have to do after the party? (Clean up, send thank-you notes)
- What jobs do you like to do?

5. *Creating a Climate of Appreciation*

Christmas

1. *Creating a Climate of Acceptance*
2. *Creating a Bridge to Reality*

   - What special holiday falls in December?
   - Does everyone like to celebrate Christmas?
   - What colors do you associate with Christmas?
   - Poem: "Silent Night," "Little Drummer Boy," or "The Night Before Christmas"

3. *Sharing the World We Live In*

   - What does Christmas mean to you now? When you were young?
   - What was Christmas like when you were young?
   - Whom do you spend Christmas with?
   - Where do you celebrate Christmas?
   - What songs remind you of Christmas?
   - Do you remember having a very special or favorite Christmas?
   - What was the best Christmas gift you ever received?
   - What are some of the symbols of Christmas? (Christmas stockings, Christmas tree, Nativity scene, holly, mistletoe, and poinsettias)
   - What are some of the foods we prepare for Christmas? (Fruitcake, cookies, eggnog, figgy pudding)
   - What do you like best about Christmas?
   - Props: Christmas ornaments, Christmas stockings, pinecones, Nativity scene, cards and postcards, mistletoe, holly, and poinsettias, sleighbells, Christmas wreaths.

4. *Appreciating the World of Work*

   - What are some of the jobs we have to do at Christmas? (Make cookies, make decorations, decorate the tree and house, buy and wrap presents, write and send out Christmas cards).
   - What job(s) do you like to do?
   - After Christmas what are some of the jobs we have to do? (Take down the tree, put away the decorations).

5. *Creating a Climate of Appreciation*

10

Sharing Memories: Reminiscing

Reminiscence was once discouraged and thought of as a sign of senility. Nostalgia was seen as living in the past and was often regarded as trival, meaningless, or irritating. Largely due to the work of Dr. Robert Butler and others, reminiscence has come to be accepted as a necessary and healthy part of a normal life review process. Reminiscence is unrelated to intellectual decline and may in fact sharpen mental acuity.

It is very important for the elderly to have an opportunity to look back, reflect, and find meaning in their life experiences. Retrieving memories of the past can help an individual to work through unresolved conflicts and feelings of guilt, reconcile family relationships, and provide a legacy for future generations. Each person approaching the close of life needs to see him- or herself as having made a meaningful contribution.

Reminiscence is particularly therapeutic to those older adults with a dementing illness. It is an activity they can enjoy as their memory of the past usually remains much clearer than their memory of recent events. Old memories aren't going to be judged for accuracy. The capacity to remember events of the distant past with great clarity can be a source of pride and satisfaction. The ability to retain long-term memory can be used to enhance the confused older adult's self-esteem. Memories provide material for conversation and entertainment and may be one of the few things the confused person feels she or he has left to contribute. Reminiscing can provide the mentally impaired elder with an effective means of interacting and communicating with others.

Reminiscence has many benefits for the older adult. It can provide a sense of continuity and security, pride in accomplishments, stimulate personal awareness, and increase self-esteem by providing confirmation of one's uniqueness. Studies suggest that reminiscence helps one adapt to change and cope with stress. There appears to be a positive relationship between frequency of pleasant reminiscing and one's satisfaction with life.

Reminiscence is also a way for older adults to contribute their knowledge of the past. Sharing memories provides many benefits for the young: a heightened awareness of their cultural heritage, solutions for dealing with grief and loss, and models for growing older successfully. Children make great audiences because stories of the past are new to them, and their curiosity and interest enhance the older adult's self-esteem.

Reminiscence can be useful in learning more about a person's past, accomplishments, ways of communicating, values, relationships, strengths, losses, and fears. Memories can help expand or clarify assessment data because they provide clues to feelings and behaviors.

Older people need opportunities to reminiscence and cultivate the life review process. Life review is greatly enhanced by listeners who can personally bear witness to life stories.

There are a few precautions regarding the use of reminiscence. For some, the past is painful. If an older adult resists and finds life review disturbing rather than rewarding, do not push him or her to talk about the past.

GROUP REMINISCING

Group reminiscing can provide a sense of belonging and may instill a sense of solidarity and importance not available to those who are alone. The elderly may have few opportunities to affiliate with their peers. Group reminiscence increases the opportunity to socialize by capitalizing on the exchange of memories. The group becomes exclusive as they share memories of a time long past and unknown to youth. Sharing memories is an easier method of participating in a group than drawing from a specific base of knowledge or expertise. Group participation is potentially positive, therapeutic, and growth producing as well as being recreational and enjoyable.

The goals for a reminiscence group may include:

- Helping the older adult accept what has been
- Helping to identify past strengths to sustain confidence in future abilities
- To develop alternate views of past failures
- To provide an opportunity for expression of individual experiences and accomplishments
- To reaffirm the participants' individuality
- To increase self-esteem by having others recognize one's life experiences
- To increase socialization, interaction, and the ability to share meaningful memories with others
- To heighten awareness among group members of each individual's uniqueness and accomplishments
- To provide an opportunity for learning by sharing

Reminiscence groups can be either structured or unstructured. Structured reminiscence groups provide specific ideas or topics; memories are fitted around a specific person, place, or event. Structured groups may be particularly useful if the group members need help to start them talking. A structured group may be more appropriate for a group of mentally impaired adults. Unstructured groups may begin with stimulation from the leader but then follow group direction. An important benefit of an unstructured group is that it provides individuals with control to accentuate the events that are the most meaningful and important to them.

SUGGESTIONS FOR IMPLEMENTING A GROUP REMINISCENCE ACTIVITY

Greet the participants by name as they arrive and welcome them with a handshake or a hug. Audio or visual displays such as posters, pictures, music, or antiques can help gain the participants' attention and stimulate interest. Relaxation exercises and music are also conducive to reminiscence. Participants can be guided to the discussion topic by using a story, poem, pictures, or other device to trigger memories. A specific memorable event, person, or object and related questions helps the participants to focus on the topic. The participants' memories are the main ingredient of any reminiscence group. To help stimulate reaction and participation, the group leader needs to listen attentively, praise the participants for sharing, and validate the memories they share.

The most conducive atmosphere for reminiscence is one that is low key and unpressured. Be patient and willing to wait for a response. Tapping the past is elusive; it may take some time for memories to flow freely. Remind the older adult that you yourself will benefit from hearing stories from that person's past. Family members can use their knowledge about an individual's background to find an area of interest that will release memories.

It is better to deal in generalities rather than ask specific questions. For example, it may be easier for an older adult to remember a time frame such as before school started instead of age in years.

Increasing age offers more stages of life about which to reminisce, and older people do not dwell disproportionately upon their childhood. Older persons report reminiscing more about the last years of their careers and middle age. This being true, it is important to focus discussions on all the stages of one's life not just the early years.

Ideas to Stimulate Memories and the Senses

Sight: Pictures, trigger films, slides, books, maps, posters, travel brochures, souvenirs, antiques and old-time objects, magazine articles, animals

Sound: Music: records, tapes, radio, instruments, sing-alongs; poetry readings, book readings; sound effects such as animals, trains, the ocean

Taste: Food and beverages such as popcorn, ice cream, taffy, lemonade

Touch: Clothing, animals, souvenirs, antiques and old-time objects

Smell: Food, incense, perfumes, oils, spices, flowers

For example, a discussion centering around remembering the circus could use old circus posters, circus music, freshly popped popcorn, and visits from a clown to help stimulate long forgotten memories.

REMINISCENCE ACTIVITIES

Interviews

Interviews can be conducted by staff, students, and volunteers. A good listener is needed as well as a good questioner. By showing interest, you can encourage the sharing of memories. Be careful to take an active part in the conversation without dominating it. Know what questions you want to ask, but don't be afraid to let the individual go off on a tangent. Give the person plenty of time to respond, and don't be uncomfortable with long periods of silence. Using props such as pictures or scrapbooks can help to stimulate memories. Cut off the interview if the person becomes restless or fatigued. Each interview should be a pleasant experience—not a chore.

Family Folklore

Family folklore is made up of the traditional beliefs, legends, and stories that are a part of every family. Many older adults like to tell stories about their past and can be encouraged to describe the many things they have experienced. The most productive family folklore interviews are those that take place in the natural context of the family. Family dinners, picnics, reunions, holidays, and even funerals provide a setting that is very conducive to the telling of family stories. The interaction that occurs at such gatherings can help spark memories. The older adult's life history can be written or recorded and given to the individual to provide tangible evidence of the validity of her or his life experiences.

Family folklore can be interesting to the participants of a reminiscence group as well as to other family members. Use a set of questions that focus on specific topics and encourage older adults to tell it the way they remember it. Here are some questions to help elicit memories of the past.

1. *Names*
   Tell me about your family's surname? Do you know what it means? What is the country of origin? Has your surname ever been changed? Does your family have any traditional first names, middle names, or nicknames?
2. *Ancestors*
   What do you know about your parents? Grandparents? Other relatives? What was their life like: their childhood, schooling, children, work, interests? How did they come to meet and marry? Do you have any black sheep, colorful characters, or famous persons in your family? Has any other person been made part of your family? Were the persons given a family title such as aunt?

3. *History*
   How has your family been affected by important historic events such as World War II, the Great Depression, or President Kennedy's assassination? How long ago did your family come to this country? How did they get here? Why did they come?
4. *Traditions/Stories*
   Are there any stories about your family? How are holidays celebrated in your family? What holidays are the most important? Does your family hold reunions: when, where, and how often are they held? Who is invited and who comes? Have any recipes, jewelry, or other family property been preserved and passed on from one generation to another? Are there stories connected with them? Is there a family cemetery or burial place? Is there a family homestead?

The following are descriptions of specific ways around which reminiscence can be discussed.

Timeline

The timeline uses important historical and personal dates to jog memories. Draw a line across or down a sheet of paper. At the top indicate the person's year of birth. Put the current year on the bottom. On one side fill in important life events, including important firsts: marriages, deaths, births, and the like. On the other side of the line, add important events taking place in the world at the same time, such as the Great Depression.

Timeline

	1917	
	1927	
Wall Street Crash		
		High school graduation
Hindenburg explodes	1937	
Pearl Harbor		Marriage, husband goes to war
		First child born
	1947	
Korean War		Second child born
		Mother dies
Sputnik in space		
	1957	
		Father dies
Kennedy assassinated		
		First grandchild born
	1967	
		Husband dies
Nixon resigns		
	1977	
	1987	

Maps

Focusing on a specific country or area can help stimulate reminiscence. Have each person give birthplace and country of origin and tell what he or she knows or remembers about them. Ask him to close his eyes and picture his home and neighborhood at a certain age. Talk about the limits or boundaries of each place, such as how far he was allowed to go, or family travels.

Family Trees

Discussions surrounding the family tree will bring out many anecdotes.

Draw a family tree. Begin with names and add births, deaths, marriages, and children. Missing information can be obtained from a family member.

Memorabilia

Looking at old family photograph albums, scrapbooks, correspondence, and other memorabilia is a pleasant way of stimulating memories for the confused older adult. Using materials that are familiar helps to put the individual at ease. Reviewing past events and persons involved in the individual's life is a relevant, meaningful, and concrete task for the confused older adult to focus on.

Books, Magazines, and Newspapers

Looking at old magazines, newspapers, or history books can help stir up memories of events long past. Books on an individual's country of origin or places lived or visited can be used as a focal point to help the confused older adult remember the places and events depicted. Publications with lots of illustrations are the most useful.

GROUP ACTIVITIES

Art and Reminiscing

After discussing past events and retelling old stories, ask the participants to draw a picture. The old skating pond, childhood home, or favorite pet are some examples of places or things that could be drawn.

Treasure Chest

The treasure chest activity can highlight individuals and make them feel important. Ask each participant to bring a cherished belonging to a group meeting. Families may need to be involved to bring or send the item to the reminiscence group. The belonging can be shown to the group and the story behind it told. Bringing in family treasures is a great icebreaker and way to learn more about each other.

Intergenerational Oral History Class

Children and older adults can team up in a fun exchange of history and ideas. Children come prepared to ask specific questions about a predetermined weekly topic, such as an old fashioned Christmas, clothing and fashions, or historical events. The elderly use their own memories and experiences to "teach" the class. Pictures or related activities, such as stringing popcorn, can be used to stimulate interest. The children can write up a summary of the class to be passed out to all the participants. While this kind of activity takes a lot of coordination, its potential benefits to both generations are worth the investment.

Given the opportunity, it is natural to have the elderly pass on their knowledge and experiences to a younger generation. The children's interest can help validate the older adult's life experiences.

OTHER IDEAS

Newsletter

The stories and memories talked about in the reminiscence group can be featured in a newsletter. The feature can be called "Memories" or something similar. Seeing one's name or story in print is always an ego booster.

Memoirs

Group memories can be compiled into a book of reminiscences and thoughts about life. An individual's memoirs can be collected and given as a gift to members of one's family. This sharing can help to strengthen family ties.

Recordings

A videotape or tape recording of the memories of a historic event, tradition, profession, or trade could be used (with the individual's permission) as the focus for a special program for other older adults or as part of a school program.

Discussion Topics

Theme Memories. Choose a theme and trace that topic through a lifetime. How did this affect you and your family? Friends, schools, jobs, religion, and travel are possible themes.

Person Memories. Name the most important people in your life. Who was the most influential person in your life? Why? What person(s) had a significant influence on your life—either positive or negative? Choices can include friends, teachers, bosses, parents, children, spouses, co-workers or relatives. When was the last time you saw him or her? Would you like to see him or her again? Is there anything you would like to tell him or her?

Important Life Events. Significant events in a person's life, historic and personal, are good discussion topics. Explore the feelings, images, dreams, objects, and persons associated with the event.

Following Are Some Questions to Stimulate Memories:

What . . .

- is the first memory you can recall?
- was your greatest achievement in life?
- was the happiest year or period in your life? Why?
- is your fondest memory?
- events helped to shape the course of your life?
- lessons of life would you like to pass on?
- would you do differently if you could?
- would you like to change about your past?
- is the greatest lesson life has taught you?

Do you remember . . .

- your youth—proms, games, punishments?
- your graduation day?
- your most embarassing moment?
- an event in which you needed/demonstrated courage?

- your biggest disappointment?
- your proudest day?
- your most fearful experience?
- a turning point in your life?
- a special friendship?
- your most exciting experience?
- when and where you met your husband/wife?
- the birth of your first child?
- the best surprise you ever had?
- ever getting lost?

Place memories. Tell me about . . .
- all the places you have lived
- the neighborhood where you grew up
- your childhood kitchen, bedroom
- your childhood home
- your hometown
- schools you attended
- favorite places lived, visited
- places visited, worked
- churches or Sunday schools attended

Tell me about your . . .
- family: parents, grandparents, siblings, or other relatives
- husband, wife, children
- first sweetheart
- most memorable valentine
- boyfriends, girlfriends, and great loves of your life
- wedding day
- best friend
- hobbies or interests
- favorite sports or games

Who or what was your favorite . . .
- stage, screen, and radio star?
- book, play, and movie?
- object or toy from childhood?
- teacher?
- names?
- birthday, Christmas, and/or other gifts?
- item of clothing?
- childhood friend?

First, best, worst, and/or most unusual . . .
- job?
- pet or animal?
- teacher?
- school?
- trips/vacations?
- car?
- home you lived in?
- birthday?
- Christmas, Hanukkah, and other holidays?

MEMORABLE EVENTS

These memorable events usually bring back a flood of memories and are great topics to stimulate reminiscence.

1920   Prohibition; first radio broadcasting service
1927   Charles Lindbergh flies the *Spirit of St. Louis* across the Atlantic; the first "talkie," *The Jazz Singer,* is released.
1929   Wall Street Crash: Black Tuesday, the most catastrophic day in the history of the stock market, becomes the forerunner of the Great Depression.
1932   Franklin Delano Roosevelt is elected president by a landslide over Herbert Hoover; Amelia Earhart becomes the first woman to make a transatlantic flight.
1933   FDR announces his New Deal; Adolph Hitler becomes Chancellor of Germany.
1936   A Black American, Jesse Owens, wins 11 gold medals at the Summer Olympics in Berlin.
1937   The German dirigible, the *Hindenberg,* explodes, killing 36 persons; Joe Lewis becomes World Heavyweight Boxing champ; nylon stockings are invented.
1939   The German invasion of Poland begins World War II.
1941   Japanese attack Pearl Harbor; "Remember Pearl Harbor" becomes a rallying cry; U.S. declares war on Japan.
1945   Roosevelt dies; the atomic bomb is dropped on Hiroshima; Japan and Germany surrender; rationing ends.
1948   Goldmark invents the long-playing phonograph record; Harry S Truman wins a surprise victory over Thomas E. Dewey; Gandhi is assassinated.
1950   The Korean War begins.
1953   The polio epidemic of 1952 leads to the development of the polio vaccine by Jonas Salk.
1957   The first satellite, *Sputnik,* is launched into space by the Soviet Union.
1962   The Cuban missile crisis.
1963   President John F. Kennedy is assassinated in Dallas, Texas, by Lee Harvey Oswald.
1965   President Lyndon B. Johnson authorizes the bombing of North Vietnam; U.S. Marine combat forces land in Vietnam.
1968   Dr. Martin Luther King, Jr., is assassinated by James Earl Ray.
1969   Neil Armstrong becomes the first man to walk on the moon from *Apollo II* with the words, "One small step for man, a giant leap for mankind."
1974   President Richard M. Nixon resigns from office over the Watergate affair.

Chapter 11 focuses on sensory stimulation. Reminiscence and sensory stimulation are very good activities for even the most confused older person. Sensory activities are very useful for stimulating reminiscence.

11

Stimulating the Senses

Our senses help to provide an awareness of our physical environment. As people grow older, their senses decline; this interferes with the ability to perceive the environment. The older adult with a dementing illness has even more difficulty making sense out of the environment. A variety of sensory inputs and experiences is needed to help the confused individual maintain contact with reality and feel in control.

Sensory deprivation can be a real problem to many elderly, especially the confused, blind, hearing impaired, institutionalized, and bedfast. A lack of touch and affection, being deprived of conversation and mental stimulation, and sensory impairments may result in boredom, withdrawal, somatic complaints, visual distortions, hallucinations, and delusions. The need for sensory stimulation is very important.

On the other hand, too much stimulation can cause fear, anxiety, irritability, or panic. Determining how much stimulation is too much can be difficult. It depends on the individual. Appropriate levels of sensory stimulation can expand the individual's awareness of the environment, increase social interactions, stimulate conversation, spark familiarity, and elicit memories.

It is important to keep as many sensory channels open and stimulated as possible. Take cues from the person as to the kinds and intensity of stimuli needed. Use a variety of sensations to stimulate all of the senses. Encourage the individual to use his or her senses and explain sensory events that are taking place. Explain unfamiliar sights, sounds, tastes, odors, and medications. Avoid unnecessary and confusing stimuli. As the severity of the dementia increases, emphasize only familiar sensory stimuli.

Sensory stimulation can be incorporated into any activity. Encourage the individual or group to touch, taste, smell, listen, and look at the materials you are working with. Point out interesting facts and objects in the environment. Help the individual to foster an appreciation of the world around him.

MATERIALS FOR SENSORY STIMULATION

Include a variety of unusual but familiar items and common household objects. Many categories overlap in the senses they stimulate. For example, popcorn can be smelled, tasted, touched, looked at, and, as it pops, listened to. Following are some materials for sensory stimulation activities.

Visual Stimuli

Comb, brush, screwdriver, hammer, safety pin, ruler, spool of thread, spoon, knife, fork, batteries, buttons, rubber bands, toothbrush, steel wool, paper clips, key, thimble, clothespin, coins, jewelry, flowers, pictures, rabbit's foot, harmonica, lipstick, and zipper.

Olfactory Stimuli

Before using a scented oil, powder, or perfume, make sure that no one is allergic to the product. It is best to present only four to six smells at a time. Cologne, spices (vanilla, pumpkin pie spice, cinnamon, garlic, nutmeg, and cloves are all familiar), flowers, potpourri, extracts (vanilla, lemon, peppermint, almond), vinegar, fresh bread, coffee, tobacco, wet wool, sawdust, cedar chips, freshly mown grass, alcohol (rum, whiskey, beer, gin, wine), and fresh fruits. Scented candles and oils can be used to imitate a variety of familiar scents, but care must be taken that no one accidentally drinks the scented oils.

Auditory Stimuli

Cowbells, whistles, marbles rolling in a box, sleigh bells, alarm clock, cuckoo clock, tambourine, maracas, and other percussion instruments, music, animal sounds, and sound effects (such as a baby crying, a telephone ringing, a train).

Tactile Stimuli

Use contrasting materials such as hard and soft, wet and dry, shapes (such as pyramids and rectangles), fruit, animal fur, fabrics (felt, velvet, satin, wool, burlap, corduroy), cotton balls, sandpaper, wood, rope, glass, metal, paper, stones, cork, feathers, powder puff, coins, box of marbles, shells, wet sponge, a peeled hard-boiled egg, coffee grounds, oatmeal, cereals, rice, seeds, macaroni, popcorn, birdseed, and sand.

Gustatory Stimuli

Choose items that are sweet, tart, sharp, sour, and spicy. Use contrasting tastes such as sweet and sour or group-related items such as condiments. Crackers, candy, fruit, pickles, peanut butter, salt, pepper, sugar, honey, coffee, tea, mustard, ketchup, marshmallows, licorice, chocolate, wintergreen, peppermint, spearmint, and Jello-O can be tasted and identified.

SENSORY STIMULATION ACTIVITIES

These activities can increase the individual's awareness of the surroundings and stimulate conversation and memories.

• Select an object from the materials suggested or of your own choosing. Pass it around and encourage everyone to look, feel, smell, taste, touch, and describe it. Ask questions to stimulate discussion.
What is it?
What color is it?
What does it remind you of?
What does it feel like? Is it cool or warm?
What shape is it?
Who uses it?
How is it used?

• An object can be placed in a clean sock or piece of material and the participants can try to guess what it is from touching and smelling it.

• Place six to eight objects on a tray. Identify and talk about each item. Remove one of the items and ask the participants to guess which one has been removed.

• Give each participant a bag that contains four to eight different materials. Ask the participants to remove one article from the bag just by feeling for it. Show them the article you want them to find. When everyone has found the object, a group discussion can follow about the different uses of the item.

• Fill four to six containers with different scents. Ask each participant to smell the scent and guess what it is. After everyone has had a turn, a discussion about the scent and its uses can follow.

• Discuss what items you usually take on a picnic. Fill a box with items you would take on a picnic (such as plastic utensils, napkins, paper plates, and a fly swatter). Ask the participants to put their hand in the box and identify each object.

• Bring in 6 to 10 different kinds of flowers or plants. Ask the participants to identify what they are. Encourage everyone to touch, smell, and describe each flower and what they like about it. Flowers and plants can bring back many memories of the past.

• Have the participants rub colored crayons over different kinds of sandpaper. Encourage everyone to feel the texture of the sandpaper and rub on pieces of wood.

• Arrange similar or related items together for a discussion:
Grass, dirt, flowers (outdoor smells)
Hot dogs, mustard, onions, lemonade (picnic smells)
Holly, star, pine bough, pinecones (Christmas decorations)

• Fill several buckets with different materials such as sand, rice, and birdseed. Have the participants run their hands through the materials and identify what they are.

• Select a wide variety of fabrics with different textures. Ask the participants to identify each type of fabric, using guiding questions:
Is it smooth or rough?
Does it have any bumps on it?
Does the pile move when you touch it?
Is it easy to fold?
Does it make noise when it moves?
Ask if any of the participants ever had something made out of the material.

• Different sound effects can be made or played on a tape recorder.

Ask the participants to identify each sound, its origin, when and where this sound may occur, and how an individual would respond to it. Ask the participants if the sound brings back any memories.

• Make everyday sounds such as pouring water, clinking ice in a glass, tearing paper, and jingling coins together. Ask the individual or group to identify what each sound is.

• Purchase plastic pipes in different shapes and sizes. Demonstrate how they are screwed into each other. The piping can be kept in a large box for individuals to use.

• Rocking in a rocking chair, porch swing, or glider and riding in a car can be relaxing and pleasurable sensory activities.

• Make a soft patchwork cloth to feel and fold, using a variety of different materials, colors, and patterns. The cloth can be made into an oblong shape, a continuous loop, or like a book with pages to flip. This activity can be very comforting.

• Ask the participants to make their own sounds: clap hands, snap fingers, stomp feet, rub palms together, whistle, cough, cry, laugh, hum, and imitate sounds.

• Soft rubber puzzles with simple patterns provide tactile stimulation and are easy to manipulate. Many confused older persons enjoy putting the pieces of these puzzles together.

• Massaging and applying hand or body lotion can be very soothing and stimulating. Touch is very important as a means of communication.

SENSORY CRAFTS

Sensory crafts combine craft projects and sensory stimuli. The individual should be encouraged to use his senses while creating a craft.

Scented Pinecones

Materials

• Quart-size disposable containers
• Pinecones
• Ground cinnamon
• Waxed paper
• Basket
• White glue
• Water

Procedure

1. Mix equal amounts of glue and water in the containers.
2. Dip pinecones into the glue/water mixture.

3. Sprinkle each cone with the cinnamon.
4. Set the cones on waxed paper to dry.
5. Place the dried pinecones in a lined basket or decorative container.

Scented Oranges

Materials

- Oranges
- Whole cloves (one box for each orange)
- Ribbon or string

Procedure

1. Pour the cloves into a shallow dish. Ask the participants to smell them.
2. Poke the sharp ends of the clove into the oranges. The more cloves used, the stronger the aroma.
3. Tie ribbons around the orange and fasten them in place with the cloves.
4. Let the scented balls dry in the sun or near heat for 3 or 4 days.

Scented Cutting Board

Materials

- Cardboard
- Wood design contact paper
- Glue
- Herbs and spices such as whole cloves, cinnamon sticks, bay leaves, and star anise

Procedure

1. Prepare the cardboard by cutting it into the shape of a cutting board.
2. Attach the contact paper to the cardboard.
3. Glue pieces or a small bunch of spice to the contact paper. Attach about six different spices to each cutting board.
4. Punch a hole in the handle of the cutting board to hang it by.

Fragrant Greeting Cards

Materials

- Used greeting cards
- Construction paper, 5″ × 8″ or 10″ × 7″
- Facial tissues
- Scented oil
- Glue
- Hat pin
- Envelopes

Procedure

1. Cut out pictures and verses from the greeting cards.
2. Fold the construction paper in half.
3. Glue verses on one side of the construction paper or leave it blank.
4. Apply one to two drops of scented oil to one piece of facial tissue.
5. Fold the tissue a little smaller than the picture.
6. Place glue on the back of the cutout picture.
7. Place the tissue between the cutout picture and the construction paper.
8. Press the picture onto the construction paper.
9. Prick small holes with a hat pin into the picture to release the fragrance. Closely supervise the confused person's use of the hat pin.

Note: A discussion about greeting cards can follow. Each participant can send his card to a friend or loved one.

Potpourri

Materials

- One quart of dried flower petals or herbs (honeysuckle, bay leaves, lavender, lemon verbena, lilac, mint, rose geranium, roses, violets. Any flower petals can be used, since they do not have to hold their own fragrance.)
- Scented oil, several drops
- 1 ¼ tablespoons of fixative
- 1 tablespoon ground spice (cinnamon, cloves, nutmeg, mace) optional
- Small baby food jars with lids for each participant

Procedure

1. Mix together the dried flower petals and/or herbs, fixative, a few drops of the scented oil, and the spice.
2. Fill the jars with the mixture and close the lid.
3. Let the mixture set in the closed jars for 2 to 4 weeks.
4. Shake the jar daily to blend the scent.

Note: After the potpourri is ready, it can be kept in the jar and the lid removed whenever one wants to enjoy the fragrance. The jars can be decorated in advance. The potpourri can also be used in a sachet.

Sachets

Materials

- Two 3″ square pieces of muslin
- One 2″ square piece of polyester fiberfill
- Glue
- Scented oils or perfume
- Cotton swabs
- Four 4″ pieces of ribbon or lace

Procedure

1. Apply a drop of scented oil or perfume to the fiberfill.
2. Place a dab of glue in the middle of one of the squares. Lay the scented fiberfill in the center of the square.
3. Apply glue around the edges of the square.
4. Lay the ribbon on the glue on the square, leaving the edges of the ribbon extending beyond the edge of the square.
5. Apply glue to the inner edge of ribbon.
6. Place the other square on top of the ribbon, pressing the edges together. Let the glue dry.

Note: A discussion about the uses for sachets can follow. Ask the participants if they ever made, bought, or received a sachet for a gift. The muslin can be decorated or painted with a design in advance.

FOOD PREPARATION ACTIVITIES

Cooking as a recreational activity is informal, fun, and contains something for nearly everybody to do. It provides a lot of opportunity to stimulate the senses and be creative. The sights and smells of cooking stimulate interest and participation.

Cooking and baking, especially for women, draw on old skills and roles. Many memories of the past surface when the confused person is involved in a familiar activity such as cooking. Unfortunately, because many older adults with a dementing illness can no longer cook independently, their families often take over this responsibility completely. Women who have spent most of their lives preparing food find the loss of ability and opportunity to cook very sad and frustrating. Cooking and baking are activities that the confused person can continue to participate in when they are modified, supervised, and simplified.

Cooking is an activity the individual can do at home. It is also a great group project because it creates a pleasant, sociable atmosphere and gives everyone something to look forward to (the finished product). Cooking allows the participants to display their knowledge and skills. Cooking also provides immediate gratification—almost everybody likes to eat!

How to Implement Cooking as an Activity

Allow the group to decide what they would like to make and select a recipe in advance. At home, give individuals a choice: "Do you want carrots or peas?" The prepared food can be served as a snack or meal, sold, or made as a gift for others. Consideration must be given to an individual's dietary restrictions.

Choose recipes that can be prepared at the table. Use large-print recipes for each person or small group. With very simple, one- and two-step recipes, each small group can make the dish. With a more complicated recipe, a large group can divide the work and allocate jobs to subgroups.

Prepare for the activity by getting all the supplies and equipment ready in advance. Make sure that everyone has clean hands. Watch that the participants don't sneeze or cough into the food. Individuals can assist in cleanup.

The leader or caregiver can bake or cook the food, so that the confused person doesn't have to use the stove or be in contact with hot food. Whoever is unable to use a paring knife safely shouldn't be asked to chop or slice. A butter knife can be used to cut soft foods like bananas. All in all, it's best to avoid using sharp objects.

Encourage everyone to talk about the ingredients being used and the food being prepared. Ask everyone to touch and smell the ingredients. Talk about other ways the ingredients can be used and any memories the food being made evokes.

Suggested Cooking Activities

Participants can shell peas, tear lettuce, snap the ends of beans and asparagus, cream and mix batters, mash food, fill and level off measuring cups, knead and roll out dough, churn butter, crank an ice cream machine, layer ingredients, cut out biscuits and cookies, fill muffin tins, drop dough on baking sheets, and ice and decorate cookies and cakes. The foods that have worked best in a group cooking activity include (from scratch):

Fruit salad	Breads
Tossed salad	Ice cream
Pizza	Butter
Strombolis	Punches
Pies	Noodles
Cakes	Soups/Vegetable soups
Cookies	Muffins

Music is another very effective sensory activity that can be used to stimulate the mentally impaired older adult.

12

Music: How to Make Magic

Music is an important part of any activities program. It is one of the best means of communication—eliciting response from even the most confused person. Music is very versatile, because it can be engaged in at every level, from simple to complex. It conveys feelings and emotions without the need for complicated language. Music is universally appealing and has meaning for people of all ages.

Music is particularly important for the older adult with a dementing illness. The portions of the brain that respond to music are often the last to deteriorate. Even the most withdrawn, confused person is responsive to music. Music and singing are good ways of increasing awareness, interest, and responsiveness. Music can calm, arouse, orient, and motivate—even if only temporarily.

Listening to old familiar music is pleasurable and relaxing—and it doesn't require intellectual skills. Nostalgic music creates a feeling of security as the words to familiar songs are more easily remembered. Music stirs up memories and prompts the older adult to reminisce.

Music is magic. It creates an overall feeling of well-being. Music releases tensions and alleviates stress. Music encourages the body to move, promoting the expression of feelings and an awareness of the body. Musical activities provide opportunities for social interaction and communication with others. Music stimulates the senses and adds to the individual's quality of life.

SUGGESTIONS FOR IMPLEMENTING A MUSICAL PROGRAM

• Music can be used to affect mood. Begin with musical selections that parallel the group's mood and proceed gradually to lift its spirits. It is important to begin where the group is rather than where you want it to be.

• Use music as a way to enhance other activities such as exercise, games, discussion groups, and art activities.

• Begin by greeting each participant and saying his or her name in a song. Finish with an appropriate closing song such as "Till We Meet Again." Encourage members to sing or hum along and to say goodbye to each other.

• Choose songs that are familiar and have repetitive lines. This gives everyone a chance to join in.

• There is less stress and confusion when the songs and activities follow a predictable pattern. Repetition reduces disorientation. Use the same opening and closing remarks and songs each time to signal the beginning and the end of the program. By following the same routine and maintaining the same activities, it is easier to observe changes in participant responses. When the same songs are repeated, the words and tunes become easier to remember, however; a few different songs can add interest and variety.

• Use music that is relevant to the events going on (reality orientation). Recognize holidays, seasons, special events, the weather—whatever is going on in the world at the time. If it is raining, play songs like "Singin' in the Rain" and "April Showers."

• When someone dies, say something about the person. A prayer or moment of silence and playing a special song as a memorial to the deceased will let the others know they will be remembered when they die.

• Create opportunities for the participants to interact with one another. Introduce persons sitting next to each other and encourage everyone to shake hands. Encourage them to look at each other's movements to develop an awareness and recognition of others.

• Use humor to make the activity fun and help people to laugh.

Play songs that are funny and tell a few jokes. Create a relaxed, informal, and pleasant atmosphere.

• Encourage and compliment the members' participation. Use physical contact to provide reassurance and stimulation.

• Use music to stimulate reminiscence. Ask questions related to the music and activity:

Do you remember this song?

Do you remember the first time you heard it?

Does this song remind you of a particular person or place?

Do you know who wrote this song? What other songs did he/she write?

Did you ever play an instrument? Has anyone in your family ever played an instrument?

Do you remember when this song was popular?

• Use different music for different activities and to create different moods. Slow music calms. Strongly rhythmic music encourages the confused, disoriented person to move to the music. Changing tempos add interest. Smooth transitions from one song or activity to another help to sustain attention.

ACTIVITIES WITH MUSIC

Musical activities are a wonderful way to create an awareness of the environment and lift the spirit.

Listening to and Appreciating Music

Older people enjoy listening to their favorite songs, musicals, classics, performing artists, and composers. A discussion about the history of music or reminiscence about the songs and their artists can follow. A program can also feature the works from a famous musical celebrity composer or show.

Moving to Music

Music can be used to encourage dancing, exercise, and other physical movement. Moving to music stimulates the senses and increases self-awareness. Dance and body movements can be part of a sing-along, rhythm band, or other musical activity. Many older adults love to dance and they welcome the opportunity to do so. People in wheelchairs can participate, too. Batons, scarves, fans, and pompoms can be used as props to add interest and create a special mood.

Musical Games

Remember This Song? It is very satisfying for the confused older adult to be able to remember the words to old tunes.

Use familiar old songs, jingles, waltzes, and hymns. Play the first or several lines of a song on the piano or recorder. Ask the participants to:

- give the next line of the song
- identify the title
- identify the composer

Name Game. This activity may be too difficult for some people. It might be helpful to give a hint by saying the first few words.

Ask the participants to list names of songs:

- with various words in the title *(love, God, moon, sunshine)*
- that begin with *I*
- that have a girl's name in it
- that have a boy's name in it

Singo. This game, a variation on bingo, is more complicated and is appropriate for one who is only mildly mentally impaired. Make a bingo card with 9, 16, or 25 squares on it. Place the names of different song titles in each block, making sure that no two cards are exactly alike. The pianist plays a tune from a master list of songs. The participants use markers to cover the squares where they have the songs being played. The first one to cover a row wins.

What is This Instrument? This activity is best for people with musical backgrounds. Listen to recordings of different instrumental sounds. Ask the participants to identify what instrument is being played.

What is This Dance? The music to these dances are great for stimulating memories.

Listen to different dances: the waltz, tango, disco, cha-cha, fox trot, minuet, bunny hop, alley cat, conga, and the Mexican hat dance. Ask the participants to identify the dance.

Sounds to Move By. This is another difficult activity, so keep it lighthearted and fun.

Match a specific movement to a specific sound. When the participants hear the sound, they should make the movement. For example, whenever the drum is played in a song, everyone should clap. When the drum stops, the participants stop.

Rhythm Bands

Rhythm bands promote physical activity and movement. Different instruments make different sounds and require different body movements. The sound produced is not as important as the enjoyment and satisfaction of participation. A pianist and group band leader are needed to lead the rhythm band. The leader can make suggestions on what instruments to use.

Use a variety of music with different rhythms such as marches or waltzes. Lively songs with a quick steady beat are the easiest to follow. Ask the participants to play loud and soft, and fast and slow.

Standard rhythm instruments are available from musical stores or supply companies. Rhythm instruments include rhythm sticks, kazoos, harmonicas, handbells, drums, cymbals, triangles, maracas, tambourines, shakers, and wood blocks.

Use a little bit of imagination to make homemade rhythm instruments. Shakers can be made by filling gourds with small stones or a plastic jug with dried corn, beans, or rice. Hat boxes and oatmeal boxes hit with pencils or dowels can substitute for drums. A rattle can be made by covering a light bulb with papier-mâché strips and breaking the glass inside once the papier-mâché dries. Bells can be made by suspending empty clay flowerpots or aluminum containers from a rope and hitting them with a metal striker. Sandpaper can be glued to wooden blocks and rubbed together or a spoon can be rubbed against a washboard to create different sounds. Two pie plates can be filled with dried beans and laced together to make a tambourine.

Sing-Alongs

Singing is the most popular musical activity. It is almost always successful with good leadership. The pleasure of singing, not the quality of one's voice, should be emphasized. The confused older adult may be able to sing old songs better than talk and will enjoy being able to communicate and participate.

Use large-print song sheets or song slides. Try using song sheets with the words to several songs written on each page to avoid having to turn the pages as often. Simple accompaniments are best. Accompaniments that are too fancy can hinder participation because participants will listen rather than sing.

Musical Performances

Almost everyone enjoys watching and listening to musical performances. Soloists and groups such as a barbership quartet, "Sweet Adelines," choirs, and bands can provide interesting and stimulating performances. Local schools, colleges, senior centers, clubs, symphonies, and musical societies can provide information on available resources in the community.

Nostalgic Songs

The elderly particularly seem to enjoy old nostalgic American songs, hymns, and spirituals and ethnic music that enhances their cultural and religious heritage. Some songs that are popular and familiar are:

Old-Time Favorites

After the Ball	Alouette
Ain't She Sweet?	America
Ain't We Got Fun?	America the Beautiful
All the Nice Girls Love a Sailor	April Showers
	Aura Lee
Baby Face	Bill Bailey
The Band Played On	Billy Boy
Beautiful Dreamer	By the Light of the Silvery Moon
Bicycle Built for Two	By the Beautiful Sea
Carolina in the Morning	Clementine
California Here I Come	Cruising Down the River
Casey Jones	Cuddle Up a Little Closer
Daisy, Daisy	Dixie
Danny Boy	Do-Re-Mi
Darling Nellie Gray	Down by the Old Millstream
Dinah Won't You Blow Your Horn?	Drink to Me Only with Thine Eyes
Easter Parade	Edelweiss
Five Foot Two, Eyes of Blue	For Me and My Gal
Get Me to the Church	God Bless America
Gimme a Little Kiss	Goodnight, Irene
Give My Regards to Broadway	Goodnight, Ladies

Happy Days Are Here Again
Heart of My Heart
Hello Dolly

I Can't Give You Anything but Love
I Could Have Danced All Night
I Dream of Jeannie with the Light Brown
Hair
If You Knew Susie
I'm Forever Blowing Bubbles
I'm Looking Over a Four Leaf Clover
In a Shanty in Old Shanty Town
In the Good Old Summertime

Johnny Comes Marching Home

Keep the Home Fires Burning

Let a Smile Be Your Umbrella
Lilli Marlene

The Man on the Flying Trapeze
Marching Along Together
Mary
Meet Me in St. Louis
Memories
Mockin' Bird Hill

Nellie Gray

O Dear! What Can the Matter Be!
O Susanna
Oh Johnny
Oh, You Beautiful Doll!

Peg O' My Heart

Roll Out the Barrel

Sailing, Sailing
Second Hand Rose
She'll Be Coming Around the Mountain
Shine on Harvest Moon
Side by Side
Silver Threads Among the Gold
Singing in the Rain

Take Me Out to the Ballgame
That Old Gang of Mine
This Land is Your Land
Till We Meet Again

Wait Till the Sun Shines, Nellie
Way Down Upon the Swanee River
When It's Springtime in the Rockies

Yankee Doodle Dandy
Yellow Rose of Texas

Home on the Range
Home, Sweet Home

In the Shade of the Old Apple Tree
Irish Eyes

It's A Long, Long Way to Tipperary
It's Only A Paper Moon
I've Been Working on the Railroad
I've Got Sixpence
I Want A Girl
I Want To Be Happy

King of the Road

Let Me Call You Sweetheart

Moon River
Moonlight Bay
My Bonnie Lies Over the Ocean
My Country 'Tis Of Thee
My Gal Sal
My Wild Irish Rose

Old Mill Stream
On Top of Old Smoky
Over There!

Polly Wollie Doodle

Row, Row, Row Your Boat

Smiles
Springtime in the Rockies
Sunny Side of the Street
Sunrise, Sunset
Sweet Adeline
Sweet Rosie O'Grady

Tennessee Waltz
Tiptoe Through the Tulips
Toot, Toot, Tootsie

When You and I Were Young Maggie
When You're Smiling
While Strolling Through the Park
You Are My Sunshine

Hymns and Spirituals

Amazing Grace	Let There Be Peace on Earth
Battle Hymn of the Republic	Michael, Row the Boat Ashore
Down by the Riverside	Onward Christian Soldiers
He's Got the Whole World in His Hand	The Old Rugged Cross
In the Garden	Rock-a-My-Soul
Just as I Am	Swing Low, Sweet Chariot
Kum Ba Yah	When the Saints Go Marching In

Chapter 13 focuses on exercise and physical activities. Music can be used to enhance any fitness program.

13

Use It or Lose It: Exercise and Physical Activities

Exercise is a key factor in keeping fit, both physically and mentally. It is important for good health and particularly beneficial for the older adult with a dementing illness. Being fit improves self-esteem and mitigates the loss of mental abilities. Physical fitness helps to create a sense of well-being by helping the individual feel good about him- or herself and the surrounding world. People who exercise regularly report they feel happier, healthier, and more energetic and often require less sleep.

Life-style, inadequate exercise, poor nutrition, and failure to take care of oneself are the cause of many health problems. A systematic program of exercise can dramatically improve fitness and increase the odds for good health. Exercise maintains and improves functional health and wellness, enabling the older adult to live a more active, independent life.

There are many reasons people give for not exercising. The elderly, in particular, have developed many negative attitudes about exercise and fitness, believing they need less exercise as they age. The risks involved in vigorous exercise are often exaggerated, and the benefits of light, sporadic exercise are often overrated. The elderly also tend to underestimate their own abilities. Many older people wrongfully assume they cannot or should not participate in physical activities because they are too ill or handicapped and believe they must take things easy. Caregivers and older adults who share these attitudes may avoid participating in an exercise program. Exercise relieves the tension and stress of caregiving, enabling the caregiver to feel more relaxed, energetic, and better able to deal with daily problems.

BENEFITS OF EXERCISE AND PHYSICAL ACTIVITY

Exercise is an adult activity that the older person can enjoy. Physical activities such as walking, dancing, and exercise are a good way to keep the mentally impaired person active.

Exercise may not increase longevity, but there is proof that it can improve the quality of life. Regular exercise helps older adults to maintain their abilities, prevents functional decline, and provides opportunities for social interaction. A moderate exercise program provides psychological, social, and physiological benefits. These benefits include but are not limited to the following:

- Weight control is aided. Exercise improves the eating habits of individuals with poor appetites and moderates the appetite of overeaters. Exercise improves digestion, aids elimination, and prevents constipation.
- Through aerobic exercise cardiovascular endurance is enhanced. An effective exercise program can reduce the risk of cardiovascular disease, improve circulation and breathing, strengthen the heart beat, and lower blood pressure.
- Muscular strength and tone are improved. Without exercise muscles will quickly atrophy. Exercise improves muscular endurance, which enhances the older adult's ability to perform the tasks of daily living.
- Flexibility of joints and muscles and range of motion are improved, and the body is kept limber. The person who exercises feels healthier and experiences fewer aches and pains. The physical effort needed to perform routine tasks is minimized.
- Balance, coordination, and agility are improved.
- The efficiency and effectiveness of body organs and systems are improved.

- Posture and appearance are improved, which contributes to an improved self-image.
- Fatigue, even with adequate sleep, may be caused by a lack of physical activity. Exercise contributes to increased energy and is one of the best antedotes for chronic fatigue.
- Restlessness and agitation that may result from boredom and the need to express pent-up feelings are decreased. This may help to alleviate the need for tranquilizing medications.
- Individuals are helped to relax and feel less tense. Exercise improves the quality of sleep; it is a natural sleep producer and tranquilizer. Exercise can help to alleviate insomnia and night-time agitation.
- Emotional stress such as anger, fear, worry, tension, or depression is relieved. Exercise reduces mental fatigue, aids relaxation, and helps individuals cope with daily pressures.
- Mental health, is enhanced, and one achieves a feeling of well-being. Exercise helps to build confidence by helping the individual to understand and appreciate her or his abilities. Participation in an exercise program can provide a sense of satisfaction and accomplishment.
- Dance and other physical activities provide an opportunity for intimacy and sensory experiences, so often missing in the life of the impaired person.
- Group exercise activities provide participants with an opportunity to socialize and work toward a common goal. Group activities heighten enthusiasm and interest in participation. Exercise programs for institutionalized geriatric patients showed among the participants motivation toward self-care and improvement in orientation, social skills, and cognition.

GUIDELINES FOR DEVELOPING AN EXERCISE PROGRAM

An individual exercise program should be tailored to meet the older adult's needs and fitness level, a program that is comfortable, enjoyable, and within the person's limitations. Everyone should have a complete medical evaluation before starting an exercise program. An activity program should be based on past patterns of physical activity and current health status. A program can be developed using common sense and the guidance of a professional knowledgeable about exercise and physical fitness.

Following are some suggestions for developing and implementing an effective exercise program for the mentally impaired elderly:

- Exercise with the impaired person and encourage his or her actions. It may be necessary to guide his movements with your hands if verbal cues don't work. Make it fun by imitating his movements and having him imitate yours.
- Consider activities that the individual has enjoyed and find ways to modify them so that they can continue. Avoid complicated dance steps and sequences.
- If the individual has a catastrophic reaction, stop and try again later or direct the person to another activity.
- Select a routine time for exercise and be consistent. Exercise at the same time each day.
- Follow the same sequence of exercise. Start from the head and work down toward the feet.
- To be effective, exercise must be rhythmic, regular, reasonably vigorous, and continuous for at least 20 minutes or more. Exercise at least three times a week, preferably every other day. It is important to perform each exercise correctly.
- Start out slowly at a low level. Set a comfortable pace and build up gradually. Start out with 20 to 30 minute workouts, three times a week.
- Warm up. Begin each day's exercise with up to 20 minutes of stretching and conditioning exercises. Perform stretching exercises very slowly.
- Encourage individuals not to hold their breath while exercising but to breathe deeply and rhythmically.
- Wear loose-fitting clothing to allow for freedom of movement is needed.
- Avoid bouncy and quick, jerky movements. Perform all exercises in moderation. Pause briefly before changing direction to avoid dizziness. Take short rest periods throughout.
- Cool down. Allow 5 to 20 minutes to cool down after exercising by slowly walking and stretching. Slow down gradually.
- Avoid strenuous exercise immediately after a large meal.
- Don't allow participants to tire themselves. Stop immediately at any sign of undue stress or fatigue (marked shortness of breath, pain in the chest or elsewhere, nausea, trembling, pounding in the head, dizziness, or prolonged weakness). If you can keep up a conversation while exercising, it is generally not too strenuous. Body pains are good warning signals that the exercises are being

overdone. Discontinue the exercise if pain or discomfort is experienced and consult a physician.

- Periodically monitor the participant's response to exercise for signs of undue stress.
- If the exercise program is interrupted for any reason for more than a week, physical activity should be resumed gradually at fewer repetitions.
- Map out an emergency plan to follow in the event of cardiac arrest or other accidents. Physical activities should be adequately supervised.
- Make the exercise time fun and enjoyable. Exercise to music. Music helps to stimulate and guide movement and enhances body rhythm. Music helps to create the right mood. Use slower, soothing music during warm-up and cool-down. A wide variety of music, including jazz marches, ballads, classical, and country-western can be used. Children's music is inappropriate. Old familiar tunes can evoke memories and add to the enjoyment of the activity program. Use scarves, bicycle inner tubes, or wooden dowels to encourage movement to the music.
- Provide verbal encouragement. Positive reinforcement helps the participants to feel good about themselves. Recognize individual achievements and compliment everyone for participating.

EXERCISE AND PHYSICAL ACTIVITIES

Walking

Walking is one of the simplest and best all-around exercises. It can be done almost anywhere at any time. All that is required is a good pair of walking shoes. Walking is particularly suitable for the older adult with a dementing illness, because it's pleasurable and doesn't require a lot of mental activity.

- Lightweight clothes and comfortable low-heeled shoes that provide good support are needed for walking. Watch for signs of blisters or calluses. Walking generates a lot of body heat. In cold weather several layers of light clothing to trap body heat should be worn.
- Have a definite walking plan and distance to cover. Walk the same route daily. Point out scenery, people, and smells as you walk to help keep the confused person oriented to the environment.

- Warm up by walking slowly for 5 minutes. Walk briskly for 5 to 30 minutes. Build up this time gradually, increasing the distance walked and decreasing the time. Cool down by walking slowly for 5 minutes.
- Stop and rest at any sign of tiredness. Don't overdo it.
- A bath, shower, cup of tea, massage, or foot rubs may feel refreshing after a long walk and may serve as incentives to take more walks.

IDEAS FOR PHYSICAL FITNESS THROUGH EVERYDAY ACTIVITIES

- Take advantage of everyday activities to find opportunities for exercise and movement. Sweeping the yard, gardening, raking leaves, grocery shopping, and walking stairs are a few examples. Park the car several blocks from your destination to encourage walking.
- Maintain old interests. If the individual has played a sport such as golf, she or he may be able to continue to play and enjoy it. Rules may be forgotten and scores not kept, but the physical activity can be continued. Dancing is an activity many older adults enjoy.
- Wandering and walking can be an excellent exercise for the person with a dementing illness. Provide a safe area to wander and move freely.
- Rocking in a rocking chair is soothing and has many physical benefits.

Exercise Through Everyday Activities

Ask the participants to pretend they are performing these activities. Familiar movements are easier for a confused person to perform.

- *Scratch Your Back:* Reach behind and scratch your back. Repeat.
- *Putting on Your Shoes:* Lift up your foot to put on your shoes and tie them.
- *Swimming:* Imagine you are swimming. Do the crawl stroke and the breast stroke.
- *Open and Shut the Door:* Pretend you are opening and shutting a door. Turn the knob, pull open the door, and slam it shut.
- *Play the Piano:* Pretend you are playing the piano. Move up and down the keyboard. Pretend you are playing other musical instruments.

- *Massage:* Massage your face and hands. Pretend to wash your face.
- *Picking Apples:* Pick apples off the tree and put them in a basket.
- *Pick Up:* While seated, pick up an object from the floor. Sit up. Return it to the floor.
- *Conduct an Orchestra:* Use both hands to conduct an orchestra.
- *March in Place:* Start with left foot and march up and down, using arms and legs.
- *Shoulder Shrugs:* Shrug your shoulders as if to say, "I don't know."
- *Punching Bag:* Hit a punching bag. Clench your fists and start swinging in a round, rolling motion.
- *Chop Wood:* Pretend to hold an axe overhead and begin to chop wood.
- *Make Soup:* Stir a large kettle of soup with your right arm. Repeat with the left arm.
- *Rock the Baby:* Clasp hands together. Raise arms to shoulder level. Swing arms from side to side as if rocking a baby.
- *Flying Exercises:* Spread your wings and fly, alternating arms at first, then do both arms.
- *Lasso:* Make a circle overhead with each arm.
- *Make Faces:* Chew, squint, open eyes wide, open mouth wide as if to scream, tighten and relax face, make a big smile, say "Shhh," wrinkle nose as if smelling something.
- *Say the Vowels:* A-E-I-O-U. Clap at the same time.
- *Hug Yourself:* Cross arms in front of body and hug yourself.
- *Pretend You're Mad:* Stamp your feet, strike out, and look mad.
- *Be a Flower:* Make yourself small and slowly stretch yourself as if you were growing into a flower. Grow leaves and stretch in all directions.
- *Play Sports:* Imitate a sport and the way participants would move: Play tennis, cast for fish, throw a football, hit a golf ball, dribble a basketball, or catch a baseball.
- *Row the Boat:* Pretend you are rowing a boat.

A DAILY EXERCISE PROGRAM

Suggestions for Exercising

- Exercise sitting in a chair. Exercises are effective even if they are performed sitting down. Sitting while exercising places less strain on the lower back, feet, legs, and heart than standing exercises. The mentally confused older adult seems to feel more steady and confident when sitting while exercising. Use comfortable sturdy chairs, facing each other or placed in a circle. Sit straight, feet slightly apart.
- The exercise leader should explain what is to be done and demonstrate the exercise.
- Start with no more than five repetitions. The number of repetitions can be increased gradually at each individual's pace. Pause between exercises to enhance relaxation.

These exercises can be performed at home or in a group setting. Individuals that are in various stages of dementia with a mild to moderate level of impairment can participate. Choose those exercises that the individual or group enjoys doing.

Warm-Up. Warm-up exercises prepare the body for the work to come. Start with slow, relaxing movements. A 2-minute walk can also be useful as a warm-up activity.

EXERCISES

These exercises should be done while sitting in a chair.

Head Tip

1. Tip the head forward slowly, trying to touch the chin to the chest.
2. Tip the head back slowly, tilting only slightly back.
3. Tilt the head slowly to the right, keeping the shoulders down, ear to shoulder.
4. Repeat to the left.

Shaking Exercise

1. Stretch or extend arms forward and shake the hands out.
2. With arms to the side, shake out the hands.

Stretching Exercise

1. Raise the right arm overhead, bend the elbow, and reach the right hand to the back of the neck.
2. Stretch up.
3. Repeat with the left arm.

Shoulders and Arms

Shoulder Shrug
1. Place hands on the thighs.
2. Shrug the right shoulder up toward the ear and down.
3. Repeat with the left shoulder.
4. Shrug both shoulders up and down.
5. Bring shoulders forward and back.

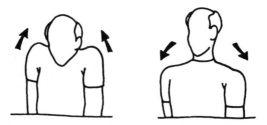

Arm Lifts
1. Close the fists and bend the elbows.
2. Keep elbows close to the side with the closed fists touching the shoulders.
3. Stretch the right arm above the head and try to reach the ceiling.
4. Bring the right arm back to the shoulder with elbows bent.
5. Repeat with the left arm.
6. Stretch the left arm to the left and the right arm to the right. Bring arms back to the shoulder.
7. Stretch both arms overhead, lower, and repeat.
8. Stretch arms out in front and open the palms toward the ceiling.

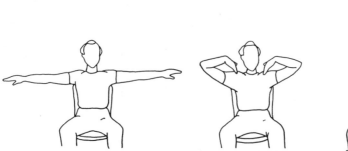

Arm Jogging
1. Move arms briskly forward and backward as if you were walking.

Swing Exercise
1. Keep arms to the side.
2. Swing the right arm forward and backward and then back to the side.
3. Repeat with the left arm.
4. Swing both arms upward, over the head, and then back to the side.

Crisscross
1. Extend the right and left arm out horizontally, keeping the arms at shoulder level.
2. Move arms forward and crisscross.

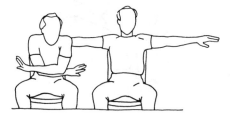

Arm Circles
1. Stretch arms out to the side, elbows straight and palms down.
2. Rotate both arms forward from the shoulders, making very small and slow circles.
3. Repeat, circling backward.

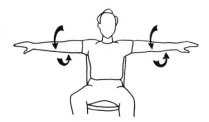

Pulling Exercise

1. Extend arms forward at shoulder level, palms up and make a fist.
2. Draw elbows close to the chest and move hands toward the shoulders in a pulling motion.

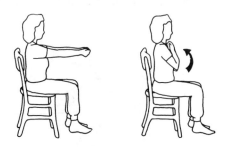

Clasp Hands

1. Place clasped hands behind the head.
2. Turn toward the right. Return to the center.
3. Repeat to the left.

Touch Elbows

1. Place hands on the shoulders.
2. Bring elbows forward and touch them together.

Hands, Wrist, and Fingers

Hand Exercises
1. Extend arms forward.
2. Close fists tightly, then extend fingers, opening and closing fists.

Hand Circles

1. Grasp the right wrist underneath with the left hand.
2. Slowly rotate the right hand making large, complete clockwise circles, palms facing down.
3. Repeat counterclockwise.
4. Repeat with the opposite hand.

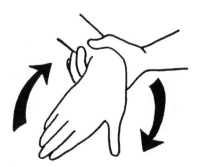

Palm Stretch

1. Clasp hands together in front of the chest.
2. Extend arms fully, turning palms away from the body.
3. Return to the starting position and repeat.

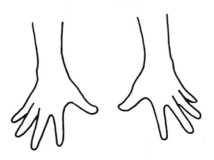

Thumb Circles

1. Rotate the right thumb forward and backward slowly.
2. Repeat with the left thumb.
3. Rotate both thumbs forward and backward.

Finger Fans

1. Extend arms forward, palms down.
2. Spread fingers wide apart and then bring them together.
3. Face palms out with fingers tightly touching each other.
4. Spread fingers widely apart. Repeat.

Clap Hands

1. Clap hands in time to the music.
2. Circle hands clockwise while clapping.
3. Repeat counterclockwise.

Torso

Torso Twist

1. Clasp hands at chin level.
2. Twist to the left. Return to the starting position.
3. Repeat to the right.

Side Bender

1. Stretch a scarf or dowel overhead, hands shoulder width apart.
2. Bend to the left. Return to the starting position.
3. Repeat to the right.

Side Reaches

1. Sit with feet spread wide apart and arms extended at shoulder height.
2. Reach as far as you can to the right.
3. Repeat to the left.

Side Bends

1. Sit with arms at sides, feet flat on the floor.
2. Reach the right arm up into the air and keep it close to the head.
3. Bend to the left. Bring the right arm over head and stretch.
4. Repeat on the other side.

Waist Whittler

1. Place hands on the waist.
2. Twist from side to side.

Side Pulls

1. Drop the right hand toward the floor, arms at sides.
2. Let the weight pull the body down to the right.
3. Repeat on the left side.

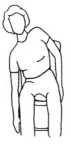

Feet, Ankles, and Legs

Foot Rotations

1. Lift the right leg slightly. Draw big clockwise circles with the toes.
2. Reverse direction.
3. Repeat with the left foot.

Ankle Flex

1. Extend the right leg and flex the ankle toward the shin. Extend forward.
2. Repeat with the left ankle.
3. Repeat with both ankles.

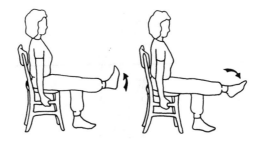

Ankle Benders

1. Put both feet together flat on the floor.
2. Lift heels off the floor. Return to the starting position.

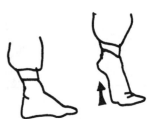

Foot Slides

1. Hold onto the chair with feet together, flat on the floor.
2. Slide one foot forward along the floor and the other foot backward toward the chair.
3. Reverse direction.
4. Put both feet together. Move the right foot all the way to the right and the left foot to the left. Do this in cadence.

Heel to Toe

1. Hold onto the sides of the chair and lift legs off the floor.
2. Point toes toward each other.
3. Bring heels together.

Crossovers

1. Extend legs forward.
2. Cross the right leg over the left, then the left leg over the right.

Leg Rotations

1. Extend the right leg forward and make a complete circle in the air with the foot.
2. Reverse direction.
3. Repeat with the left leg.
4. Hold onto the chair. Rotate both legs at the same time.
5. Reverse direction.

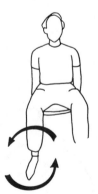

Thigh Exercises

1. Place hands on the outside of the knees, feet flat on the floor and knees separated.
2. Push against the hands with the knees to a slow count of five.
3. Place hands on the inside of the knees.
4. Bring the knees together while pushing against the hands slowly to a count of five.

 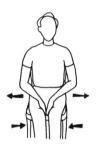

Double Leg Lift

1. Hold the sides of the chair with feet together.
2. Lift both feet off the floor and extend legs forward.
3. Return to the starting position.

Cool-Down

Cool-down is designed to gradually return the body to a nonexercising state. Relaxing exercises such as these should be emphasized:

Rag Doll

1. Sit toward the front of the chair, legs 12″ apart.
2. Lift both hands overhead as if reaching for the ceiling.
3. Bend slowly forward from the waist, keeping the knees straight. Let the arms and hands hang down as far as possible toward the toes. Relax like a rag doll, keeping the chin to the chest.
4. Breathe in and let the air float you back up slowly.
5. Repeat.

Deep Breathing

1. Place hands on the rib cage.
2. Deep breathe in through the nose and out through the nose.
3. Repeat three times.
4. Hold breath for a count of three.
5. Repeat three times.

FUN FINALES FOR EXERCISE GROUPS

Soccer

Materials:
Nerf soccerball, music.

Procedure:
Participants should sit in a large circle facing the group leader. The leader begins by kicking the ball to one of the participants. Each person is to kick the ball when it lands at his or her feet. The ball can be kicked around the circle or kicked to the opposite side of the circle.

Parachute Toss

Materials:
Parachute, music.

Procedure:
Participants should sit in a large circle. Each participant grabs onto the parachute with both hands and moves it up and down. Place a ball in the center and move it all around. Make waves with the parachute. Move the parachute in time to different music.

Clasp Hands

Participants should sit in a large circle, holding hands. Swing arms forward to the mood of the music. Lean toward the right while holding hands. Return to the starting position. Repeat to the left. Bend forward and back while holding hands.

Balloon Volleyball

Materials:
Large balloon or beachball; cord, net, or a 3″ ribbon of crepe paper suspended between two poles or walls, approximately 4 feet from the ground. Chalk, string, or other markers can be used to mark the side boundaries. Divide the participants into two teams of equal size.

Rules of Play:

1. Server tips the ball to get it over the net.
2. Ball is out of play if it does not go over the net in three tips, if it touches the floor, if it goes over the boundary, or if the same player hits it twice in a row.
3. If the serving team puts the ball out of play, the serve goes to the other team and no points are scored.
4. If the receiving team puts the ball out of play, the serving team scores a point and serves the ball.
5. The winning score is 21 points for a team.

Rules are made to be broken. The game can be simplified to suit the needs of the participants.

Toss and Catch

Materials:
Large nerf ball or inflatable beach ball.

Procedure:
Participants should sit in a large circle. The leader can toss the ball back and forth to each person in the circle. The participants can also toss the ball to each other or pass the ball around the circle.

Exercise with Scarves

Materials:
Large, brightly colored scarves, music.

Procedure:
Participants should sit in a large circle. The leader uses the scarves to move to the mood of the music and encourages the participants to follow her or his lead.

The Wave

Participants should sit in a circle and hold hands with the persons on both sides. Everyone should lean to the left, then to the right, back to the left, and so on. Repeat.

Games like these can make exercise more fun and enjoyable. Chapter 14 includes games that are fun and mentally challenging.

14

Games

Games are entertaining and fun to play. Games arouse interest and encourage social interaction. Playing a game helps the confused older person stay alert and oriented. Being able to play a game or give an answer to a quiz helps to build confidence and self-esteem.

SUGGESTIONS FOR INTRODUCING AND PLAYING GAMES

Games should be adult in type and presentation. The activity should be adapted to the ability level of the individual or group. Simplification is essential! The leader should be flexible and willing to modify the game as needed. In a group activity, the leader may need assistance to help and encourage the individual players to participate.

When introducing a game, the leader should name it, explain it briefly, and demonstrate how it is played. If the leader is enthusiastic, the players will be, too. Games can be played in teams, so that individual players are not threatened by lack of skill or knowledge. Players should not be singled out to respond or asked to take a turn. Play should be stopped before the players lose interest so the group will be enthusiastic for the next activity. Points can be given and prizes or awards presented to the winner or winning team at the game's finale.

Questions related to an individual's past history make it easier for the confused person to respond. Historic events are more easily retained than current events. Use familiar names and phrases to evoke old memories and stimulate conversation. Provide clues to help individuals respond. Material that was memorized, such as multiplication tables and prayers, are often easily recalled.

Large-print playing cards and bingo games, rubber horseshoes, a felt dartboard with nerf darts, nerf balls, foam rubber puzzles, and other adaptive games that are easy to use can be purchased. Contests such as guessing the number of beans in a jar or predicting the first snowfall, a baby's birthday and weight, or the weather are also fun.

GAMES

Famous Persons

Prepare a list of famous persons. The leader states the first or last part of their name and the participants fill in the rest of the name. Give hints. You can also use categories such as U.S. presidents or movie stars.

Famous Americans

George	**Washington**	Abraham	**Lincoln**
Christopher	**Columbus**	Davy	**Crockett**
Annie	**Oakley**	Daniel	**Boone**
Buffalo Bill	**Cody**	Benjamin	**Franklin**
Calamity	**Jane**	Benedict	**Arnold**
Francis Scott	**Key**	John Paul	**Jones**
John Quincy	**Adams**	Andrew	**Jackson**
Elizabeth Cady	**Stanton**	Millard	**Fillmore**
Jefferson	**Davis**	Robert E.	**Lee**
Ulysses S.	**Grant**	Harriet	**Tubman**
General George S.	**Custer**	Grover	**Cleveland**
Booker T.	**Washington**	Franklin Delano	**Roosevelt**
Helen	**Keller**	Frank Lloyd	**Wright**
George Washington	**Carver**	Susan B.	**Anthony**
Warren G.	**Harding**	Calvin	**Coolidge**
F. Scott	**Fitzgerald**	Charles A.	**Lindbergh**
Herbert	**Hoover**	Amelia	**Earhart**
Eleanor	**Roosevelt**	Ernest	**Hemingway**
General Douglas	**MacArthur**	Harry S	**Truman**
Adlai E.	**Stevenson**	Dwight D.	**Eisenhower**
Dr. Jonas	**Salk**	Henry Cabot	**Lodge**
Martin Luther	**King**	John F.	**Kennedy**
Malcolm	**X**	Richard Milhous	**Nixon**

Famous Others

Benito	**Mussolini**	Adolph	**Hitler**
Genghis	**Khan**	Charles	**DeGaulle**
Napoleon	**Bonaparte**	Bing	**Crosby**
Zsa Zsa	**Gabor**	Mitch	**Miller**
Babe	**Ruth**	Count	**Basie**
Duke	**Ellington**	Greta	**Garbo**
Lucille	**Ball**	Cary	**Grant**
Erroll	**Flynn**	Rita	**Hayworth**
Clark	**Gable**	W. C.	**Fields**
Mae	**West**		

Who Am I?*

Who is the "Father of Our Country"? **George Washington**
What was William Frederick Cody's nickname? **Buffalo Bill**
Who was known as the "Lone Eagle" who flew the *Spirit of St. Louis* from New York to Paris? **Charles Lindbergh**
What was Samuel Clemens's pen name? **Mark Twain**
Who was called "Old Hickory" by his soldiers? **Andrew Jackson**
Who was a "Rough Rider" and a U.S. president? **Teddy Roosevelt**
Who formulated the theory of relativity? **Albert Einstein**
Who was the "Greatest Showman on Earth"? **P. T. Barnum**
Who said, "Give me liberty or give me death"? **Patrick Henry**
Who was nicknamed "Silent Cal"? **Calvin Coolidge**
Who was called "Schnozzola" because of his big nose? **Jimmy Durante**
What notorious gangster was known as "Pretty Boy ___"? **Floyd**
Who was sent to Alcatraz for income tax evasion after being kingpin of the Underworld? **Al Capone**
Who invented the telephone? **Alexander Graham Bell**
Who was nicknamed "The Brown Bomber"? **Joe Louis**
Who is famous for the line, "Come up'n see me sometime"? **Mae West**
Who was nicknamed "Blood and Guts"? **General George Patton**
Who was the labor leader and president of the UMWA who organized the Congress of Industrialized Organizations? **John L. Lewis**
Who developed the polio vaccine? **Dr. Jonas Salk**
Who was the first man to walk on the moon? **Neil Armstrong**

*Adapted from T. Merrill *Activities for the Aged and Infirm* A Handbook for the Untrained Worker © 1979. Courtesy of Charles C Thomas, Publisher, Springfield, IL.

Famous Duos*

Abbott and Costello
Laurel and Hardy
Fred Astaire and Ginger Rogers
Pat and Mike
Romeo and Juliet
Adam and Eve
Cain and Abel
Gilbert and Sullivan

George Burns and Gracie Allen
Amos and Andy
Rogers and Hammerstein
Edgar Bergen and Charlie McCarthy
Sacco and Vanzetti
Samson and Delilah
Spencer Tracy and Katherine Hepburn
Jimmy Durante and Mrs. Calabash
Scarlett O'Hara and Rhett Butler
Fibber McGee and Molly
Punch and Judy
Daisy Mae and Lil' Abner

*Adapted from J. Lacy *The Games Older People Play.*

Famous Quotes*

"Honor thy father and thy mother."	**The Bible (Exodus)**
"Nice guys finish last."	**Leo Durocher**
"Frankly, my dear, I don't give a damn."	**Rhett Butler *(Gone with the Wind)***
"There's a sucker born every minute."	**P. T. Barnum**
"I'm only thirty-nine."	**Jack Benny**
"The public be damned!"	**William Vanderbilt**
"One small step for man, one giant leap for mankind."	**Neil Armstrong**
"Ask not what your country can do for you; ask what you can do for your country."	**John F. Kennedy**
"We have nothing to fear but fear itself."	**Franklin Delano Roosevelt**
"The buck stops here."	**Harry S Truman**
"A rose is a rose is a rose."	**Gertrude Stein**
"Good night, Mrs. Calabash, wherever you are."	**Jimmy Durante**

INVENTIONS

Who Invented the Following?

The inventor may not be known, but the invention will be.

Sleeping car	**Pullman**
Electric razor	**Schick**
Safety razor	**Gillette**
The elevator	**Otis**
The telephone	**Bell**
The carpet sweeper	**Bissell**
Vulcanized rubber	**Goodyear**
Mercury thermometer	**Farenheit**

Nylon stockings	**DuPont**
Sewing machine	**Howe**
Dynamite	**Nobel**

TRADES

Name the person who has this type of job:

Carries the mail	**Mailcarrier**
Takes care of sick animals	**Veterinarian**
Keeps buildings clean	**Custodian, janitor**
Keeps law and order	**Police officer**
Fills prescriptions	**Pharmacist**
Fights for a country	**Soldier**
Works on your teeth	**Dentist**
Takes care of young children	**Nanny, Babysitter**
Sells flowers	**Florist**
Fights fires	**Fire fighter**
Teaches school	**Teacher**
Drives a bus	**Bus driver**
Serves food in a restaurant	**Waiter, Waitress**
Reports the news	**Newscaster, Reporter**
Flies an airplane	**Pilot**
Types letters and files	**Secretary**
Cuts men's hair	**Barber**
Gives legal advice	**Lawyer**
Teaches at a college level	**Professor**

TOOLS OF THE TRADE*

A colander is used by a	**cook**
An auger is used by a	**carpenter**
A T square is used by a	**draftsman**
A conduit is used by an	**electrician**
A cultivator is used by a	**farmer**
A trowel is used by a	**mason**
A scalpel is used by a	**surgeon**
Spigots are used by a	**plumber**
A drill is used by a	**dentist**
A ledger is used by a	**accountant**
An easel is used by a	**painter**

Adapted from T. Merrill *Activities for the Aged and Infirm,* A Handbook for the Untrained Worker, © 1979. Courtesy of Charles C Thomas, Publisher, Springfield, IL.

WEIGHTS AND MEASUREMENTS

| How many cups in a quart? | **4** | How many cups in a pint? | **2** |
| How many ounces in a cup? | **8** | How many inches in a foot? | **12** |

How many pounds in a ton?	**2,000**	How many feet in a yard?	**3**
How many ounces in a pound?	**16**	How many inches in a yard?	**36**
How many pints in a quart?	**2**	How many feet in a mile?	**5,280**

WHERE WOULD YOU BE IF . . .

You see herds of zebras, giraffes, and elephants?	**Africa**
You are greeted by an "Aloha" and a lei of fresh flowers?	**Hawaii**
You see the Eiffel Tower?	**Paris, France**
You travel through the streets of this city in a gondola?	**Venice, Italy**
You're in the "City of Brotherly Love"?	**Philadelphia, PA**
You're at the Mardi Gras?	**New Orleans, LA**
You're at the Kentucky Derby?	**Louisville, KY**
You're crossing the Golden Gate Bridge?	**San Francisco, CA**
You see the Statue of Liberty?	**New York City**
You see a lot of movie stars and the famous Walk of Stars?	**Hollywood, CA**
You see Big Ben?	**London, England**
You're at the White House, home of the President of the U.S.?	**Washington, DC**
You're in "Mile High City"?	**Denver, CO**
You see a penguin?	**Antarctica**
You see tulips and people wearing wooden shoes?	**Holland**
You see the pyramids?	**Egypt**
You see a bullfight?	**Spain or Mexico**
You are "down under"?	**Australia**
You are on the "Great Wall"?	**China**

ONE, TWO . . . THREE*

Lock, stock, and **barrel**
Tic tac, **toe**
Eat, drink, and **be merry**
Sugar and spice and **everything nice**
Ear, nose, and **throat**
Healthy, wealthy, and **wise**
Tall, dark, and **handsome**
Faith, hope, and **charity**
Wynken, Blynken, and **Nod**
Stop, look, and **listen**
Hook, line, and **sinker**
Animal, vegetable, and **mineral**

Love, honor, and **obey**
Niña, Pinta, and **the Santa Maria**

Baubles, bangles, and **beads**

Ready, set, **go**
Hear no evil, see no evil, **speak no evil**
Snips and snails and **puppy dog tails**
Ready, willing, and **able**
Reading, writing, and **arithmetic**
Wine, women, and **song**
Tom, Dick, and **Harry**
Kukla, Fran, and **Ollie**
Friends, Romans, **Countrymen**
Hop, skip, and **jump**
Larry, Moe, and **Curly**
Life, liberty, and **the pursuit of happiness**
Acheson, Topeka, and **the Santa Fe**
The butcher, the baker, and **the candlestick maker**
Fair, fat, and **forty**

*Adapted from "The Games Older People Play."

PROVERBS

The leader reads half a proverb and the participants finish it. These familiar sayings are easily remembered:

Experience is the	**mother of learning**
Familiarity breeds	**contempt**
Music hath charms to	**soothe the savage beast**
Appearances are	**deceitful**
It takes two to make a bargain	**or a quarrel**
It is better to be safe	**than sorry**
Never cry over	**spilled milk**
A watched pot	**never boils**
Fine feathers	**make fine birds**
Possession is nine tenths	**of the law**
Wherever there is smoke,	**there's fire**
Necessity is the	**mother of invention**
Speech is silver,	**silence is golden**
Never put off until tomorrow	**what you can do today**
Nothing ventured,	**nothing gained**
Honesty is the	**best policy**
You can lead a horse to water	**but you can't make him drink**
Brevity is the	**soul of wit**
Manners make the	**man**
Every rose has its	**thorn**
Better late than	**never**
Easy come,	**easy go**
Marry in haste,	**repent at leisure**
Paddle your	**own canoe**
Spare the rod,	**spoil the child**
Out of sight,	**out of mind**
All is fair	**in love and war**
People who live in glass houses	**shouldn't throw stones**
An apple a day	**keeps the doctor away**
A stitch in time	**saves nine**
A bird in the hand	**is worth two in the bush**
Practice makes	**perfect**
Absence makes	**the heart grow fonder**
Misery loves	**company**
A fool and his money	**are soon parted**
All things come to him	**who waits**
The early bird	**catches the worm**
Birds of a feather	**flock together**
Too many cooks	**spoil the broth**
Actions speak louder	**than words**
When the cat's away,	**the mice will play**
You can't have your cake	**and eat it, too**
You've made your bed,	**now lie in it**
A rolling stone	**gathers no moss**
A miss is as good	**as a mile**
Don't count your chickens	**before they are hatched**

Children should be seen	**and not heard**
Every cloud	**has a silver lining**
Cleanliness is next to	**godliness**
The pen is mightier	**than the sword**
What goes up	**must come down**
A penny saved is	**a penny earned**
Time flies	**when you are having fun**
If you can't fight them	**join them**
Don't throw the baby	**out with the bathwater**
Life is just a	**bowl of cherries**
The best things in life	**are free**
It's not the company, it's	**the hour**
The truth	**hurts**
When in Rome,	**do as the Romans do**
Curiosity	**killed the cat**

SIMILES*

Deaf as a **post.**	Dumb as a **doorbell.**
Bright as a **star.**	Smart as a **whip.**
Blind as a **bat.**	Brown as a **berry.**
Busy as a **bee.**	Clean as a **whistle.**
Clear as a **bell (mud).**	Crazy as a **loon.**
Cross as a **bear.**	Dead as a **mackerel (doornail).**
Dry as a **bone.**	Fat as a **pig.**
Fit as a **fiddle.**	Flat as a **pancake.**
Happy as a **lark.**	Hard as a **nail (rock).**
Light as a **feather.**	Mad as a **hornet.**
Neat as a **pin.**	Nervous as a **cat's tail.**
Playful as a **kitten.**	Pretty as a **picture.**
Proud as a **peacock.**	Pure as a **lily.**
Quick as a **flash (wink).**	Poor as a **churchmouse.**
Red as a **rose.**	Sharp as a **tack.**
Slippery as an **eel.**	Sly as a **fox.**
Sound as a **bell.**	Sore as a **boil.**
Sour as a **lemon.**	Stiff as a **poker (board).**
Strong as an **ox or mule.**	Quiet as a **mouse.**
Pale as a **ghost.**	Brave as a **lion.**
Ugly as **sin.**	Fair as a **maiden.**
Limp as a **dishrag.**	Higher than a **kite.**
Slick as a **whistle.**	Straight as an **arrow.**
Dirty as a **pig.**	Tired as a **dog.**
Bitter as **gall.**	Spry as a **spring chicken.**
Pure as an **angel.**	Wise as an **owl.**
Thin as a **dime.**	Fresh as a **daisy.**

Adapted from T. Merrill *Activities for the Aged and Infirm*, A Handbook for the Untrained Worker, © 1979. Courtesy of Charles C Thomas, Publisher, Springfield, IL.

SUPERSTITIONS

What does it mean when:

A black cat crosses your path?	**Bad luck**
Your foot is itchy?	**You're walking on strange ground.**
You drop a fork?	**A woman is coming to visit.**
You drop a knife?	**A man is coming to visit.**
There is a bird in the house?	**Death.**
Your palm is itchy?	**You will receive money.**
You break a mirror?	**Seven years bad luck.**
You open an umbrella in the house?	**Bad luck.**
You walk under a ladder?	**Bad luck.**
Your nose is itchy?	**You will hear news.**
Your ears are burning?	**Someone is talking about you.**

WHAT DO YOU USE:

To dry the dishes?	**Dish towel**
To weigh yourself?	**Scale**
To hear the news?	**Radio, television**
To store clothing?	**Closet**
To dig a hole?	**Shovel**
To wash your clothing?	**Washing machine**
For seasoning food?	**Salt, pepper, herbs, spices**
To fix your hair?	**Comb, brush**
To cook the dinner?	**Stove**
To sit on?	**Chair**
To tell the time?	**Clock**
To take pictures?	**Camera**
To cut paper?	**Scissors**
To keep food cold?	**Refrigerator**
To take your temperature?	**Thermometer**
To sew on buttons?	**Needle and thread**
To wipe up a spill?	**Mop**
To light a fire?	**Match**
To cut the grass?	**Lawnmower**
To measure height?	**Tape measure**

COMPLETE THIS:

Bread and _____	Up and _____
In and _____	Yes and _____
Horse and _____	Cream and _____
Fork and _____	Down and _____
Stop and _____	Brother and _____
Cause and _____	Bacon and _____

Cat and _____

Shoes and _____

Boy and _____

Supply and _____

Paper and _____

Cigarette and _____

Needle and _____

Soap and _____

Salt and _____

Black and _____

Mutt and _____

A young _____

A lot of _____

A tank of _____

A glass of _____

Peanut butter and _____

North and _____

Dollars and _____

Time to wake _____

Love and _____

Hot and _____

You and _____

Old and _____

Pen and _____

Fire and _____

Night and _____

Comb and _____

Milk and _____

Meat and _____

A new _____

A cup of _____

A bowl of _____

A batch of _____

A box of _____

Nickels and _____

Good and _____

As hungry as a _____

How are _____

Soup and _____

Heaven and _____

Give an appropriate word to complete the sentence:

Please be _____.

She is my best _____.

How much do you think it will _____?

She's asleep on the _____.

He's as strong as an _____.

He wore a shirt and _____.

I ate much too _____.

It cost 25 _____.

I need an answer to my _____.

The children are making too much _____.

It's on the tip of my _____.

It's too good to be _____.

Three strikes and you're _____.

His daughter is in the fourth _____.

After Tuesday comes _____.

I will teach them a good _____.

His house is not for _____.

They set the wood on _____.

Have a Happy New _____.

She works until 4:00 _____.

They are like two peas in a _____.

As hungry as a _____.

How are _____?

Take a deep _____.

Love and _____.

COLOR QUIZ*

A kind of:

Scissors	**Pinking** shears
Flower	**Bluebell**
Wartime lights-out	**Black**out
Member of the Nazi party	**Brown**shirt
21—the card game	**Black**jack
Sign of surrender	**White**flag
List of undesirables	**Black**list
Government bureaucracy	**Red** tape
First prize	**Blue** ribbon
Place where flowers grow	**Green**house
Snowy Christmas	**White** Christmas
Little (fifth) finger	**Pink**ie
Factory worker	**Blue** collar
Professional worker	**White** collar
Extortion	**Black**mail
Robin	**Red**breast
American Indian	**Red**skin
Spiced bread and apple pudding	**Brown** Betty
Aristocrats	**Blue**bloods
A skillful gardener	**Green** thumb
Giant trees of California	**Red**woods
Paint the town	**Red**
Sailor	**Blue**jacket
Object without value	**White** elephant
Building plans	**Blue**prints
Go	**Green** light
Where the President lives	**White** House
Communist sympathizer	**Pink**o
Novice	**Green**horn
Waltz	**Blue** Danube
"_____ Rose of Texas"	**Yellow**
"By the Light of the	**Silvery** Moon"

Adapted from "The Games Older People Play."

ANIMAL QUIZ

What is the largest bird in the world?	**Ostrich**
What is the plural of moose?	**Moose**
What is the largest land mammal?	**Elephant**
What is the tallest animal?	**Giraffe**
What is the largest mammal?	**Blue whale**
What animal lives the longest?	**Turtle/Tortoise**

Animal	Male	Female	Young	Group
Cat	Tom	Puss	Kitten	Clowder
Cow	Bull	Cow	Calf	Herd
Deer	Buck/Stag	Doe	Fawn	Herd
Dog	Dog	Bitch	Pup	Kennel
Goat	Billy	Nanny	Kid	Herd
Goose	Gander	Goose	Gosling	Gaggle/Flock
Horse	Stallion/Stud	Dam/Mare	Foal	Herd
			Colt (m.)	
			Filly (f.)	
Lion	Lion	Lioness	Cub	Pride
Sheep	Buck	Dam	Lamb	Flock
	Ram	Ewe	Lambkin	Herd
Turkey	Gobbler/Tom	Hen	Poult	Flock
Pig	Boar	Sow	Piglet	
Frog			Tadpole	
Whale	Bull	Cow	Calf	Pod
Seal	Bull	Cow	Pup	Herd
Duck	Drake	Gander	Duckling	Flock
Bear	Boar	Sow	Cub	
Elephant	Bull	Cow	Calf	Family/Herd
Donkey	Jackass	Jennie	Foal/Colt	Herd
Rabbit	Buck	Doe	Kitten	

NUMBERS QUIZ*

Fill in the correct number.

His better **half.**
Seven-Year Itch.
House of **Seven** Gables.
The **Three** Musketeers.
The **three** Rs.
Seventh inning stretch.
The **13** colonies.
Three wise men.
Cat-o'-**nine**-tails.
Three blind mice.
Friday the **thirteenth.**
Around the World in **Eighty** Days.
Four and **twenty** blackbirds.
The Armistice, **eleventh** hour,
eleventh month, and **eleventh** day.
A cat has **nine** lives.
Rain before **seven,** dry before
eleven.

At the stroke of **Twelve.**

Thousand Island dressing.
Pieces of **eight.**
The Gay **Nineties.**
Fair, fat, and **forty.**
He sailed the **seven** seas.
Tea for **two.**
Twelfth Night.
Seven men on a dead man's chest.
Two is company, **three's** a crowd.
Seven wonders of the world.
Ali Baba and the **Forty** Thieves.
Three cheers.
The roaring **twenties.**

Seven years of bad luck.
Drawn and **quartered.**

"The night has a **thousand** eyes, the
day but **one.**"
The first **100** years are the hardest.

How many states in the Union? **50**

How many days in a year? **365**

How many cookies in a baker's dozen? **13**

How many weeks in a year? **52**

*Adapted from T. Merrill *Activities for the Aged and Infirm*, A Handbook for the Untrained Worker, © 1979. Courtesy of Charles C Thomas, Publisher, Springfield, IL.

ADVERTISING SLOGANS*

Keep that schoolgirl complexion. **Palmolive**
Chases dirt. **Old Dutch**
When it rains it pours. **Morton's Salt**
Good to the last drop. **Maxwell House Coffee**
Hasn't scratched yet. **Bon Ami**
From contented cows. **Carnation Milk**
Cover the earth. **Sherwin William's Paint**
The flavor lasts. **Wrigley's Chewing Gum**
His master's voice. **RCA Victor**
The instrument of immortals. **Steinway Piano**
A clean tooth never decays. **Colgate**
There's a reason. **Postum**
For economical transportation. **Greyhound**
The skin you love to touch. **Woodbury**
The name that means everything in electricity. **General Electric**
Melts in your mouth, not in your hand. **M&M's**

Note: Pictures of the products can be shown to stimulate recall.

*Adapted from T. Merrill *Activities for the Aged and Infirm*, A Handbook for the Untrained Worker, © 1979. Courtesy of Charles C Thomas, Publisher, Springfield, IL.)

MUSICAL QUIZ*

What did I hold "on my knee" when "I went to Alabama" to see Susanna?   **Banjo**
"You may search everywhere but none can compare" with what?
    "My Wild Irish Rose"
What color was "the bonnet with the blue ribbons on it"?   **Gray**
What time of the year am I "coming back to you" in the Rockies?   **Springtime**
What did Dinah blow?   **Horn**
Who was in the kitchen with Dinah?   **Someone**
What is the famous World War I song written by George M. Cohan?
    "Over There"
How old was "My village queen, down by the old mill stream?"   **Sixteen**
"Give my regards to   **Broadway."**
In the "Good Old Summertime," the young lady is referred to as
    "your tootsie-wootsie."

What kind of horse did the man bet his money on at the Camptown Races?
"Bobtailed nag"
What kind of flowers do you "tiptoe thru"?   **Tulips**

*Adapted from T. Merrill *Activities for the Aged and Infirm,* A Handbook for the Untrained Worker, © 1979. Courtesy of Charles C Thomas, Publisher, Springfield, IL.)*

SPORTS QUIZ

Who was the only man to knock out Jack Dempsey during his years as champion?   **No one**
Who did knock out John L. Sullivan?   **Jim Corbett**
Who won the heavyweight boxing crown by a foul decision?   **Jack Sharkey**
Where is a "spot shot" used?   **Pool**
In what sport was there a "Louisville Slugger?"   **Baseball**
Who gave Joe Louis the worst beating in his entire career?   **Max Schmelling**
Who were the two great pitching brothers in the early '30's?   **Dizzy and Paul Dean**
Who was the "Beer Barrel"?   **Tony Galento**
Who made top records in speedboat racing and "sweet music"?
        Guy Lombardo
Who was "Slinging Sammy"?   **Sammy Baugh**
Who established football as a great sport?   **Walter Camp**
Who was the greatest billiard player of all time?   **Willie Hoppe**
What is the NFL?
        National Football League
How many players are on a football team?   **Eleven**
How many points are scored for a touchdown in football?   **Six**
What is the professional association for basketball?
        National Basketball Association
In baseball what does RBI stand for?   **Runs batted in**
Name the two New York City baseball teams.   **Mets and Yankees**

GAMES FOR SPORTSMEN*

Name the game in which the following expressions are used:

Fore	**Golf**	Checkmate	**Chess**
Slide	**Baseball**	Double	**Baseball**
Break	**Boxing**	Tallyho	**Fox Hunting**
Serve	**Tennis**	Fifteen two	**Cribbage**
Sweep	**Hockey**	First down	**Football**

Name the game which is started in each of the following ways:

Jump at center	**Basketball**	Face off	**Lacrosse**
Kick off	**Football**	Tee off	**Golf**

Play for serve	**Tennis**	Bell rings	**Boxing**
	Poker	On the mark	**Racing**
Break the balls	**Pool**	Batter up	**Baseball**

Name the sport in which each of the following is forbidden or illegal:

Reneging	**Cards**	Moving into check	**Chess**
Feet past limit	**Bowling**	Touching net	**Tennis**
Moistening ball	**Baseball**		

Name the sport in which each of the following is used:

Épée	**Fencing**	Brassie	**Golf**
Bird	**Badminton**	Silks	**Racing**
Rosin bag	**Baseball**	Eight ball	**Pool**
Fly	**Fishing**	Touching net	**Basketball**

Name the game which is measured off by each of the following:

Rounds	**Boxing**	Periods	**Basketball**
Innings	**Baseball**	Sets	**Tennis**
Frames	**Bowling**	18 holes	**Golf**
Quarters	**Football**	120 holes	**Cribbage**

CHAMPIONSHIP QUIZ

Match the sport to its championship.

World Cup	**Soccer**
Super Bowl	**Football**
World Series	**Baseball**
Championship	**Basketball**
U.S. Open	**Golf**
Stanley Cup	**Hockey**

Reprinted with permission from T. Merrill *Activities for the Aged and Infirm*, A Handbook for the Untrained Worker, © 1979. Courtesy of Charles C Thomas, Publisher, Springfield, IL.

DO YOU KNOW:

What suits of regular playing cards have one-eyed jacks?   **Hearts and spades**
Does the red or green light appear on top of a traffic signal?   **Red**
Whose face appears on a five-dollar bill?   **Abe Lincoln**
How many keys are there on a standard typewriter?   **Forty-two**
Do buttonholes of a man's shirt run vertically or horizontally?   **Vertically**
Do men's coats button to the right or the left?   **Right**
On which side is the bow on a man's hat?   **Left**
Whose face appears on a ten-dollar bill?   **Alexander Hamilton**
Which stripe appears at the top of the American flag, the red or the white?   **Red**
On which side of the sink is the hot water usually found?   **Left**
In which hand does the Statue of Liberty hold her torch?   **Right**
Does the eagle's head face right or left on a quarter?   **Left**
What is the national holiday of Canada?   **Dominion Day**
What is a southpaw?   **A left-handed person**
What does IQ stand for?   **Intelligence Quotient**
What is the national sport of Spain?   **Bullfighting**
What great city in the United States is built on seven hills?   **Seattle**
What is the name of the day celebrated by planting trees in a great many states?   **Arbor Day**
In what one state are the highest and lowest points in the United States?
     California
How many sides does a hexagon have?   **Six**
How many sides does an octagon have?   **Eight**

GESTURES

Make a gesture for each of these common phrases:

Yes.
No.
Hello.
Goodbye.
Come here.
I don't know.
Sit down.
Give it to me.
Go away.
Stand up.
Take it away.
Turn it on.
Turn it off.
Thank you.
Good to see you.
Doesn't matter.
Quiet, please.
I'll do it.

Let's go.
Make a phone call.
Open the window.
Close the window.
Open the door.
Close the door.
Who is it?
What time is it?
Where is it?
What is this?
How?
That's right.
That's it.
That's wrong.
This is dirty.
I'll watch TV.
Listen to the radio.
Cut the meat.

I'm finished.
Comb my hair.

PANTOMIME

Name or show the participants each of the objects and have them pantomime what *one does* with each one.

Knife	Fork	Spoon
Cup	Plate	Napkin
Pillow	Blanket	Chair
Door	Window	Lamp
Scissors	String	Telephone
Pencil	Key	Watch
Matches	Cigarette	Hammer
Broom	Saw	Water faucet
Salt or pepper shaker	Credit card	Calendar
Thermometer	Shoelace	Thimble
Aspirin	Flashlight	Toothpick
Ashtray	Calculator	Binoculars
Typewriter	Alarm clock	Checkbook
Bobby pin	Suitcase	Umbrella
Vacuum cleaner	Clothes hanger	Lawnmower
Cigarette lighter	Bowling ball	Coffeepot
Mirror	Drinking fountain	Thumbtack
Rolling pin	Bottle opener	Clothes brush
Hair dryer	Letter opener	Pencil sharpener
Footstool	Tape measure	Ironing board
Sewing machine	Bathroom scales	Bandage
Facial tissue	Eyeglasses	Hearing aid
Deodorant	Shampoo	Shoes
Nail file	Razor	Robe
Wallet	Socks	Gloves
Hat	Belt	
Ring	Sweater	
Slippers		

Men:

Aftershave	Shirt	Trousers
Tie	Pajamas	

Women:

Lipstick	Powder	Eyeshadow
Perfume	Blouse	Slacks
Nightgown	Stockings	Bra
Earrings	Necklace	Bracelet
Purse	Apron	

HOW MANY WORDS CAN YOU MAKE?

Pick a word or combination of letters such as *apple, green, foot, sun, east, new, pen,* or *non-*. See how many words the participants can make using that word or the letters in it. For example, apple: apple pie, applesauce, apple cider, apple strudel, apple juice.

ANIMAL GAMES

Choose an animal such as a dog, cat, or bird. See how many different kinds of each can be identified. For example, dog: St. Bernard, poodle, dalmatian.

NAME FIVE

Ask the participants to name five (or any number) of each of the following: Songs, jobs, books, magazines, TV shows, movie stars, articles of clothing, U.S. presidents, or desserts. Name five things someone might say to you if they were any of the following: waitress, maid, bartender, store clerk, door-to-door salesman, preacher, teacher, traffic officer, secretary, or mail carrier.

ALPHABET GAME

Make a large poster with each letter of the alphabet on it. Mount it on the wall. Choose a category. Work through the alphabet and find a word in that category for each letter. This can be done as a group, with participants calling out their suggestions. Multiple responses can be recorded for each letter. Suggested categories: Birds, animals, flowers, boys' or girls' names, fruits and vegetables, occupations, song titles, cities, places, street names, famous people, articles of clothing, and foods.

CATEGORIES

Make a grid with 25, 36, or 49 squares. At the top of the grid write in a word (there should be no double letters in the word). On the left side of the grid, write in a category for each line. Players are asked to name words in each category, beginning with the letter at the top of the grid. Using the example shown, ask the participants to name a word that begins with the letter *C*.

Example:

	C	A	T

Cars
Animals
Cities

RHYMING GAME

One participant says a word, and the group tries to see how many words they can think of that rhyme with the original word.

ASSOCIATION

The first person names a place, object, or something else. The next person say the first word that he or she associates with the original word. Continue around the group.

CROSSWORD PUZZLE

Pick a short, simple puzzle. Enlarge the puzzle to approximately 3′ square or larger. Fill in the crossword numbers and blank spaces from the original puzzle. Post it where it can be seen by all. Read the clues to the group and have them give you the answers.

WHEEL OF FORTUNE

Materials

- Letters of the alphabet. These can be made or purchased. Scrabble board letters can be used. If the letters are made, be sure to make several of each vowel and other frequently used letters.
- Container

Procedure

Choose a category and select a word or phrase from it. Print the category and a dash for each letter in the word(s). Each player selects a letter from the container. If the letter appears in the word or phrase, that space is filled in with the letter. The game continues until the phrase is completed or someone guesses the answer.

Example: Holidays   — — — — — — — — —
                       C H R I S T M A S

WHAT DO I NEED?

Choose a topic such as going on a picnic, going on a trip, having a baby, or building a house. Ask the participants to list the items needed to get ready for the event.

PICTURE BINGO

Bingo cards can be made using pictures in place of the bingo numbers. Pictures of familiar items are best. Nine, sixteen, or twenty-five squares can be used. The leader calls out the item and shows a picture of it. The first player to cover all the pictures in a row wins.

SUPERMARKET

Make a list of items found in a supermarket. Write the first letter of each item and a blank for the other letters. Describe the item and ask the participants to fill in the blanks.

Example: A porterhouse S — — — —
                           T E A K

CONCENTRATION (card game)

Materials

- Two decks of playing cards of the same design, purchased or made, or buy the game Concentration.

Procedure

Lay out all the cards, face down, in even rows. Each player takes a turn and turns over two cards, trying to get a matched pair. If the cards match, the player keeps them and tries again. If the cards don't match, the cards are turned over again. The player with the most pairs is the winner.

THE PRICE IS RIGHT

Materials

- Pictures of cars, pianos, large appliances and other household items cut from catalogs. Mount on cardboard. Place the article's description and suggested retail price in large print on the back of each item.
- Prizes

Procedure

Participants can be divided into small groups or they can play individually. Each participant or group is shown a picture of an object and the item is described. The players make a bid for the item and the bids are recorded. The closest bidder, who does not go over the list price, wins. If all the bids are over the designated price, the bids are erased and everyone has a second bid.

Variations

Use pictures from old catalogs for items used many years ago. Instead of pictures, plants, food, and other prizes can be used to bid on. Attach a large price tag, covered by an envelope, for each item. The closest bidder wins the item.

FAMILY FEUD

Divide the participants into two teams. The Family Feud game or other trivia questions can be used. The team that gives the correct answer scores one point. One team wins when it gets the required number of points (the number is arbitrary).

STATES AND THEIR CAPITALS

Materials

- Draw a large map of the United States with each state outlined. Post it where everyone can see it. Make a list of all the states and their capitals.

Procedure

Ask the participants to identify where each state belongs on the map. After all the states are identified, the participants can try to guess the capital city of each state.

Variations

Talk about each state. Ask if any of the participants ever lived or visited there. You can also identify the state flower, bird, or motto.

HORSE RACING

Materials

- Racing track. The track can be made oval shaped or straight. Divide the track so there are 6 vertical lines and 20 sections. If oval shaped, the start and finish lines are at the same place. Otherwise, the finish line is at the opposite end of the starting line. Number the vertical sections 1 to 6.
- Horses
- Dice

Procedure

Each player is given a horse and a die. The players take turns rolling the die and moving their horses the number of spaces rolled on the die. The first player to cross the finish line wins.

Variations

One pair of dice is used, each die representing a horse. Each player takes a turn throwing the dice. If a 3 and a 6 are thrown, horses number 3 and 6 move one space each. If doubles are thrown, that horse moves two spaces (if double 6s are thrown, horse number 6 moves two spaces). Hurdles can be drawn midway along the track. When the horses reach the hurdle, a double must be rolled to get the horse over it (horse number 1 must roll double ones to get over the hurdle).

COVERALL

Materials

- Divide a piece of paper into 12 blocks numbered 2 through 12 with 1 free block. Make copies for each player.
- Dice
- Markers

Procedure

Each player rolls the dice and places a marker over the number rolled. The player continues to roll until rolling a number that was already covered. The dice are passed around to each player until one person covers a card and wins.

TIC-TAC-THROW

Materials

- Beanbags
- Tic-tac-toe grid. Draw a large grid on a 36″ square piece of paper
- Xs and Os cut from construction paper

Procedure

Divide the participants into two teams: X team and O team. Have them sit in a circle around the grid. Each team takes a turn throwing the ball. If the Xs hit a square, they put an X on that square and vice versa. The first team to get three Xs or Os in a row wins.

Variations

If a team hits a square that is already occupied by the other team, the square is negated and is no longer occupied.

TARGET BEANBAG

Materials

- Target—Mark 3 concentric circles on the floor or on a large piece of paper. Label the circles 20 for the outer circle, 50 for the middle, and 100 for the bull's-eye. The circles can be color coded for easier identification.
- Beanbags

Procedure

Players sit around the target and throw three beanbags each. The number of turns each player gets can vary but should be established in advance. The player with the most points wins. In case of a tie, a play-off can be held.

Variations

Change the shape of the target and/or the point values. A box, basket, or other container can be used as a target. Toss the beanbags into pails with different point values. In the fall of the year, beanbags can be tossed into a hollowed-out pumpkin. Styrofoam or nerf balls can be used in place of beanbags. Have the participants knock over cones or other objects.

HOT POTATO

Seat the participants in a circle. Start music. Have the participants pass a beanbag "potato" around the circle. When the music stops, applaud the participant who is holding the bag.

RELAY RACE

Divide the players into two teams, facing each other. Each team has a pitcher who stands in the middle and throws the beanbag to the team members. The pitchers toss the beanbag to each player and that player throws it back to the pitcher. The first team to reach the end of the line of players wins.

TABLE BEACH BALL

Seat the participants around a table. Place a beach ball on the table. The players hit the ball to one another and try to keep it from going off the table.

15

The Art and Craft of Creative Expression

Arts and crafts encourage the confused older adult to use leisure time in a sociable, productive manner. Well-done projects can be a source of great pride and pleasure. Arts and crafts can renew interest in life by providing a means of creative self-expression and the opportunity for individual achievement. The end product is a tangible, visible example of an individual's ability. It is something of which the person can say, "Look at what I made today." Arts and crafts can be soothing and relaxing. They can stimulate the senses and improve coordination and dexterity. A group project can enhance an individual's sense of self-esteem and feeling of belonging.

As there are many good craft books available, only a limited selection of crafts have been included. By using the guidelines that follow, many arts and crafts activities can be adapted for use by the elderly person with a dementing illness. Also, a variety of easy, inexpensive, and attractive kits are available from crafts supply stores.

GUIDELINES FOR IMPLEMENTING AN ARTS AND CRAFTS PROGRAM

- BE PREPARED. Have all of the supplies and materials ready in advance. Cover the tables with newspaper or plastic. Provide a hard surface to work on.

- Keep the projects SIMPLE. Use simple but good-quality materials. Choose activities that are repetitive.

- Make something USEFUL. No one wants to spend time making useless objects. The projects can be used for decorations, as prizes, to sell at a fund raiser, to give as a gift, or as a service project for others. Select crafts that are interesting and build on old skills.

- Use only NONTOXIC MATERIALS. Avoid putting craft materials in food containers. Watch that no one accidentally ingests inedible materials. Use small groups to provide maximum supervision.

- Work at a SLOW PACE and GIVE INSTRUCTIONS ONE STEP AT A TIME. Don't give out too much information or materials at one time. Break the project down into short, simple steps. Provide a sample of the completed project. Let everyone *work at his or her own pace* and according to his or her capabilities. Try to put workers at the same ability level together.

- CREATE AN ENVIRONMENT THAT SUPPORTS THE PARTICIPANTS' STRENGTHS. Avoid using small, fragile pieces. Simple adaptations such as adding food coloring to white glue to make it easier to see and providing a dark tablecloth under white paper can make it easier for individuals to participate. Make sure the work area is well ventilated.

- Help the participants complete the project without telling them what to do. *Avoid giving too much assistance.* Never do someone else's work because you can do it easier or better. It is the effort that counts, not the finished project.

- ANY PART OF THE PROJECT THAT IS POTENTIALLY HAZARDOUS SHOULD BE COMPLETED BY A STAFF PERSON OR THE CAREGIVER. Avoid having the participants use sharp tools.

- PROVIDE ENCOURAGEMENT. Try to find something positive to say to everyone, but never lie. If the project is not very attractive, praise the effort involved. Never correct anyone, criticize, or make fun of the work.

- MOUNT, MAT, or DISPLAY THE COMPLETED ARTWORK. People are very proud to have their work exhibited.

- REPEAT SUCCESSFUL ACTIVITIES. Once you know what the individual or group enjoys doing, the activity can be repeated. The activity will become easier to do with practice.

ARTS AND CRAFTS PROJECTS

Drawings

Materials

- Drawing paper
- Colored chalk, markers, pastels, oil crayons, watercolors, or crayons
- Clear finishing spray

Procedure

1. Ask the participants to draw a design on the paper. Still lifes, self-portraits, and landscapes are good subjects for beginners.
2. Spray the completed drawing with the finishing spray to protect it from smudging.

Variations

- Ask the participants to draw only circles, lines, squares, or other simple shapes.
- Play music and ask everyone to draw to the beat and mood of the music.
- Use a picture, drawing, or still life arrangement to draw from. If a painting is used, talk about it. Ask everyone what she or he sees in the picture. Ask what they like or dislike about it.

Paintings

Materials

- Nontoxic tempera watercolor paint or ink
- Heavy-stock drawing paper
- Large brushes, Q-Tips,® sponges, foam brushes, or toothbrushes

Variations

- Add dry soap flakes to tempera paint. The mixture should be thick, so add water only if necessary.
- Make sparkle paint by mixing equal parts of flour, salt, and water. Food coloring can be added to this mixture to give the paint some color. When the paint dries, the salt gives the picture a glistening quality. Tempera paint can also be mixed with liquid starch and salt to make sparkle paint.
- Paint on different surfaces such as glass, wood, corrugated cardboard, or tissue paper.
- Use a sponge dipped in watercolors to create different designs.

Activities

- Draw large-print letters and numbers on heavy white paper with a permanent marker. Fill in the letters with tempera paints. It doesn't matter if the paint goes outside the lines because the letters can be cut out for use on signs.

- Make designs by folding a sheet of paper in half and applying different colors of paint to one side. Fold the paper over and press the two sides together. Let the paint dry.
- Place small blobs of tempera paint on the paper. Create designs with the straw by blowing into the straw and moving the paint around the paper. You must be careful with this activity, as some people will try to suck on the straws.
- Fold a piece of paper in half, then reopen it. Cut string into different lengths. Dip the string into different colors of tempera paint. Arrange the string in a design on one half of the paper. Fold the paper again and smooth it over the string. Open the paper and remove the string. Repeat this using a different color string. Or remove the string while the paper is still folded. This method makes attractive wrapping paper. Cover the strings on the wrapping paper with newspaper to create a design instead of folding the wrapping paper.
- Glue several buttons on a piece of paper. Use tempera paint or markers to create a picture of flowers (the buttons form the center of the flower).
- Hang a large piece of paper on the wall. Choose a theme such as Christmas. Ask everyone to draw or paint something that reminds him or her of the theme. Or ask everyone to draw a circle or a specific design. When everyone is finished, the leader can use markers or paint to add a few finishing touches to tie the picture together.
- Create a series of stripes by very lightly pressing masking tape onto the paper. Paint between the strips of tape. After the paint dries, remove the tape. This can be used for wrapping paper.
- Make a spatter paint print. Use stencils or cutouts to cover the part of the picture you do not want painted. Cover the paper with a piece of window screen, about 8″ square. Dip an old toothbrush into paint or ink. Rub the toothbrush across the screen to spatter the paint. Allow the paint to dry.

Window Paintings

Materials

- Drawing paper, 8 ½″ × 11″
- Tempera paints
- Plastic sandwich bags

Procedure

1. Paint a design on the paper using the tempera paints. Let the paint dry. Or use paints and straws to create a design.
2. Place a few drops of paint in a plastic sandwich bag. Seal the bag and press the sides together to form a design with the paint in the bag.
3. Cut a 4″ circle on the paper and tape the colored bag to the back of the paper.

Watercolors and Rubber Cement

Materials

- Watercolors
- Water
- Brushes
- White drawing paper
- Rubber cement

Procedure

1. Prepare the paper in advance by painting a design with rubber cement on the paper. Allow to dry.
2. Paint over the design with the watercolors.
3. After the paint dries, rub the rubber cement off the painting to reveal the design underneath.

Snow Resist

Materials

- Colored construction paper
- Crayons the same color as the paper
- Brush
- White tempera paint
- Container for water

Procedure

1. Draw a picture of a winter or Christmas scene, pressing hard with the crayon.
2. Mix the white paint with water.
3. Brush lightly over the drawing with the paint mixture until the entire paper is covered. The crayon will resist the white paint and a snow scene will appear.

Note: Talk about the winters and Christmases from the past to stimulate interest in the project.

Stencils

Materials

- Stencils
- Tempera paint, watercolors, stencil paint or stencil markers
- Drawing paper
- Sponges or brushes

Procedure

1. Have everyone choose a stencil. Tape the stencil into place over the paper.
2. Dip the sponge or brush into the paint and dab it all over the open areas of the stencil.
3. Carefully lift the stencil off the paper and wipe off the excess paint.
4. The pattern can be repeated several times across the paper to form a design. Let the paint dry.

Variations

- Use fabric, wood, plaster, or metal instead of paper.
- Use the cutout from the stencil to create an interesting design. We stenciled geese in a pattern on the paper. Cutouts of the geese were placed on the paper to form an attractive design. Eyes and a ribbon were drawn on the cutout geese with markers. The geese were partially covered with a calico print "jacket."
- Use stencils to make greeting cards.

Stencils on Wood

Materials

- Stencils
- Stencil paint
- Wooden plaque, box, plate, rack, tray, basket, paddleboard, or shelf
- Foam brushes
- Stencil brush
- Sandpaper, coarse and fine
- Wood stain
- Shellac

Procedure

1. Sand the wood until it is smooth, first with coarse sandpaper, then with fine.
2. Use the foam brush to apply wood stain to the wood. Apply a second coat if necessary. Let the stain dry between coats.
3. Stencil a design on the wood. Let the paint dry.
4. Apply shellac with the foam brush. Let the shellac dry.
5. Apply as many coats of shellac as needed to achieve the desired effect.

Printing

Materials

- Plain wrapping paper, newsprint, drawing paper, greeting cards, stationery, or tissue paper
- Tempera paint or ink
- Brush
- Printer (see below)
- Stylus or sharp knife

Procedure

1. Paint the printer with the paint, allowing it to become saturated. Or saturate a foam rubber pad with ink or paint and press the printer into the pad.
2. Press the printer down slowly and evenly onto the paper.
3. Reapply paint as needed.

Printers

A variety of items can be used for printers. Most of these should be cut in advance, as they are too delicate to be cut by someone who is mentally impaired.

- Cut a potato in half. The edges of the potato can be trimmed to form a design. Other fruits and vegetables can also be used: cabbage wedges, artichoke halves, lemon slices, and Bermuda onions.
- Stamps can be purchased or a design can be cut from an art gum eraser with a sharp knife.
- Cover a block of wood or a tin can with string, crisscrossing the string to create a raised pattern. Glue or tack the ends of the string in place.
- Empty thread spools can be used for printing. Cut nicks and lines into the end of the spool of thread to create a design.
- Make designs using kitchen utensils such as wire whisks and cookie cutters.
- Use different width rollers to create bold stripes and checkerboard and plaid patterns.
- Cut a design into art foam paper. Make sure that words or numbers are written backward, so they print correctly. Cover the design with paint. Press a piece of paper onto the paint.

Leaf Print

Materials

- Freshly picked leaves with well-defined veins
- Brayers

- Drawing paper, greeting cards, or stationery
- Tempera paint or ink
- Scrap paper or waxed paper

Procedure

1. Lay the leaf flat and ink it or paint it with a brayer. Or place the leaf, vein side down, into an inking plate. Cover it with scrap paper or waxed paper and roll over it with a clean brayer, place a weight on it, or gently rub it to print the leaf.
2. Carefully place the leaf on the paper. Cover it with scrap paper and roll over it with the clean brayer. Be careful not to move the leaf. Make a design with the leaf prints.
3. Allow the leaf print to dry.

Variations

- Negative leaf prints can be made using the spatter technique. Put one or more leaves in position on the paper and weigh them down. Dip an old toothbrush into the paint and shake off the excess drops. Hold the toothbrush about 1 ½" from the paper with the bristles pointing down and flick the bristles using a pencil or fingertip. Repeat until the paper is attractively sprinkled. Carefully remove the leaves and allow the paint to dry.

Greeting Cards

Materials

- Card-stock paper folded to make a card
- Envelopes
- Glue
- Scissors
- Old greeting cards
- Small pieces of fabric, yarn, ribbon, or lace
- Markers
- Paint
- Brushes
- Art foil
- Tissue paper, cut into assorted shapes
- Paper doilies
- Stencils

Activities

- Cover the outside of the card with scraps of fabric. Decorate the fabric-covered card with pieces of ribbon and lace.
- Paint the outside of the card with rubber cement. Allow it to get slightly tacky. Apply tissue paper shapes to the rubber cement. Overlap the tissue until the outside of the card is covered. Allow to dry. Trim any excess.
- Cut pictures from old greeting cards and glue them to the card. Use paper doilies to decorate the cards.
- Draw, paint, stencil, or print designs on the card.
- Cut out the message from old greeting cards or print a message. A simple, one-line greeting or a poem is appropriate. Have the participant sign the card and send it to a friend or relative.

Collages

A collage is a picture made by gluing all sorts of things together to create a pattern or an overall design. A collage can be done individually or as a group project.

Materials

- White glue
- Pictures, postage stamps, greeting cards, foil, advertisements, colored paper or tissue paper cut into assorted shapes, fabric scraps, leaves, wallpaper, or gift wrapping
- Posterboard
- Brushes

Procedure

1. Cut out pictures for the collage.
2. Arrange the collage pieces in a pattern and glue them to the posterboard.
3. When the posterboard is dry, brush white glue over all the cutouts. The white glue dries clear and will protect the collage.
4. A second coat can be applied after the first one dries.

Variations

- Choose a theme such as Christmas or babies
- Use a lighter weight paper and use the collage to cover coffee cans or wastebaskets

- Make a scrapbook on a theme, such as the four seasons
- Make a candle collage. Apply glue to a small area of a clear glass candlehold-er. Arrange cutout pieces of tissue paper over the glue. Continue the process until the whole candleholder is covered. After the glue dries, seal the tissue paper onto the glass with a coat of white glue. After this dries, a scented candle can be placed in the holder.

Paper Designs

Materials

- Colored paper, including wrapping paper or tissue paper
- Glue
- Markers
- Clear, adhesive-backed plastic film (optional)
- Drawing paper

Procedure

1. Have pieces of colored paper or colored tissue paper precut in various shapes, such as flower petals, leaves, butterflies, triangles, or baskets.
2. Paste the cutouts on the drawing paper to create a flower arrangement or other design.
3. Use the markers to add details.
4. Cut the sheet of film slightly larger than the picture to be covered. Cover the picture with the film. Trim the edges.

Variations

- Crumble up different-colored tissue paper. Glue the tissue paper onto the center of the flowers. Don't cover this with the film.
- Make a calendar. Choose a motif such as animals. Cut out enough pieces of colored paper or colored tissue paper to make 12 pictures. The cutouts can be placed in the same spot or in different spots. The days of the month are applied using instant transfer lettering, which is held over the area to be printed and rubbed on. Cover the entire surface with the adhesive film. Use a heavyweight paper or cardboard for the backing.
- Make individualized place mats. Cut posterboard into a 14" × 18" rectangle. Create a design or make a collage out of colored paper or colored tissue paper. Seal it with the plastic film.
- Instead of using paper, use a variety of solid and printed fabrics or felt. Cut the fabric into shapes to create a design. For example, use a solid-colored fabric for background. Attach it to a piece of cardboard. Cut a basket and flowers out

of printed fabric. Glue the basket to the background material and then glue the flowers into the basket. Buttons, feathers, eyes, lace, and ribbons can be applied to give the picture a finishing touch.

Decoupage

Materials

- Pictures
- Wooden plaque or box
- Sandpaper
- Wood stain or paint
- Foam brushes
- Clear decoupage finish
- Crystal clear glitter (optional)

Procedure

1. If the wood is not new, prepare it by cleaning the surface with paint or varnish remover.
2. Sand the rough edges of the wood and clean the sand off the wood.
3. Stain the wood with wood stain or paint it. Let it dry.
4. Have the participants choose a picture and glue it onto the wood.
5. Using a foam brush, cover the picture with several coats of decoupage finish.
6. Sprinkle on the glitter for a sparkling finish (optional).
7. Let the clear finish dry.

Sand Painting

Materials

- Colored sand
- Glue
- Brushes
- Large-design pictures
- Large container

Procedure

1. Apply glue to one area of the design.
2. Sprinkle sand over the glue. Let the glue dry.
3. Shake off the excess sand into a container.
4. Repeat the process until all of the design is covered with the sand.

Mosaics

Materials

- Seeds, seashells, rice, peas, corn, birdseed, tapioca, beans, macaroni, and the like.
- Plywood
- Glue
- Markers
- Clear plastic spray film

Procedure

1. Prepare the plywood by drawing a simple design on paper and tracing it onto the plywood.
2. Draw the outline of the design with a bold-lined marker.
3. Spread glue in the defined area, working in one small area at a time.
4. Press the seeds down into the glue and let the glue dry.
5. After the seeds have dried for several days, spray them with a clear plastic film.

Variations

- Fill in the spaces with coffee, tea, or herbs.
- Trivets can be purchased. Fill the trivets with ceramic tiles and glue them into place. Fill in the spaces between the tiles with grout. After the grout dries, rub the excess grout off the tiles.
- Apply seashells or seeds to a picture frame or piece of heavy cardboard cut into the shape of a picture frame.

Coffee Mug Recipe Holder

Materials

- Dried, silk, or plastic flowers, fruits, or vegetables
- Artificial bee or butterfly (optional)
- Coffee mug
- Styrofoam (cut to fit inside the mug)
- Moss
- Plastic plant cardholder
- Recipe card

Procedures

1. Place the Styrofoam in the mug and cover it with moss.
2. Insert the flowers into the moss-covered Styrofoam.
3. Attach the bee to a wire and insert it into the arrangement.
4. Place the plant cardholder into the arrangement.
5. Attach a recipe card to the plastic cardholder.

Note: A cracked or damaged mug can be repaired and used for the recipe holder. Apply a coat of gesso over the entire mug, particularly over the cracks. Spray the mug with several coats of spray paint.

Decorative Flower Pots

Materials

- Clay flower pot or plastic pot
- Glue
- Seashells, in assorted shapes and sizes

Procedures

1. Apply glue to small areas of the pot.
2. Glue the shells on the outside of the pot. Let the glue dry.

Variations

- Make a patchwork pot. Cut small pieces of multicolor and print fabrics. Glue the fabric swatches in a patchwork design on the outside of the pot. After the glue dries, apply a clear acrylic finish or a white glue and water wash over the fabric.

Dough Sculpture

Materials

- Dough (recipe follows)
- Foil-covered cookie sheets
- Butter knife, fork, spoon
- Toothpicks

- Watercolors or acrylic or tempera paint
- Clear gloss or acrylic lacquer

Procedure

1. Prepare the dough:
   2 cups flour
   1 cup salt
   1 cup water
   Combine flour and salt in a large flat-bottomed bowl, and mix well with spoon. Next, add water (a little at a time), mixing as you pour to form a ball. *Note:* Additional water may be needed, depending on humidity. Take care not to add so much water that the dough becomes sticky.

   Knead 7 to 10 minutes until dough has a smooth, yet firm, consistency.

   Place dough in a plastic bag to prevent drying.

   The dough can be made in advance and kept in a plastic bag in a refrigerator for up to 5 days. If the dough dries out, add a little more water and knead it back to its original consistency. If the dough becomes sticky, just add more flour.

   Flour hands and work surfaces to keep the dough from sticking on them.
2. Roll out the dough until it is ¼" thick. Use cookie cutters to cut out the basic shapes. Eyes, nose, cheeks, and buttons can be made by rolling small pieces of dough into a ball. A mouth can be formed by rolling dough into a curve. Hair can be made by rolling dough into a spaghetti shape or pressing it through a sieve to make strands to be used for hair and fringe. To join any two pieces of dough together, moisten both edges with tap water and press together. A fork or knife can be used to form the fingers. Make a small hole at the top for the ribbon to hang it by.
3. To harden the sculpture, the dough can be air dried or baked. To air dry, place the sculpture on a screen and let it dry for at least 48 hours (until it turns rock hard and white). To bake it, place the sculpture on a foil-covered cookie sheet. Bake at 325°F ½ hour for each ¼" of dough thickness or until the surface turns a light golden brown. Place the dough in the oven soon after making the sculpture to prevent crumbling. If the sculpture puffs up, reduce the oven temperature by 50°F and poke a hole in it to release the air. To prevent large pieces from curling up, the edges can be weighed down with a heavy object after the surface has been cooked long enough not to leave indentations.
4. The hardened sculpture can be finished in a variety of ways:
   - Coat the sculpture with two coats of acrylic lacquer or clear gloss.
   - Paint the sculpture with watercolors before applying varnish.
   - Acrylic paints can be used to seal a sculpture instead of varnish.

Variations

Ideas for sculptures:

- Christmas tree ornaments
- Place cards

- Key ring decorations
- Lapel pins (glue a pin on the back)
- Mirrors (glue air-dried cookie cutter shapes on a mirror)
- Plaques
- Wreaths
- Picture frames

Ceramics

Materials

- Potter's clay or greenware (unfired clay objects are called greenware)
- Underglazes (to decorate ceramic objects before they are glazed)
- Overglazes (decorative finishes applied over a fired glaze finish)
- Stains (for ceramic objects that have first been bisque fired. No additional firing is needed. Bisque firing means that the cleaned piece of greenware has been placed in a ceramic kiln and fired to a very high temperature to make it hard and suitable for decorating).
- Modeling tools

Procedure

There are two methods of doing ceramics. If you are lucky enough to have access to a kiln, objects can be made out of the potter's clay. The clay must first be wedged or kneaded to work out any air bubbles. Some suggestions for projects include:

- Cookie cutter shapes
- Mobiles
- Bowls
- Plates
- Easter eggs
- Baskets
- Flower pots
- Ashtrays
- Plaques
- Beads—for necklaces, wall hangings, etc.
- Picture frames
- Coil pots (made by forming the clay into long coils which are layered to form the sides of the pot).

Allow the finished shapes to dry before they are bisque fired. Make sure the edges and seams are clean and smooth. After they are bisque fired, glazes are applied and they are fired again.

The other alternative is to purchase pieces that have been bisque fired and paint them with stains. A large variety of bisque-fired pieces are available for sale at pottery stores.

Ceramic objects make attractive, useful craft projects. Ceramic pots can be used as containers for horticulture projects—the subject of Chapter 16.

16

Horticulture: Activities with Plants and Flowers

Horticulture therapy uses the propagation and cultivation of plants, gardening, flower arranging, and plant materials in craft projects as an aid to rehabilitation. Horticultural activities provide many benefits for the elderly in general and to the confused person in particular.

In a study conducted for the National Council on Aging, older U.S. citizens rated growing vegetables and flowers as the number one choice of physical activity. Gardening and raising plants ranked second, after socializing with friends, as the recreational activity of choice. When people enjoy an activity, they are motivated to participate.

THE BENEFITS OF A HORTICULTURE PROGRAM

Horticultural activities are inexpensive, meaningful, adult activities. They are easy, fun, and rewarding. The end results—fresh garden vegetables and herbs and beautiful flowers and plants—provide the impaired older adult with a sense of pride and achievement. Horticulture promotes interest, enthusiasm, and anticipation. Individuals recognize that despite their impairments they can still grow and take care of new life. Horticulture is a form of physical and emotional therapy that helps reduce stress, is soothing, and boosts self-esteem and confidence. The colors, smells, textures, and shapes of plants and flowers enhance the environment and create a more restful, serene atmosphere.

Horticulture provides many older adults with the opportunity to use existing skills derived from a lifetime of gardening experience. Gardening is an activity that usually evokes many fond memories. Horticulture also provides an opportunity for many elderly to develop new skills and interests.

Horticulture is an excellent activity to stimulate the senses and arouse curiosity. It helps to create an awareness of and sensitivity to the environment. It provides an outlet for self-expression and creativity. For groups, horticulture can be a very social activity.

Gardening is also good exercise. It can help to develop or improve basic motor skills and provides a constructive outlet for anxiety and boredom.

HOW TO DEVELOP A HORTICULTURE THERAPY PROGRAM

A horticulture therapy program needs to have someone who knows how to care for and maintain plants and provide the proper growing conditions. The local agriculture extension service can be contacted for information on times for planting and harvesting and suggestions for growing and fertilizing fruits, vegetables, and other plants.

A full range of horticultural activities are available, making it possible to plan a year-round program of activities. Many projects can be done at any time of the year. A demonstration of the activity can help alleviate the fear of failure from people who don't have a "green thumb." The leader should determine the participants' past interests, knowledge of horticultural activities, and need for adaptive equipment.

A horticultural therapy program should encourage social interaction among participants and give them the opportunity to help one another. Nature crafts, plants, and flower arrangements can all be used as gifts for others. Participants enjoy giving gifts and this helps to make them feel good about themselves.

Almost everyone has grown something at one time or another, so horticultural activities are a perfect catalyst for reminiscence and discussion. Ask the participants about their gardening and farming experiences.

Adaptive Equipment and Tools

The most common difficulties experienced by the elderly while they are gardening are difficulty in bending, poor balance, weak grip, impaired vision, and decreased arm span. A variety of special equipment and tools are available to make gardening easier. Garden tools can also be adapted to make them easier to use. An occupational therapist can help make suggestions for adaptive devices. The horticultural activities described here can easily be completed when they are broken down step by step.

- Raised garden beds and other containers allow the older adult to work more comfortably and provide access for people in wheelchairs.
- Watering wands in various lengths make watering plants easier. Lightweight water cans with a spout can also be used.
- Seed tape or large seeds make it easier to see where the seeds are being planted. Seeds can also be mixed with sand and sown into the garden using a shaker can. The sand helps the gardener to see where the seed is falling.
- Stools with handles on each side and a soft kneeling cushion help the older adult to raise and lower him- or herself to ground level.
- The handles of tools can be elongated to eliminate the need for stooping.
- Velcro wristbands can be attached to standard hand tools in order to strap tools on the hands of those with a weak grip. Handles can be padded by applying putty on the tool handles and molding the putty to the shape of the hand. Foam rubber can also be used on handles to make tools easier to grip.

OUTDOOR GARDENING PROJECTS

Where no outdoor garden space exists, containers can be used. Window boxes, wall pots, tubs, barrels, raised beds, hanging baskets, and many other kinds of containers can be used for gardening. Almost any plant can be grown in a container.

Small outdoor containers should be filled with soilless mixes. After transplanting plants into an outdoor container, water them thoroughly until the water comes out of the drainage holes. Water the container thoroughly whenever the soil is dry. Use concentrated, water soluble fertilizers to fertilize containers. Mulching can help conserve moisture and cool the soil during hot weather. Special seeds are available for small-container gardening.

Plant fragrant plants to help stimulate the senses. Sweet alyssum, heliotrope, lily of the valley, scented geranium, peony, lavender, rosemary, and thyme are some examples of fragrant plants.

Plants can be purchased or started from seeds sown indoors or outdoors. Sow seeds indoors about 1 to 2 months before the last frost date. Seeds or transplants must be sown once the danger of frost has passed.

Annuals—Growing Flowers for Fresh and Dried Bouquets

Materials

- Bone meal
- Flower seeds (annuals)
- Compost, peat moss, or potting soil
- Mulch (straw, shredded bark, leaves, or newspapers)
- Foliar fertilizer
- Labels and waterproof markers

Procedure

1. Use bone meal to define minibeds in the garden. Sow seeds inside the beds (you can plan the design of the garden in advance, considering the height and color of the plants).
2. Cover seeds lightly with a layer of compost, peat moss, or potting soil. Press down gently.
3. After planting, label each bed and water thoroughly. Keep the garden slightly moist at all times.
4. Thin out the seedlings—leave only the healthiest and sturdiest plants. Pull out seedlings that are growing too close together. Space according to the instructions on the seed package. Pinch back young plants when they are 2" to 4" tall. Snip off the tip of the plant just below the top pair of leaves.
5. Mulch the seedlings when they are several inches high. Cover the seedlings with a thick layer of mulch to smother any weeds and increase soil moisture.
6. Fertilize the flowers by spraying them with a foliar fertilizer once every other week.

7. Most annuals look and grow better when dead blossoms are removed.
8. Cut the flowers for arrangements. Remove dead, dying, or deformed blooms from the plants. The more the flowers are cut, the more blooms you will have.

Vegetable Gardening

Producing your own food is a rewarding activity. Select plants for the garden that the participants want to grow and like to eat. Participants enjoy all the gardening activities from preparing the soil to harvesting the vegetables. They can help rake leaves, till the earth, dig holes for planting, weed, water the plants, and pick the fresh fruits, vegetables, and flowers. When the fruits and vegetables are picked, the participants should be encouraged to touch, smell, and taste them. A discussion about the fruits or vegetables and ways they are used can follow.

INDOOR GARDENING PROJECTS

Potentially Harmful Plants

These indoor plants may be harmful if eaten. Use caution and provide supervision if using them.*

Asparagus Fern	Gold-toothed Aloe
Azalea	Ivy
Bird of Paradise	Jerusalem Cherry
Caladium	Lily of the Valley
Creeping Charlie	Marble Queen
Crown of Thorns	Meadow of Saffron
Daffodil	Nephthytis
Dumb Cane	Philodendron
Elephant Ear	Pothos
	Umbrella Plant

*Reprinted with permission from *Horticultural Therapy Projects for Senior Centers, Nursing Homes, Retirement Living* by Eugene A. Rothert, Jr. and James R. Daubert, © 1981 by the Chicago Horticultural Society.

Plant Propagation

Stock plants are needed for plant propagation activities. Each participant will need at least one large, healthy stock plant to take cuttings from. Aluminum plants, artillery plants, devil's ivy, coleus, begonias, spider plants, strawberry begonias, wandering jews, English ivy, and Swedish ivy are all easy and reliable plants to use for starting new plants.

ZIP-LOCK METHOD OF PLANT PROPAGATION*

Materials

* Zip-Lock bags, 1 gallon size
* Labels and waterproof markers
* Rooting materials (can be purchased, or mix equal parts of peat moss, perlite, and vermiculite)
* Plant cuttings or runners
* Hand clippers or sharp scissors for making the cuttings
* Spray bottle to mist plants
* Rooting compound

Procedure

1. Label each bag and fill it ¼ full of moist rooting material.
2. Cut plants 3″ to 6″ from the top of the longest shoot, about ¼″ below a leaf joint. Remove the leaves from the bottom 1″ to 2″ of the stem. For runners, cut the plantlets free from the mother plant. Dip the cut end in rooting powder and tap off excess.
3. Insert two or three cuttings or plantlets 1″ to 2″ inches deep. To prevent rot, space plantlets so that the leaves do not touch.
4. Water just enough to wet the leaves. Blow air into the bag and seal it.
5. Keep the bag in bright, indirect light. Open the bag for several hours if mold or excess moisture develops. Do not add more water.
6. Open the bag after roots are observed through the side of the bag (2 to 6 weeks). Roll down the sides of the bag and water the cuttings.
7. After several days, gently loosen the soil by squeezing the bottom of the bag. Pot the new plants and water immediately. Cover with a plastic bag if the new plant begins to wilt.

Alternatives: Plant in a clear-plastic shoe box or plastic/glass aquarium with a cover.

*Adapted from *Horticultural Therapy for Senior Centers, Nursing Homes, Retirement Living* by Eugene A. Rothert, Jr. and James R. Daubert, © 1981 by the Chicago Horticultural Society.

PLANT PROPAGATION FROM SEEDS*

Flowers, vegetables, and some indoor plants can be started indoors from seeds. Growing plants from seeds are easy, but they do require daily care.

Materials

- Potting soil
- Vermiculite
- Containers (clay and plastic pots, seed flats, compressed peat pellets, peat containers, food containers, Styrofoam cups, old egg cartons, muffin tins, milk cartons or bottles)
- Labels and waterproof markers
- Seeds

Procedure

1. Place drainage holes in the bottom of each container. Fill each container with moist potting soil. Label each container with the date, participant's name, and plant name.
2. Sow seeds according to package directions. Firm the soil over the seeds. Place a ¼" layer of vermiculite over the top. Lightly water the soil. (Do not cover seeds if the seed package instructs otherwise.)
3. Cover each container with plastic. Place the container in bright, indirect light. Keep the seeds at a temperature of 70°F to 75°F.
4. Remove the plastic cover after the seeds sprout. Place in a sunny window or about 6" from artificial lights that are kept on 18 hours per day. Water as needed. Mist the seedlings frequently.

*Adapted from *Horticultural Therapy for Senior Centers, Nursing Homes, Retirement Living* by Eugene A. Rothert, Jr. and James R. Daubert, © 1981 by the Chicago Horticulturial Society.

COMPRESSED PEAT PELLET METHOD OF PLANT PROPAGATION*

Compressed peat pellets expand when watered to form a complete growing unit (pot nutrients and soil). Seeds and rooted cuttings can be transplanted pot and all.

Materials

- Compressed peat pellets
- Plastic tray

* Labels and waterproof markers
* Seeds or plant cuttings

Procedure

1. Prepare the pellets according to directions.
2. To root cuttings: Poke a pencil-size hole about 1″ deep in the top of the pellet. Place the cutting into the hole and firm the medium around the stem.
3. To plant seeds: Place several holes in the pellet. Put two seeds in each hole and cover (follow package directions on how deep to plant each seed).
4. Cover with plastic.
5. Place cuttings in bright, indirect light. It should not be necessary to water cuttings.
6. Place seeds in a warm area (70°F to 75°F). When the plants begin to appear, place the container in a sunny window. Prop the plastic cover open 1″ to let air in. Water as needed, being careful not to overwater. Empty out excess water.
7. Keep only the most sturdy plant in each pellet. After 7 to 10 days, carefully remove the remaining plants by cutting them (don't pull them out).
8. Transplant plants, pellet and all, when they are 2″ to 3″ tall or when the roots grow through the sides of the pellet. Bury the pellet completely and water it.

*Adapted from *Horticultural Therapy for Senior Centers, Nursing Homes, Retirement Living* by Eugene A. Rothert, Jr. and James R. Daubert, © 1981 by the Chicago Horticultural Society.

TRANSPLANTING A PLANT

If the roots show through the draining hole or if the roots are matted on the outside of the root ball, it's time to repot.

Materials

* Potted plant
* Potting soil
* Spoon
* Newspaper
* Water in watering can
* Container
* Coarse sand and granulated charcoal (optional)

Procedure

1. Remove plant from existing pot by squeezing sides and turning plant upside down. Shake plant gently to remove large clumps of soil.
2. Place a small amount of soil in the new container using a spoon or scoop. For

containers without drainage holes, prevent soil from souring by spreading a ½" to 1" layer of coarse sand mixed with granulated charcoal.

3. Hold plant in the new pot with the rim of the pot being even with the base of the plant's foliage.
4. Fill the container with soil. Press soil firmly around the plant so that the plant is upright.
5. Water the plant thoroughly. Place newly transplanted pots in a shady location for a day or two to help them get through the shock of transplanting.

Related Activity: Cover or decorate pots; plant several plants in a montage.

PEANUT PLANTS

Peanuts grow fast and are fun to watch. The peanuts will grow on the underground shoots.

Materials

- Small plastic container with a transparent cover
- Cotton balls
- *Raw* peanuts, shelled with the red skin covering the peanut intact
- Potting soil
- Container

Procedure

1. Fill the container to ½" from the top with the cotton balls.
2. Moisten the cotton balls until they are damp but don't soak them.
3. Place the shelled peanuts one to two for a small container, more for a larger container) on the cotton and put on the cover.
4. Place the container in a shady area.
5. After a few days, shoots will emerge from the nuts. When they are about 1" long, remove the cover.
6. Transplant the nuts, cotton and all, when the shoots are about 3" or 4" tall and have leaves. Transplant them into a container filled with potting soil.
7. Place the container in a sunny location and water the plants daily.

TERRARIUM*

Materials

- Containers (any clear, closed container, such as an aquarium, bottles, fish bowl, or 1 or 2 liter soft drink bottle)
- Potting soil
- Drainage material: gravel, clay chips, or sand
- Activated charcoal (to absorb by-products and prevent bacterial growth and odors)
- Decorations, such as colored stones, shells, or driftwood (can be collected on a field trip or brought from home)
- Plants (slow-growing plants that require high humidity and low light, such as African violet, aluminum plant, artillery plant, asparagus fern, Creeping Charlie, false aralia, peperomia, strawberry begonia, wax plant)

Procedure

1. Place ½" of drainage material on the bottom of the container.
2. Place a ⅛" to ¼" thick layer of charcoal over the drainage material.
3. Add moistened soil to approximately one-fourth to one-third the height of the container.
4. Arrange plants and accessories on the table top to form a pleasing arrangement. Each participant selects a plant to contribute to the terrarium.
5. Dig holes in the soil for each plant. Gently remove the plants from their pots and place them in the holes. Pat the soil gently around the roots.
6. Add the accessories.

*Adapted from *Horticultural Therapy for Senior Centers, Nursing Homes, Retirement Living* by Eugene A. Rother, Jr. and James R. Daubert, 158 1981 by the Chicago Horticultural Society.

CITRUS SEED PLANTS*

Materials

- Citrus seeds (oranges, lemons, limes, grapefruit)
- Potting soil
- 5" pots
- Labels and waterproof markers

Procedure

1. Wash the fruit off the seeds. Soak the seeds in water if they cannot be planted right away.
2. Fill pots with moist soil to within 1½" of the top. Scatter three to four seeds over the soil. Cover with another ¾" of soil. Water thoroughly.
3. Cover the pot with plastic.
4. Place the pot in bright, indirect light.
5. After the seeds sprout, remove the plastic cover and move the pot to a sunny window.
6. Allow soil to dry between waterings. Transplant plants into their own pot when they are 3" high (about 5 weeks).

Note: The fruit can be used to make a snack: fruit salad, lemonade, limeade, juice, or sorbet. Pass the fruit around and have everyone smell it and talk about how it can be used.

*Adapted from *Horticultural Therapy for Senior Centers, Nursing Homes, Retirement Living* by Eugene A. Rothert, Jr. and James R. Daubert, © 1981 by the Chicago Horticultural Society.

SWEET POTATO PLANTS*

Materials

- Sweet potato (with the buds beginning to sprout)
- Clear plastic jar or glass
- Toothpicks

Procedure

1. Stick four toothpicks around the middle of the potato. Place the potato in the container with the pointed end down.
2. Fill the container with water until the bottom one-third of the potato is covered. Place in a warm, dark location.
3. After the roots appear (in about 3 weeks), place the container in bright, indirect sunlight. Keep the roots covered with water. The potato can also be transplanted into a large container filled with potting soil.

Note: This may be a good reminiscence activity, as many people have grown sweet potato vines on their windowsills.

*Adapted from *Horticultural Therapy for Senior Centers, Nursing Homes, Retirement Living* by Eugene A. Rothert, Jr. and James R. Daubert, © 1981 by the Chicago Horticultural Society.

AVOCADO SEED PLANTS*

Materials

- Avocado seed
- Potting soil
- 6″ pot

Procedure

1. Wash the seed and place it in a warm place to dry. Remove the brown covering from the seed.
2. Fill the pot half full with wet potting soil.
3. Place the large end of the seed down in the soil. Add more soil, but leave the top one-third of the seed exposed. Soak the soil and cover it with plastic.
4. Set the pot in bright light (not sunlight). Water the soil as needed. After the seed sprouts (this may take up to 5 months), fertilize it.
5. Keep the plant in bright, indirect sunlight.

Note: The avocado can be put in a salad or used in a dip (guacamole).

*Adapted from *Horticultural Therapy for Senior Centers, Nursing Homes, Retirement Living* by Eugene A. Rothert, Jr. and James R. Daubert, © 1981 by the Chicago Horticultural Society.

HERBS

Herbs need at least 4 hours of direct sunlight each day. Herbs should be fertilized with every watering. These herbs can be grown indoors from seed and can be used for sensory stimulation and for a variety of cooking and craft projects: basil, chives, mint, dill, marjoram, oregano, parsley, peppermint, rosemary, sage, savory, spearmint, tarragon, and thyme. Lavender, lemon balm, lemon verbena, and pineapple sage can also be used in scented craft projects. Participants can rub the herbs between their fingers and try to identify what they are by smelling them.

Dried Herbs

Dried herbs can be stored and used for cooking, sachets, pillows, potpourri, and gifts. Tie the herbs in small bunches so they will dry quickly and retain their color and fragrance. Hang them to dry in a well-ventilated, moderately warm place. Avoid direct sunlight. In 3 to 7 days, the herbs will be dry enough to crumble. Store them in an airtight container.

SPROUTS*

Growing sprouts is an easy, edible activity.

Materials:

- Wide-mouthed, quart-size jar
- Square of cheesecloth
- Labels and waterproof markers
- Seeds (soybeans, wheat, buckwheat, and garbanzo)—available at health food stores.

Procedure

1. Place one-fourth cup of seeds in a jar. Cover with cheesecloth secured with a rubber band.
2. Add enough water to cover the seeds. Shake to wash off seeds. Pour off the water. Repeat two to three times.
3. Add water to cover the seeds and let soak 12 to 16 hours (8 to 10 hours for soybeans).
4. After soaking, pour off the water and place the jar on its side in a warm, dark place for 2 to 5 days.
5. Rinse and drain the seeds twice a day (in the morning and afternoon).
6. Place the jar in indirect light (the last 1 to 2 days).

Uses: Sprouts can be eaten raw in a salad, on a sandwich, alone as a snack, or in Chinese cooking.

Other Types of Sprouts

Follow the same procedures as above.

- Alfalfa Red Clover: 1 rounded teaspoon, soak 5 to 8 hours for 5 to 7 days.
- Mung or lentil: 1 rounded tablespoon, soak 12 to 16 hours for 3 to 4 days.

*Adapted from *Horticultural Therapy Projects for Senior Centers, Nursing Homes, Retirement Living* by Eugene A. Rothert, Jr. and James R. Daubert, © 1981 by the Chicago Horticultural Society.

HORTICULTURAL CRAFT PROJECTS

Fresh Flower Arranging

Flower arranging is a simple but effective activity. Flowers can be obtained from the garden, florist, or a funeral home. Flower arranging stimulates the senses and provides an outlet for self-expression and creativity. The end result is attractive and appealing. Encourage the participants to touch, smell, and describe the flowers.

Materials

- Containers: Almost anything that holds water can be used, including purchased pots, bowls, vases, teacups, teapots, and sugar bowls. Plastic food containers, Styrofoam cups, or tin cans can be decorated, painted, or covered with florist foil and filled with gravel to make them steady (that can be a craft project). Use a container about two-fifths the size of the overall arrangement.
- Knife or round cookie cutter.
- Floral foam.
- Flowers and plant materials. Some of the best flowers for fresh bouquets are old-fashioned annual flowers that many older people will remember from their gardens.

Suggested flowers for fresh-cut flower arrangements:

Amaranth	Ferns
Asparagus	Huckleberry
Baby's breath	Juniper
Bachelor buttons	Larkspur
Calendula	Magnolia
Carnations	Parsley
Chrysanthemum	Pussy willow
Celosia	Salvia
Cattails	Snapdragon
China aster	Sanvitalia
Cleome	Thistle
Daisies	Verbena
Dahlia	Yarrow
Day lily	Zinnia

Procedure

1. Soak the floral foam in water.
2. Have each participant make or choose a container.

3. Mark lines on the foam where it is to be cut. Cut out a circle of foam to fit the container, using a butter knife or cookie cutter. Place the foam into the container and press it down until it is even with the rim.
4. Have participants choose their own plant materials and remove the lower leaves.

Each type of flower can be inserted into the arrangement. Small arrangements can be made with as few as three to five flowers and two to three pieces of greenery. Use larger, darker, heavier, and more ornate flowers toward the center of the arrangement. Use lighter, smaller flowers as you go away from the center. Use delicate plant material to help blend the arrangement together.

CHRISTMAS TABLE ARRANGEMENTS

Materials

- Mixed greens
- Miniature wired bows
- Miniature pinecones
- Miniature Christmas candies
- Miniature Christmas ornaments
- Waterproof containers
- Floral foam

Procedure

1. Cut a piece of floral foam to fit snugly in the waterproof container, extending it 1″ to 2″ above the container. Soak the foam in warm water until it is saturated.
2. Arrange the mixed greens in the container.
3. Decorate with miniature ornaments, bows, candies, and pinecones.

Note: Some people are sensitive to certain evergreens and they may need to wear gloves when handling greens.

AIR DRYING

When the natural shape of the plant must be preserved, flowers and foliage can be air dried. Plants dried in this way can be used in dried bouquets. The following are plant material for dried bouquets:

Baby's breath	Helipterum
Bells of Ireland	Herbs
Cattails	Knotweed
Celosia	Mullein

Chrysanthemum
Curled duck
Delphinium
Dusty miller
Globe amaranth
Globe thistle
Goldenrod
Grasses

Pussy willow
Blue salvia
Statice
Strawflowers
Tansy
Teasel
Yarrow
Xeranthemum

Procedure

1. Pick the plants on a warm, sunny day after the morning dew evaporates. Cut them before they are fully open.
2. Remove the leaves from the stems immediately after picking them.
3. Make small bundles. Tie the stems tightly, using a rubber band or string.
4. Hang upside down in a dark, dry, well-ventilated, dust-free area (attic or closet). Most bundles take two to three weeks to dry.

DRIED BOUQUETS

Materials

- Containers such as bowls, vases, glasses, dishes, baskets, pots, driftwood, mugs, jars
- Floral clay or Styrofoam
- Dried flowers and foliage

Procedure

Use the same basic technique as for fresh flower arranging. Arrangements can also be made inside a glass jar. Place the clay in the lid of the jar and add the dried flowers.

PRESSING PLANTS

Materials

- Plant materials: Try a variety of flowers and foliage (except for heavy, thick plants) such as ferns, grasses, Queen Anne's lace, ivy, clover, violets, pansies, and baby's breath.

- Brick
- Newspapers or tissue
- Telephone book

Procedure

1. Place the plant material between several layers of tissue or newspaper. Don't let the plants touch each other.
2. Cover the plant material with more newspaper.
3. Repeat the process until all the plant material is used.
4. Cover with a final layer of newspaper and the telephone book.
5. Place the brick on top of the telephone book to weight it down.
6. Store in a cool, dry place for 1 to 2 weeks.

PRESSED PLANT PROJECTS

Materials

- Clear contact paper, clear plastic spray, or wax paper and iron
- Glue
- Scissors
- Stationery or art paper
- Frames or mat boards
- Wooden plaques

Procedure

Used pressed plants to make bookmarks, cards, gift tags, place cards, stationery, place mats, candles, or framed pictures. Carefully arrange the plant material to create a pleasing design.

1. Use paper to create place mats, bookmarks, cards, and tags. Glue the plants in place on the paper and allow to dry. For stationery, cover only the design with clear contact paper. For other projects, cover the whole top and/or underside of the project with contact paper.
2. Place mats and bookmarks can be made by arranging the plant material between two pieces of clear contact paper for a transparent object. Arrange plants on a piece of fabric glued to cardboard to fit into a glass-covered picture frame or to be covered by a matboard frame.
3. Arrange the pressed plants between two layers of wax paper. Place sheets of newspaper underneath and on top of the wax paper and iron gently with a warm electric iron. Once the two layers of wax paper have been sealed together, trim the design to an attractive shape (round, square, heart, abstract). Supervise participants who are using the iron.

FLOWER PLAQUES

Materials

- Peat pot, cut in half, 2 ¼" in diameter
- Masking tape
- Mat board, 4" × 6", or wooden plaques
- Glue
- Pressed and/or dried flowers and leaves
- Sphagnum moss
- Ribbon

Procedure

1. Anchor the pot to the mat board using masking tape and glue.
2. Spread glue around the pot's lip and on the mat board. Place the sphagnum moss loosely around the opening.
3. Glue the plant material to the mat board. Place some of the stems through the moss.
4. Decorate the pot with a ribbon.

Note: Dried plant material can also be glued to painted or stained wooden plaques and sprayed with clear plastic spray.

OTHER IDEAS

- Grow sunflower seeds for bird seed harvesting. Make bird feeders.
- Create a garden salad. Plant lettuce, radishes, and carrots in a bushel basket.
- Grow a sack of potatoes. Fill a plastic bag halfway with compost or garden soil. Plant three cut-up potatoes with an eye in each piece. Cover with 2" of soil and water.
- Plant parsley in individual peat pots for participants to take home.
- Make herbal teas using fresh or dried herbs. Corsican mint, peppermint, spearmint, anise, and scented geranium can be used to make tea or added to regular tea to enhance the flavor.
- Pot miniature evergreens in containers decorated for Christmas. Decorate the evergreens with miniature ornaments.

17

Loving Bonds: Children and the Elderly

Many elders have only a limited opportunity to come into contact with children and young adults. Intergenerational activities give the elderly an opportunity to share their experiences, love, and wisdom with the young. Young and old can be together for their mutual benefit, sharing and enriching each other's lives.

Children can provide a sense of belonging, of loving and being loved. Being around children can help the confused older adult become more sociable, resume a caring role, and enjoy physical contact—to touch and be touched—hand holding, lap cradling, kissing, cuddling, and hugging. Children enjoy the love and attention of an adult. The affection they give in return promotes feelings of increased self-esteem and self-worth in the older adult. Children can appreciate memory-impaired older adults for what they are now, not what they've been. Children are a joy to be with. They are full of laughter, fun, and surprises. Even the simplest activity is appropriate and meaningful to the elder when it is for the children.

HOW TO IMPLEMENT AN INTERGENERATIONAL ACTIVITY

- Plan *simple activities* that are appropriate and interesting for both the young and old. Keep them short. Plan activities that capitalize on the strengths of the older adults.

- *Be prepared.* The program should be well planned and carefully implemented. The children's teachers should be aware of aging and dementia so that the teachers feel comfortable. If the teachers are uncomfortable, they will communicate this to the children. Refreshments and activities must be considered in advance so that no taboo foods or activities are planned. The staff working with the elderly must feel comfortable having the children visit.
- The elders must be comfortable having the children visit. Both the children and the elderly must be *willing participants.* Older adults must be given the option not to participate if they're not interested or don't feel like it.
- Ask the elderly for their suggestions and ideas on how to enhance the program. *Involve the participants* in the initial planning of activities.
- Plan *regular activities* with the children. Regular visits will help the elderly and the children develop closer relationships. Frequent contact provides the best opportunity for sharing.
- Make the program *environment* as pleasant, positive, festive, and comfortable as possible.
- Use *name tags* on the adults and the children to help the older adults remember and use the children's names.
- *Share food.* Eating is an activity that everyone enjoys. The children and the elders can prepare a snack or meal to enjoy together.

Resources

A variety of resources can be tapped for planning intergenerational programs.

Infants and Toddlers

- Families and friends of the elder or staff
- Day care centers
- Nursery schools

Children

- Kindergarten
- Elementary and middle school students

- Boys and girls clubs
- 4H clubs
- Scout groups
- Church choirs and groups

Young Adults

- High school and college students
- Mentally retarded young adults
- Youth summer or part-time job placements
- Volunteer placements

INTERGENERATIONAL PROGRAM ACTIVITIES

Holiday Celebrations (such as Christmas, Halloween, or Valentine's Day)

- Making decorations
- Adorning the facility
- Dressing in holiday costumes
- Exchanging cards or presents
- Discussing the holidays: plans, holidays past, expectations, and the like
- Listening or singing to holiday music
- Making holiday foods together
- Sharing holiday foods—eating together

Musical Activities

- Rhythm band
- Music appreciation
- Sing-along
- Dance

Games

- Parachute games
- Balloon volleyball

- Bowling
- Bingo
- Spelling bee
- Nerf darts
- Word games
- Trivia

Parties/Special Events

- Birthday celebrations
- Hawaiian luau
- Carnival
- Balloon release
- Scavenger hunt/Easter egg hunt

Contests

- Kite flying

Shows/Performances (by the children or elderly)

- Bands
- Choirs
- Solo performances
- Drama performances
- Magic show
- Poetry readings
- Fashion show
- Talent show
- Puppet show

Outings

- Circus
- Boat ride
- Zoo
- Picnics

Pets

- Pet show
- Pet visitation
- Demonstrations: obedience, police dog, seeing eye dogs

Arts and Crafts

- Ceramics/modeling clay
- Painting

Horticulture

- Gardening
- Flower arranging

Edible Activities

- Cooking/baking
- Preparing a snack or meal together
- Ice cream social

Spiritual Activities

- Bible history
- Bible readings
- Hymn singing

- Church visit
- Religious program

Oral Histories

- History class
- Looking at scrapbooks/pictures of historic events
- Sharing past experiences

Exercise

- Walks
- Exercise program

Other

- Sharing hobbies
- Playing Show and tell
- Exchanging letters/cards/telephone calls
- Making popcorn and watching a movie
- Conversing or assisting one on one
- Sharing a task-related activity such as setting the table
- Visiting the children's day care center or school for show and tell or to see their work, toys, and facilities
- Discussing careers

SAMPLE ACTIVITY (FROM VINTAGE ADULT DAY CARE)

Exercise Together

A group of children from a nearby child day care center visited the adult day care center. Each of the children brought a paper flower to give to an older adult "friend."

The children sat next to the seniors and participated in the daily exercise program. Afterward they sang songs together: some children's songs, some old time favorites, and some both knew. The children sang a special song to the seniors.

To end, one of the older adults thanked everyone for coming and invited the children back.

The children and the seniors enjoyed each other very much. Exercising together worked very well and prompted much discussion about energy and youth.

Chapter 18 focuses on pet programs for the elderly. Programs that include both children and pets can be fun and exciting. The elderly can enjoy watching how the youngsters respond to the animals.

18

Special Friends: Elders and Pets

Pets can help fill a void of loneliness. Animals eagerly respond to care and attention. When treated with kindness, pets can be affectionate and loyal. They have the capacity for unconditional love and acceptance. Pets seek attention from everyone. They don't reject people because they are old, sick, or impaired.

The elderly have responded favorably to pet programs by showing renewed interest in their own lives and surroundings. Those conducting pet programs have reported joyous responses and immediate emotional impact on the introduction of pets, especially in institutions. Animals can contribute to a supportive, homelike environment.

Animals can spark interest in even the most confused withdrawn person. Communication with an animal relies on close physical contact. Speech is not necessary to interact with an animal or to convey warmth and affection. The confused older person who may be experiencing sensory impairment responds to the physical nature of communication with animals.

Animals can have a soothing, calming effect on people. Studies have shown when people interact with puppies and kittens by rhythmically petting or stroking them, all measures of body tension eased below usual levels. Even watching fish in a tank or birds in a cage can reduce stress.

Pets provide companionship and decrease social isolation. Caring for a pet is rewarding: It provides a feeling of usefulness and being needed. A pet gives the confused older adult something to care about. Pets can be an incentive for engaging in activities, increasing interest, alertness, and responsiveness. Caring for an animal's needs as part of a daily routine contributes to reality orientation. Interacting with animals stimulates multiple senses: smell, touch, vision, and hearing. Walking a dog is good exercise, too.

Pets are an icebreaker for bringing people together, encouraging social interaction and communication. They provide the elderly with an opportunity to express their feelings. Pets evoke memories that can result in animated discussion of pets and animals in general.

Pets bring a spark of joy into the day. They add interest, warmth, and humor to life. Animal antics can be amusing and entertaining.

HOW TO INCORPORATE PETS INTO AN ACTIVITY PROGRAM

Basic precautions and safety procedures need to be taken with pets. The animals should be healthy, clean, and well-groomed and have all their current innoculations. Visiting animals should be friendly and unafraid of strangers. Animals should not go into food areas or nursing stations. Check with any local agency that inspects for health purposes to determine if there are any regulations concerning pets visiting or residing.

A volunteer should accompany the pet to make sure everyone who wants to see it does. A blanket can be used to keep the animal off the participants. If the participants are given treats to feed the animals, they should be humanly edible, as the participants may try to eat them.

It is important to be sensitive to and respect the wishes of individuals who do not wish to have contact with the pets. Not all people are fond of animals. Those who had a close relationship with a pet in the past probably will benefit the most from a companion animal.

ANIMALS AS PETS

Aquariums

Aquariums are colorful, visually stimulating, and require minimal care. Watching fish reduces stress and contributes to a feeling of tranquility. Overfeeding is a common problem, so feeding should be supervised.

Vivariums

Vivariums house small reptiles (lizards or snakes) or amphibians (frogs, toads, or small tortoises). They require little maintenance and are entertaining and visually stimulating. However, some older adults may be repulsed by them. The animals do require careful handling.

Small Mammals

Small mammals such as rats, mice, gerbils, and hamsters are entertaining to watch and have low maintenance requirements. They may bite if they are not used to being handled. Some people may have a strong aversion to them, especially people with a farming background. Rats can become very affectionate and attached to individuals. Rabbits and guinea pigs offer more opportunity for interaction than the smaller rodents and they are less active. They are usually calm and can be held and stroked. Rabbits can be litter trained.

Birds

Caged birds, especially finches, canaries, parakeets, cockatiels, love birds, and parrots, make suitable pets. They are vocal, colorful, entertaining, and stimulating. Small birds must be handled with extreme care. Cockatiels are affectionate and tame more easily than some others.

Bird feeders placed where they are easily seen offer the individual an opportunity to observe birds in their natural habitat. They are entertaining and visually stimulating. A window bird feeder with a one-way mirror can be purchased. A simple bird feeder can be made by tying a string around a pine cone, spreading the cone with peanut butter, and rolling it in bird seed. It can be hung near a window so that everyone can watch the birds eat.

Cats and Dogs

Cats and dogs offer the maximum pet and therapeutic potential. They are soft, cuddly, and affectionate. However, they do require the most care and supervision.

Other Pets

Small farm animals can also be used as pets, depending upon local restrictions. The African pygmy goat is affectionate and friendly and can be paper trained. Ducks in a small pond or pool are fun and interesting to watch.

ACTIVITIES WITH ANIMALS

Pet Show

A pet show can be fun and exciting. A pet itself or a photo or drawing of it can be used in the show. Awards can be given for the largest and smallest animal, most unusual, shortest tail, and longest legs. This can be an intergenerational activity if a school or scout group is involved (it can provide the pets). A kennel club or cat club can be invited to bring its animals to the pet show.

Animal Races

Animal races can be held. Small rodents can be placed in exercise balls and cheered across the floor. Turtles can also be used. Every person can be given an animal to cheer on. If there are more people than animals, the people can be divided into teams.

Animal Demonstrations

Participants enjoy watching trained animals perform. A local kennel club or Police K-9 Unit can provide an animal and a trainer to put on a special show. A Seeing Eye dog demonstration is also interesting and educational.

Farm Day

Many elders grew up on farms and they enjoy being around farm animals. A trip to a working farm is enjoyable for people from the city and country. A 4-H group can bring their show animals for a Farm Day program. All of the day's activities can revolve around farming and farm life.

PET VISITATION PROGRAMS

If a pet in residence is not possible, a pet visitation program is an alternative. Visiting animals cannot provide continuing reinforcement, love, and affection, and it is more difficult for individuals to develop a special attachment to a visiting animal. But for many elderly this may be the only contact with animals they will have. Visiting animals can be obtained from pet stores, 4-H clubs, kennel clubs, humane societies, chapters of Therapy Dogs International, zoos, and farms.

The participants can watch the animals, hold, groom, and feed them. Small puppies and kittens work well with the elderly, as they are easily held and petted. An animal that can be held is much more conducive to feelings of love and security. They may especially enjoy feeding baby animals bottled milk. An educational program about the visiting animal can be planned as part of the activity.

A discussion of pets and animals in general can also be part of the program. Animals stimulate reminiscence. The discussion can include pets owned, dislikes for various animals, and animals preferred as pets.

A pet program can add a lot of interest and variety to an activity program. Chapter 19, "Miscellaneous Activities," includes a variety of ideas to spice up an activity program.

19

Miscellaneous Activities

There are many more activities for the mentally impaired elderly than are included in this manual. It is hoped this resource will serve as a guide to help you develop many more ideas of your own. This final chapter consists of a variety of activity ideas to help make a well-rounded program.

She enjoyed grocery shopping and cooking and some TV programs. She read the newspapers but very little else. Mostly she enjoyed being with other people, entertaining them, helping them and just being with them. She was restless just sitting around when these had to be stopped or curtailed. I tried to find things for her to do with her hands. There was little or nothing she could or would do on her own. This frustrated her. I *read* to her or had her read aloud to me. I doubt that she comprehended what she was reading, but she seemed to enjoy it. I gave her a word to *spell* and she spelled it better than I could. This, too, she enjoyed. She answered prayers on key. We sang songs. She remembered most. We looked at photographs and she was able to name everyone until the last year or so. I gave her numbers to add, subtract, divide and multiply and she did them accurately. I gave her playing cards to identify and she did pretty well. We were out a part of almost every day. When she wasn't at Vintage we went shopping or visiting. She seemed to follow conversations by responding to a word or a laugh at the appropriate moment up until the very end.

ACTIVITIES FOR THE SPIRIT

The spiritual needs of a person are as important to an individual's care as the physical, emotional and social. Spiritual growth is possible throughout the life span. Religion is important to many older adults, and religious activities play an important role in an activity program. Yet spiritual activities are an often neglected dimension of activities programming.

Religion can be an important resource to the elderly, contributing to a sense of well-being and personal adjustment. An assurance of God's continuing love, relief from feelings of guilt, grief, fear, and loneliness, and a feeling of continuing usefulness were among the spiritual needs identified at the 1981 White House Conference on Aging. Religion can help the older adult face problems of old age and mental impairment. Faith in God can be comforting and reassuring.

Pastoral counseling is one way the elderly can meet their spiritual needs. Pastoral counseling can help the older adult counteract feelings of grief and loneliness and provide consolation. It gives the older adult an opportunity to express fears and concerns.

There are some basic considerations that must be taken into account when a group religious activity is planned. The need to express religion varies and will probably depend on the individual's lifelong practices. No one should be forced or feel pressured to participate in a religious activity. Religious preferences must be respected. Every participant's religious practices should be considered when planning a religious activity. For example, Hannukah should be celebrated along with Christmas when there are Jewish members in the group. The spiritual needs of the elderly can be met through intergenerational spiritual experiences.

RELIGIOUS ACTIVITIES

Bible Studies

The Bible is a source of many activities. Passages from the Bible can be read and discussed. Potentials Development for Health and Aging Services has published the book *Bible Studies for Senior Citizens* for the lay person to use. Slides or tapes of the Bible or Sunday School lessons can be used for discussions. A Bible quiz can be held to test the participants' knowledge. Other religious books such as the Torah, and the Koran, can be read and discussed.

Religious Services

Religious services can be held regularly or on special holidays. Religious leaders can be invited to conduct a nonsectarian service, or services can be held for each religious group separately.

During vesper services, every participant can light a candle at an altar. This can be followed by a religious reading and the playing of hymns. A prayer time can be held. Sometimes a person with a dementing illness will remember the words to religious songs and prayers verbatim, thus gaining a deep sense of satisfaction. If the first words or lines of a prayer are given, even the most confused person may be able to complete it (if the individual knew the prayer in the first place). Memorial services can be held to commemorate the death of a group member or for an individual's loss of loved ones.

Hymn Singing

A sing-along of spiritual songs can be a very moving, enjoyable experience. As the words to familiar hymns are often remembered, everyone can participate. Members from a local church or choir can join in or lead the hymn singing.

Service to Others

Making articles to be sold at church fairs or for foreign missionaries can be a rewarding experience. Churches may need clothing mended, newsletters folded, or envelopes stuffed. Participation in mission-related projects can help increase the older adult's sense of self-esteem and usefulness.

Bible Quiz*

Those who have a love for the Bible often are able to remember the names of characters and complete familiar phrases. Ask the participants what person from the Bible is associated with this event or term:

Adam and Eve	The Garden of Eden
Noah	The Ark
Moses	A burning bush, the Ten Commandments, the parting of the Red Sea
Jonah	A whale

Goliath	A giant
David	A slingshot
Daniel	The lion's den
Joseph	The coat of many colors
Samson	Strength from long hair
Peter	"The Rock"
Thomas	"The Doubter"
Joshua	The battle of Jericho
John the Baptist	Baptism of Jesus
Judas	Betrayal of Jesus
Jesus	Water into wine

Cain and Abel	Who are the sons of Adam and Eve?
Lot	Whose wife turned to a pillar of salt when she disobeyed God?
Delilah	Who tricked Samson into revealing the secret of his strength?
Lazarus	Who was raised from his grave by Jesus?
Forty	How many days and nights did it rain while Noah was in the Ark?
Ten	How many commandments are there?
Six	How many days did it take for God to create the world?
Two	How many men died on the cross beside Jesus?
Bethlehem	Where was Jesus born?
Apple	What fruit did Eve tempt Adam with?
Dove	What animal did Noah send out to find dry land?
Good Friday	What day did Jesus die?
Easter Sunday	What day did he rise from the dead?
Amen	What is the last word in the Bible?

Complete these phrases from the Bible:

I am the way, the **truth and the life.**

Eye for an eye, **tooth for a tooth.**

The love of money is the **root of all evil.**

It is more blessed to give **than to receive.**

No man can serve **two masters.**

It is easier for a camel to go through the eye of a needle, than for a rich man to enter into the **Kingdom of God.**

Honor thy father and **thy mother.**

Greater love hath no man than this, that a man lay down his life for his **friends.**

Give us this day **our daily bread.**

You are the salt of the **Earth.**

You are the light of the **World.**

Give thanks to the Lord **for He is good.**

Blessed are the poor in spirit, **for their's is the kingdom of heaven.**

Blessed are those who mourn, **for they will be comforted.**

Blessed are the meek, **for they will inherit the Earth.**

Blessed are the merciful, **for they will be shown Mercy.**

Blessed are the pure in heart, **for they will see God.**

Blessed are the peacemakers, **for they will be called sons of God.**

Other

Have the participants:

- make a scrapbook of religious articles and verses.
- plan a speaker: invite leaders of different religions to address the group.
- begin or conclude a religious activity with prayers, a familiar hymn, or reading.
- conduct a discussion group about religions and churches. Talk about why people need religion and why they go to church. Ask everyone what religion means to them.

*Adapted from V. Darnell, *This & That* "Trivia for Seniors," by Golden Horizons, Sullivan, Illinois.

TRIPS

Most persons with a dementing illness remain very social and enjoy being out with people. Outings are fun, provide for a needed change of scenery, and are something the older adult can look forward to. However, many impaired older adults have few opportunities to go out. The caregiver is often apprehensive about taking the confused person out in public, fearing embarrassment for both. By taking a few precautions and making preparations in advance, the caregiver can enable the confused older adult to enjoy being out in public.

- Plan to visit places or attend events when they are free from noise and overcrowding.
- Clear any travel plans with the older adult's physician.
- Purchase tickets in advance.
- Make advance arrangements to use a facility's wheelchairs and to obtain access to entrance ways and elevators that accomodate the handicapped.
- Notify the management in advance that the individual has a dementing illness that can cause him or her to be confused, or if a group will be attending, that a group of individuals with memory impairments will be coming from your organization.
- Determine if there are steps, easily accessible bathrooms, and places to sit and rest and when large crowds are expected.
- Determine if an attendant of the opposite sex will be able to help the confused person use the restroom or if an employee could help.
- On group trips have each person attended at all times. Each participant should be assigned to a staff person.
- Make sure that the confused person is carrying or wearing identifying information in case the person wanders off or gets lost.
- Watch for signs of fatigue. Allow for adequate rest times.

Dining Out

- Discreetly explain to the waiter or waitress that you will order for the person and the bill should be given to you.
- Tell the confused person you are treating her or him and you will take care of everything. Reassure him if he becomes concerned about paying the bill. It is sometimes helpful to let the confused person keep a few dollars in his wallet to alleviate this anxiety.
- Select simple foods that can be eaten neatly.
- Remove unnecessary glasses and utensils.

Shopping Trips

- Give the confused person something to do while you are shopping. Ask him or her to hold parcels or check off items from the shopping list.
- Ask for advice on what to buy to help the individual feel useful. ("Should we buy peas or corn?")
- If the confused person accidentally shoplifts, explain to the manager that the person has a dementing illness. Offer to pay for or return the item.

The Vintage Adult Day Care program participants have taken many successful trips, including:

Boat ride
Restaurants
Zoo
Aviary
Picnics
Children's day care center
Factory tour
Sporting events
Church tours
Concerts
Car rides (seasonal rides to see the foliage, view Christmas lights, visit the cemetery, out for ice cream, to tour the city and see how it has changed)

Flower show
Museums
Circus
Festivals/fairs
Incline
Senior center
Nursing home
Shopping trips
Parks
Exhibits
Drama performances
Musical comedies

Other Suggestions for Outings

- Train ride
- Fishing
- Rodeo
- Fashion show
- Horse show

- Greenhouse
- Farm
- Hayride
- Local landmarks
- Historic sites

PARTIES AND SPECIAL EVENTS*

Parties give the older adult something to look forward to. They are a reminder of former happy times. Parties and other special events give people a chance to work together: planning the program, making decorations, preparing the food, decorating, and cleaning up afterward. Planning and organization are the keys to a successful event.

- Choose a theme around which the decorations, favors, food, entertainment, and group activities can follow. Some suggested themes are:

Birthday	Ethnic group
Historic event	Fortune-telling
Holiday	Carnival
Cookout/Picnic	Circus
Fashion show	Travel/Foreign countries
Seasonal event	Country fair
Family day/Open house	Festival (strawberry festival)
Games (Bingo)	Contest/Races (horse races)
Hawaiian luau	Anniversary
Patriotic celebration (Flag Day, Fourth of July)	

- Give everyone an invitation. Consider inviting family members to some events.
- Make everyone a festive name tag or pin on a corsage or boutonniere. Make party favors such as leis for a Hawaiian luau for everyone to wear.
- Refreshments are important. Choose refreshments that reflect your theme such as mock piña coladas and pineapple fruit kabobs for a Hawaiian luau.
- Entertainment can make or break a party. It should be lots of fun—lively and upbeat. Dancing schools, school bands, church choirs, drama clubs, choral groups, musician's unions, majorettes, cheerleaders, senior centers, and schools for the performing arts are entertainment resources.
- Decorations help to carry out the theme and create a festive atmosphere.
- Use the party as an opportunity to discuss memories of past events and celebrations relating to the party's theme.

Ethnic Celebration

A country is chosen by the participants or because of its relation to another event (Ireland for St. Patrick's Day). Information on the country and its food, handicrafts, customs, music, costumes, and famous sons and daughters should be researched and prepared in advance, including:

- Slide or movie presentation
- Display of handicrafts/industry
- Posters, brochures, maps from travel agencies

- Music—songs sung or played on a record or tape
- Entertainment—ethnic dance or musical performance
- Ethnic food as refreshments
- Presentation on the country: its location, history, industries, and customs
- Display or modeling of ethnic costumes
- Ethnic decorations
- A few words or sayings in the native language to be taught
- Items pertaining to the country brought by participants to show to other participants

Tasting Parties

Invite a small group of participants to join you in a taste adventure. Tasting parties are very social, pleasant affairs that are relaxing and stimulate conversation. The table should be a focal point and set attractively. A floral centerpiece and paper lace doilies make a nice touch.

Tea Party

Serve tea in china teacups from a china teapot. Use a variety of different teas and garnish such as mint, orange and lemon slices, and honey. Scones, tea sandwiches, biscuits, or cookies can be served along with the tea. Afterward, everyone's fortune can be read from the tea leaves.

Coffee-Tasting Party

Serve different types of coffees from a silver or china coffee service. The coffee can be embellished with twists of orange and lemon, cinnamon, vanilla sugar, and whipped cream. Nutbreads, cookies, or a coffeecake can be served along with the coffee.

Unusual-Food Tasting Party

Serve a variety of unusual foods, such as rare fruits, juices, vegetables, or cheeses. Serve different ethnic foods that are not commonly available.

Wine and Cheese Party

Different grape juices, wines, or nonalcoholic sparkling beverages can be served with cubes of cheese, French bread, and fresh fruits. The drinks can be served in glass or plastic wine glasses.

Fondue Party

Fondues are lots of fun. The participants can cut the food into little cubes for dipping. Fruit, cakes, and marshmallows can be dipped into a chocolate or caramel fondue. Vegetables or bread can be dipped into a cheese fondue.

Cocktail Party

Punch or drinks can be made nonalcoholic by eliminating the alcohol. One type of drink can be made and served. After hors d'oeuvres are passed around, a new type of drink can be introduced.

Ice Cream Social

Make your own ice cream or purchase a variety of ice cream flavors. Offer a variety of toppings and let everyone make their own sundaes. Many older people enjoy an old-fashioned ice cream soda or root beer float.

Valentine's Day

Activities

- Making and/or sending valentines
- Making ceramic heart mobile
- Decorating heart cookies
- Sweetheart Dance
- Games: naming famous couples, romantic words, songs with the word *love* in the title
- Discussion topics: past romances, favorite pets, sweetheart dances, best Valentine's Day, favorite Valentine's gift

St. Patrick's Day

Activities

- Making shamrocks
- Playing and singing Irish folk songs

- Dancing to Irish folk dances
- Irish musical performance
- Giving everyone an Irish name: O'__; Mc__
- Telling Irish jokes or stories
- Dressing in green
- Making potato candy, cookies, or Irish stew
- Displaying costumes and items made in Ireland
- Discussion topics: trips to Ireland, Irish history, participants of Irish descent

Easter/Passover

Activities

- Egg dying
- Decorating Easter bonnets
- Easter egg hunt
- Playing and singing Easter and Passover songs
- Making candy
- An Easter parade
- Making a flower basket arrangement
- Displaying a Seder table
- Discussion topics: Easter and Passover celebrations of the past, old-fashioned Easter parades, spring fashions

Patriotic Celebrations

Activities

- Cookout/picnic
- Attending a fireworks display
- Singing patriotic songs
- Flag ceremony
- Relay races
- Games: quiz on flags or American history
- Discussion topics: participation in patriotic organizations, service-related stories, remembering "the war," old-fashioned fireworks displays, and patriotic events

Halloween

Activities

- Making Halloween masks
- Costume party/judging

- Carving or painting a face on a pumpkin
- Popping popcorn
- Making a mosaic using pumpkin seeds and corn kernels
- Games: name 20 items associated with Halloween, popular superstitions
- Decorating cupcakes with a pumpkin face
- Discussion topics: best costumes, funniest or scariest experiences, autumn or Halloweens past

Christmas/Hanukkah

Activities

- Making Christmas and Hanukkah decorations
- Singing Christmas carols and Hanukkah songs
- Making and sending cards
- Playing dreidel game
- Lighting a menorah
- Decorating a Christmas tree
- Making Christmas cookies
- Discussion topics: religious celebrations, old-fashioned Christmas/Hanukkah celebrations, favorite holidays, or best Christmas gift ever received/given

*Adapted from the *Complete Handbook of Activities and Recreational Programs for Nursing Homes* by Linda Emerson Hastings, © 1981, with permission of the publisher Prentice-Hall Inc., Englewood Cliffs, NJ.

Movies and TV Shows

Movies and TV programs provide opportunities for people to social-ize. The movies can be purchased, rented, or borrowed from libraries, video stores, and different companies. Cassettes of old radio shows are also available. Old-time movies and TV shows stimulate memo-ries and serve as a catalyst for conversation.

- At home, make a production of watching TV. Pop some popcorn or order a pizza.
- Serve popcorn and a drink during the movie or at intermission.
- Make sure everyone can hear the show. Seat everyone within a comfortable viewing distance.
- A poster of the movie or show or the actors and actresses can help stimulate memories and create a festive atmosphere.
- After the movie or show, plan a discussion around it. Ask questions: how everyone liked it, did they ever see it before, and what did they think of the actors. Favorite movies, the cost of old movies, old-time TV and radio pro-grams, neighborhood theatres, and favorite TV and movie stars and radio personalities can also be discussed.

EDUCATIONAL PRESENTATIONS

Programs and presentations on a variety of educational topics are enjoyed by many. Educational topics should be relatively short and simple. Health topics are always popular, and they provide older adults with an opportunity to hear about health issues and talk about their own concerns.

The registered nurse students and guest speakers have prepared presentations on a variety of topics for the Vintage Adult Day Care Program participants including nutrition, arthritis, the benefits of exercise, African art, proper use of medications, and the history and culture of Ireland. Simple handouts are prepared and distributed. Other daily activities can reflect the topic presentation such as preparing a nutritious snack and singing related songs.

DISPLAYS AND EXHIBITS

Displays and exhibits provide a visible reminder of an individual's past and accomplishments.

Photographic displays. Take a current picture of each participant and staff member. Underneath each picture place a brief personal history or humorous anecdote about the person.

Memory board. Post pictures of the participants and staff from their childhood or young adult years. Place brief descriptions about the persons and what they were doing at the time underneath the pictures.

Memorabilia. Ask each of the participants to bring in an item of memorabilia. Old family portraits, old letters, awards, medals, membership cards, and family heirlooms can be put on display.

Art exhibit. An annual exhibit of the participants' work can be held. The art exhibit can include samples of paintings, drawings, ceramics, and craft projects. The participants can act as hosts and hostesses. Refreshments can be served. Awards can be given to the best of show, best from each category, most colorful, most creative, and most unusual, so that everyone receives recognition for achievement.

TASK-ORIENTED ACTIVITIES

Everyone likes to feel useful. There are many things the confused person can help with at home or at an activity program. Simplify activities by breaking them down into steps. Provide examples or demonstrations of how they should be done.

Repetitive activities work well. For example, don't just ask the individual to set the table; Give the person four placemats and ask her or him to put them on the table, then give four plates. Always acknowledge help by expressing your thanks.

Housekeeping

- Wash dishes
- Fold laundry
- Dust furniture

- Set/clear the table
- Sweep floor/porch/yard

- Help prepare meals
- Sort silverware
- Sort clothing (e.g., socks—darks and lights)
- Polish silverware, pots, tea services
- Simple hemming and mending

Gardening

- Water plants
- Rake leaves/grass
- Turn earth in the garden
- Dig holes for planting
- Pick fruits or vegetables from the garden or an orchard

Miscellaneous

- Cut out coupons, pictures in magazines, stamps from envelopes
- Wash the car
- Chop/saw wood
- Mow the lawn
- Sand old pieces of furniture or blocks of wood
- Care for a pet: brush it, feed it, walk it, love it
- Assemble/disassemble items such as piping, an old clock, or carburator
- Unravel a knitted item and wind yarn into a ball
- Sort buttons, nails, nuts and bolts, and like items
- Wash blackboards
- Roll bandages
- Polish shoes
- Prepare craft materials

LOOKING AND FEELING GOOD

Appearance is very important to older adults and the people they come in contact with. Being well dressed and well groomed helps build self-confidence, facilitates group participation, and influences social acceptance. An attractive appearance heightens self-esteem, self-assurance, and lifts the spirit. When you fuss over someone's appearance, you are telling that person that you care how he or she looks and feels.

Personal care activities help the older adult to feel special. They provide the individual with an opportunity to be touched by the caregiver and can be very relaxing and enjoyable.

- Visit a beauty shop for a wash and set; or arrange for a beautician or barber to come to the house, residence, or facility. Finish with hair combs or decorations, if applicable.
- Soak hands and feet in warm water. Place the older adult's hand gently in water and caress it with the water. Pat the hand dry. Gently rub on hand and body lotion. Follow with a manicure or pedicure. Talk along with the individual to calm and relax her or him while you are doing this.
- A facial is relaxing and soothing. Follow with light makeup, if applicable. Talk about how beautiful or radiant the person looks. With a mirror show the confused person how nice he or she looks unless he is afraid of his own image. At Vintage, local cosmetic representatives visited the adult day care program and gave all the participants a facial and did a makeup demonstration. Everyone loved it.
- Arrange a shopping trip. Many older adults do not have many opportunities to shop for clothes. The Vintage adult day care participants take advantage of the Vintage resale shop by shopping for clothing during off-hours.
- Most people enjoy a massage. Even a simple shoulder rub feels good and is a way to communicate your love.

ONE-ON-ONE

Some people may not do well in groups or need time-out from group activity. Others need individual attention to participate. Persons who are bedfast need to be kept stimulated and active. Individualized assistance enables these individuals to participate in a variety of activities and receive the attention they need. One-on-one activities can include assistance with a craft project, walking, looking through magazines together, or just sitting quietly holding hands. Volunteers and students can help ensure that any older adult who needs one-on-one attention will get it.

CONCLUSION

I hope that throughout this book it is evident that there are many ways to enhance the life of an older adult who is mentally impaired. The least we can do is to ensure that every individual's quality of life is the best that it can be, and that means an active, varied, and full life-style.

References—Alzheimer's Disease and Related Disorders

About Alzheimer's disease. (1986). Harrisburg, PA: Pennsylvania Department of Aging.

Alzheimer's Disease. (August 3, 1983). U.S. Congress, House of Representatives. Joint Hearing, Select Committee on Aging, 98th Congress. SCOA Pub. No. 98–412. Washington, DC: U.S. Government Printing Office.

Alzheimer's disease. A description of the illness for the family and friends of patients with this disorder. Washington, DC: National Institute on Aging.

Alzheimer's disease. Early warning signs and diagnostic resources. (1986). New York: The Junior League of the City of New York, Inc.

Alzheimer's disease: An in-depth report. (1982–1983 Special Issue). *Journal of Gerontological Nursing, 9*(2), 1–69.

Alzheimer's disease. An information paper. (January 1984). U.S. House of Representatives, Select Committee on Aging, 98th Congress.

Alzheimer's disease. A scientific guide for health practitioners. Bethesda, MD: National Institute of Health.

Alzheimer's disease and related disorders. (Fall 1982—Special Issue). *Generations: Journal of the Western Gerontological Society, 7*(1), 1–72.

Alzheimer's disease: A Florida perspective. (May 19, 1984). U.S. Congress, House of Representatives, Select Committee on Aging, 98th Congress. Palm Harbor, Florida. Comm. Pub. No. 98-476. Washington, DC: U.S. Government Printing Office.

Alzheimer's disease. Report of the secretary's task force on Alzheimer's disease.

(September 1984). Washington, DC: U.S. Department of Health and Human Services.

Alzheimer's disease research. (1984). U.S. Congress, House of Representatives. Hearings before the Subcommittee on Investigation and Oversight of Committee of Science and Technology. 98th Congress. Washington, DC: U.S. Government Printing Office.

Blass, J. P. (1982, September). Dementia. *Medical Clinics of North America,* 66(5), 1143–1160.

Brown, D. S. (1984). *Handle with care: A question of Alzheimer's disease.* New York: Prometheus Books.

Burnside, I. M. (1976). *Nursing and the aged.* New York: McGraw-Hill.

Burnside, I. M. (1979, July–August). Alzheimer's disease: An overview. *Journal of Gerontological Nursing,* 5(4), 14–20.

Dahl, D. (1983, April). Diagnosis of Alzheimer's disease. *Postgraduate Medicine,* 73(4), 217–221.

Davies, P. (1983, Summer). Biological aspects of Alzheimer's disease. *ADRDA Newsletter,* 3(2).

The dementias: Hope through research. (1983). Bethesda, MD: U.S. Department of Health and Human Services. NIH Publication No. 83-2252.

Dementia—the quiet epidemic. (January 7, 1978). *British Medical Journal,* (6104).

Dietsche, L., & Pollman, J. (1982, February). Alzheimer's disease: Advances in clinical nursing. *Journal of Gerontological Nursing,* 8(2), 97–100.

Drachman, D. A. (1983, Winter). The related disorders—Non-Alzheimer's dementia. *ADRDA Newsletter,* 3(4).

Ebersole, P., & Hess, P. (1981). *Toward healthy aging—Human needs and nursing response.* St. Louis, MO: C. V. Mosby.

Emr, M. (1984, April). Facets of dementia: Research on Alzheimer's. *Journal of Gerontological Nursing,* 10(4), 38–39.

Endless night, endless mourning: Living with Alzheimer's. (September 12, 1983). Senate Hearing Before the Special Committee on Aging, 98th Congress. New York, NY. Senate Hearing 98-410. Washington, DC: U.S. Government Printing Office.

Fact sheet on Alzheimer's disease. Chicago, IL: Alzheimer's Disease and Related Disorders Association, Inc.

Fact sheet: Senile dementia (Alzheimer's disease). (1980). Rockville, MD: National Institute of Mental Health, Center for Studies of Mental Health of the Aging.

Falck, H. S., & Kane, M. *It can't be home.* Rockville, MD: U.S. Department of Health, Education and Welfare, National Institute of Mental Health, 5600 Fishers Lane, Rockville, MD 20857

Fox, P. J. (1986, Fall). Alzheimer's disease: An historical perspective. *The American Journal of Alzheimer's Care,* 1(4), 18–24.

Garcia, C. A., Reding, M. J., & Blass, J. P. (1981). Overdiagnosis of dementia. *Journal of the American Geriatric Society,* 29(9), 407–410.

Gilhooly, M., Zarit, S., & Birren, J. (Eds.). (1986). *The dementias: Policy and management.* Englewood Cliffs, N.J.: Prentice-Hall.

Hamsher, K. (1983, April). Mental status examination in adult day care. *Post Graduate Medicine, 73*(4).

Hemshorn, A. (1985, January). They call it Alzheimer's disease. *Journal of Gerontological Nursing, 11*(1), 36–38.

Henig, R. M. (1985). *The myth of senility.* Washington, DC: American Association of Retired Persons.

Hess, B. B., & Markson, E. (1980). *Aging and old age: An introduction to social gerontology.* New York: Macmillan.

Heston, L. L., & White, J. A. (1983). *Dementia: A practical guide to Alzheimer's disease and related illnesses.* New York: W. H. Freeman.

Hooker, S. (1976). *Caring for elderly people—Understanding and practical help.* London: Routledge & Kegan Paul.

LaPorte, H. J. (1982, February). Reversible causes of dementia: A nursing challenge. *Journal of Gerontological Nursing, 8*(2), 74–80.

Leroux, C. (1981). The silent epidemic. *Chicago Tribune.* Chicago, IL: Reprinted by ADRDA.

Lieberman, A., Gopinathan, G., Neophytides, A., & Goldstein, M. *Parkinson's disease handbook. A guide for patients and their families.* New York: American Parkinson's Disease Association.

Lindeman, D. A. (1984). *Alzheimer's disease handbook.* Aging Health Policy Center, University of California, San Francisco. U.S. Department of Health and Human Services, Office of Human Development Services, Administration on Aging, Volume I.

Losing a million minds: Confronting the tragedy of Alzheimer's disease and other dementias. (1987). Washington, DC: Congress of the United States, Office of Technology Assessment.

Mace, N. L. & Rabins, P., M.D. (1981). *The 36-hour day: A family guide to caring for persons with Alzheimer's disease, related dementing illnesses, and memory loss in later life.* Baltimore: The Johns Hopkins University Press.

McKinstry, D. W. (1982, June). Diagnosis, cause and treatment of Alzheimer's disease. *Research Resources Reporter, 6*(6). U.S. Department of Health and Human Services.

Merrill, S. (June 18, 1986). *Alzheimer's disease. Updated issue brief.* Science Policy Research Division, Congressional Research Service, The Library of Congress.

Minaker, K. L. (March 31, 1987). *Diagnostic approach to patient with senile dementia Alzheimer's type and related disorders.* Pittsburgh, PA: West Penn Hospital and Vintage, Inc. Second Annual Forum on Geriatric Care.

Nolen, W. (1983, August). The enigma of Alzheimer's. *50 Plus.*

Powell, L. S. & Courtice, K. (1983). *Alzheimer's disease: A guide for families.* Massachusetts: Addison-Wesley.

Prachman summarizes mini white house proceedings. (March 1981). *ADRDA Newsletter, 1*(1). New York, NY.

Progress report on senile dementia of the Alzheimer's type. (September 1981). National Institute of Health, U.S. Department of Health and Human Services, NIH Publication No. 81-2343.

Progress report on Alzheimer's disease. Volume II. (July 1984). National Institute of Health, U.S. Department of Health and Human Services, NIH Publication No. 84-2500.

Reisberg, B., M.D. (1981). *A guide to Alzheimer's disease for families, spouses and friends.* New York: The Free Press.

Reisberg, B. (February 1984). Stages of cognitive decline. *American Journal of Nursing,* 225–228.

Report of the mini conference on Alzheimer's disease. (September 28, 1980). The 1981 White House Conference on Aging, New York. U.S. Government Printing Office.

Roach, M. (1983). Another name for madness. *The New York Times.* Reprinted by ADRDA.

Santori, R. and Barrett, K. (January 1983). The tragedy of Rita Hayworth. *Ladies Home Journal.*

Schmeck, H. M. (July 31, 1979). Research attempts to fight senility. *The New York Times.*

Schmidt, G. (April 1983). Mechanisms and possible causes of Alzheimer's disease. *Postgraduate Medicine, 73*(4), 206–213.

Schneck, M. K., Reisberg, B. and Ferris, S. H. (February 1982). An overview of current concepts of Alzheimer's disease. *American Journal of Psychiatry, 139*(2), 165–173.

Senility: The last stereotype. (May 18, 1983). U.S. Congress, House of Representatives, Select Committee on Aging, 98th Congress. Comm. Pub. No. 98-390. Washington, DC: U.S. Government Printing Office.

Senility: Myth or madness. Age Page. (1980). Bethesda, MD: National Institute on Aging, U.S. Department of Health and Human Services.

Senility reconsidered. Treatment possibilities for mental impairment in the elderly. (July 18, 1980). *Journal of the American Medical Association, 244*(3), 259–263.

Shapira, J., Schlesinger, R. and Cummings, J. (1986). Distinguishing dementias. *American Journal of Nursing, 86*(6), 699–702.

Shodell, M. (October 1984). The clouded mind. *Science 84.*

Sisex, F. M. (Fall 1986). Risk of Alzheimer's disease for first degree relatives. *The American Journal of Alzheimer's Care, 1*(4), 14–17.

Terry, R. (Fall 1982). The structural changes in Alzheimer's disease. *ADRDA Newsletter, 2*(1).

Update on Alzheimer's (Special issue). (Winter 1984). *Generations: Journal of the Western Gerontological Society, 9*(2), 1–72.

Wallis, C. (July 11, 1983). Slow, steady and heartbreaking. *Time,* 56–57.

Whall, A. (October 1986). Identifying the characteristics of pseudodementia. *Journal of Gerontological Nursing, 12*(10), 34–35.

Wurtman, R. J. (January 1985). Alzheimer's disease. *Scientific American,* 62–74.

References—Creating the
Right Environment

Berger, E. (November/December 1985). The institutionalization of patients with Alzheimer's disease. *Nursing Homes.*

Bozian, M., & Clark, H. (March 1980). Counteracting sensory changes in the aging. *American Journal of Nursing, 80*(3), 473–476.

Burnette, K. Relocation and the elderly: Changing perspectives. *Journal of Gerontological Nursing, 12*(10), 6–11.

Burnside, I. M. (1976). *Nursing and the aged.* New York: McGraw-Hill Book Company.

Calkins, M. P., & Arch, M. (March/April 1987). Designing special care units: A systematic approach. *The American Journal of Alzheimer's Care and Research, 2*(2), 16–22.

Caring: A family guide to managing the Alzheimer's patient at home. (1985). New York: The New York City Alzheimer's Resource Center.

Cohen, D., & Eisdorfer, C. (1986). *The loss of self: A family resource for the care of Alzheimer's disease and related disorders.* New York: W. W. Norton.

Ebersole, P., & Hess, P. (1981). *Toward healthy aging—human needs and nursing response.* St. Louis, MO: C. V. Mosby.

Engle, V. (October 1985). Temporary relocation: Is it stressful to your patients? *Journal of Gerontological Nursing, 11*(10), 28–31.

Falck, H. S., & Kane, M. *It can't be home.* Rockville, MD: U.S. Department of Health, Education and Welfare, National Institute of Mental Health, 5600 Fishers Lane, Rockville, MD 20857

Gray, M., & McKenzie, H. (1980). *Take care of your elderly relative.* London: Allen and Unwin and Beaconsfield.

Guide to caring for the mentally impaired elderly. (1985). Washington, DC: American Association of Homes for the Aging.

Gwyther, L. P. (1986). *Care of Alzheimer's patients: A manual for nursing home staff.* American Health Care Association and Alzheimer's Disease and Related Disorders Foundation.

Hess, P., & Day, C. (1977). *Understanding the aging parent.* Bowie, MD: Robert J. Brady Company.

Hooker, S. (1976). *Caring for elderly people—understanding and practical help.* London: Routledge and Kegan Paul.

Jacobs, B. (1981). *Working with the at-risk older person: A resource manual.* Washington, DC: The National Council on the Aging, Inc.

Lindeman, D. A. (1984). *Alzheimer's disease handbook.* Aging Health Policy Center, University of California, San Francisco. U.S. Department of Health and Human Services, Office of Human Development Services, Administration on Aging, Volume I.

Losing a million minds: Confronting the tragedy of Alzheimer's disease and other dementias. (1987). Washington, DC: Congress of the United States, Office of Technology Assessment.

Mace, N. L. (October 1985). Facets of dementia. Do we need special care units for dementia patients? *Journal of Gerontological Nursing, 11*(10), 37–38.

Mace, N. L., & Rabins, P. (1981). *The 36-hour day: A family guide to caring for persons with Alzheimer's disease, related dementing illnesses, and memory loss in later life.* Baltimore, MD: The Johns Hopkins University Press.

McDowell, F. H., & Lincoln, E. M. (Ed.) (1980). *Managing the person with intellectual loss at home.* White Plains, NY: Burke Rehabilitation Center.

Nowakowski, L. (September 1985). Accent capabilities in disorientation. *Journal of Gerontological Nursing, 11*(9), 15–20.

Powell, L. S., & Courtice, K. (1983). *Alzheimer's disease: A guide for families.* Massachusetts: Addison-Wesley Publishing Company.

Preventing accidents. (July–August 1986). *Perspectives on aging, 15*(4), 17–20.

Program minimizes risk of falls in the elderly. (September 1984). *Journal of Gerontological Nursing, 10*(9).

Ravish, T. (October 1985). Prevent social isolation before it starts. *Journal of Gerontological Nursing, 11*(10), 10–13.

Schmall, V., & Cleland, M. (1985). *Helping memory impaired elders. A guide for caregivers.* Corrallio, OR: Oregon State University Extension Service.

Sincox, R. B., & Stacy-Cohen, P. (1986). *Adapting the adult day care environment for the demented older adult.* Springfield, IL: The Illinois Department on Aging.

The sixth sense. Understanding sensory changes and aging. (1985). Washington, DC: The National Council on Aging, Inc.

Small, secure and homelike environment best for Alzheimer's patients. (1984). *Aging, 347.*

Springer, D., & Brubaker, T. H. (1984). *Family caregivers and dependent elderly. Minimizing stress and maximizing independence.* Beverly Hills, CA: Sage Publications.

Thornton, S. M., & Fraser, V. (1982). *Understanding "senility"—a layperson's guide.* Buffalo, NY: Potentials Development for Health and Aging Services, Inc.

Williams, L. (February 1986). Alzheimer's: The need for caring. *Journal of Gerontological Nursing, 12*(2), 21–27.

Wolanin, M. O., & Phillips, L. (1981). *Confusion. Prevention and care.* St. Louis, MO: C. V. Mosby Co.

Zachow, K. (August 1984). Helen, can you hear me? *Journal of Gerontological Nursing, 10*(8), 18–22.

Zarit, S. H. (April 1984). Interventions for families of dementia patients. *Alzheimer's Disease Handbook.* Volume I. U.S. Department of Health and Human Services, Administration on Aging.

RESOURCES—ENVIRONMENT

Calkins, Margaret P. (1988). *Designs for Dementia Planning Environments for the Elderly and Confused* National Health Publishing. Owings Mills, M D.

"Environment: Implications for the health of older people." (Spring 1985). *Pride Institute Journal of Long Term and Home Health Care, 4*(2).

Safety for older consumers; Home safety checklist. (1985). Washington, DC: U.S. Consumer Product Safety Commission.

Webb, D. L. (1988). *Planning the Successful Adult Day Care Center.* Kansas City, MO., D. L. Webb and Associates.

References—Daily Living Skills

Alzheimer's disease: A personal care management system and trainer's guide. (1984). Rockville, MD: Alzheimer's Care Management System.

Alzheimer's disease: An in-depth report. (1982–1983 Special Issue). *Journal of Gerontological Nursing, 9*(2).

Alzheimer's disease and related disorders. (Fall 1982—Special Issue). *Generations: Journal of the Western Gerontological Society, 7*(1), 1–72.

Bell, M. F., & Bell, C. C. (1985). *Aging and senile dementia: What every Pennsylvanian needs to know about Alzheimer's disease and other types of senile dementia.* Harrisburg, PA: Pennsylvania Department of Aging.

Berger, E. (November/December 1985). The institutionalization of patients with Alzheimer's disease. *Nursing Homes.*

Bozian, M., & Clark, H. (March 1980). Counteracting sensory changes in the aging. *American Journal of Nursing, 80*(3), 473–476.

Brice, G., & Novak, C. (October 7, 1983). *Managing geriatric residents with special problems.* Seminar held at St. John's Lutheran Home, Mars, PA.

Brown, D. S. (1984). *Handle with care: a question of Alzheimer's disease.* New York: Prometheus Books.

Burnside, I. M. (1976). *Nursing and the aged.* New York: McGraw-Hill Book Company.

Campos, R. G. (February 1984). Does reality orientation work? *Journal of Gerontological Nursing, 10*(2), 53–61.

Caring: A family guide to managing the Alzheimer's patient at home. (1985). New York: The New York City Alzheimer's Resource Center.

Cohen, D., & Eisdorfer, C. (1986). *The loss of self: A family resource for the care of Alzheimer's disease and related disorders.* New York: W. W. Norton.

Ebersole, P., & Hess, P. (1981). Toward healthy aging—human needs and nursing response. St. Louis, MO: C. V. Mosby.

Falck, H. S., & Kane, M. *It can't be home.* Rockville, MD: U.S. Department of Health, Education and Welfare, National Institute of Mental Health, 5600 Fishers Lane, Rockville, MD 20857.

Fisk, A. A. (April 1983). Alzheimer's disease: A five article symposium. Management of Alzheimer's disease. *Post Graduate Medicine, 73*(4), 237–250.

Gartley, C. B. (Ed.) (1985). *Managing incontinence—a guide to living with loss of bladder control.* Ottawa, IL: Jameson Books.

Gray, M., & McKenzie, H. (1980). *Take care of your elderly relative.* London: Allen and Unwin and Beaconsfield.

Guide to caring for the mentally impaired elderly. (1985). Washington, DC: American Association of Homes for the Aging.

Gwyther, L. P. (1986). *Care of Alzheimer's patients: A manual for nursing home staff.* American Health Care Association and Alzheimer's Disease and Related Disorders Foundation.

Henderson, J. N., & Pfeiffer, E. (1984). *Mental health and aging: A curriculum guide for nursing home caregivers.* Tampa, FL: Suncoast Gerontology Center, University of South Florida.

Hess, P., & Day, C. (1977). *Understanding the aging parent.* Bowie, MD: Robert J. Brady Company.

Hooker, S. (1976). *Caring for elderly people—understanding and practical help.* London: Routledge and Kegan Paul.

Horne, J. (1985). *Caregiving—Helping an aging loved one.* Washington, DC: American Association of Retired Persons.

Huss, A. J. (January 1977). Touch with care or a caring touch: 1976 Eleanor Clarke Slagle lecture. *The American Journal of Occupational Therapy, 31*(1), 11–18.

It isn't senility. The nurse's role in Alzheimer's disease. (February 1981). *Journal of Practical Nursing, 17*–19.

Jacobs, B. (1981). *Working with the at-risk older person: A resource manual.* Washington, DC: The National Council on the Aging, Inc.

Keane, E. E. (Ed.) (June 1980). *Coping with senility: A guidebook.* COBS Society, Inc. of Pennsylvania.

Lindeman, D. A. (1984). *Alzheimer's disease handbook.* Aging Health Policy Center, University of California, San Francisco. U.S. Department of Health and Human Services, Office of Human Development Services, Administration on Aging, Volume I.

Long, M. L. (January 1985). Incontinence. *Journal of Gerontological Nursing, 11*(1), 30–41.

Losing a million minds: Confronting the tragedy of Alzheimer's disease and other dementias. (1987). Washington, DC: Congress of the United States, Office of Technology Assessment.

Mace, N. L. (September 1984). Facets of dementia: Incontinence. *Journal of Gerontological Nursing, 10*(9), 32.

Mace, N. L., & Rabins, P. (1981). *The 36-hour day: A family guide to caring for persons with Alzheimer's disease, related dementing illnesses, and memory loss in later life.* Baltimore, MD: The Johns Hopkins University Press.

McDowell, F. H., & Lincoln, E. M. (Ed.) (1980). *Managing the person with intellectual loss at home.* White Plains, NY: Burke Rehabilitation Center.

Muncy, J. H. (August 1986). Measures to rid sleeplessness. *Journal of Gerontological Nursing, 12*(8), 6–10.

Nowakowski, L. (September 1985). Accent capabilities in disorientation. *Journal of Gerontological Nursing, 11*(9), 15–20.

Pajk, M. (February 1984). Alzheimer's disease. Inpatient care. *American Journal of Nursing.*

Panella, J., Jr., & McDowell, F. H. (1983). *Day care for dementia: A manual of instruction for developing a program.* White Plains, NY: The Burke Rehabilitation Center Auxiliary.

Powell, L. S., & Courtice, K. (1983). Alzheimer's disease: A guide for families. Massachusetts: Addison-Wesley Publishing Company.

Preventing accidents. (July–August 1986). *Perspectives on aging, 15*(4), 17–20.

Program minimizes risk of falls in the elderly. (September 1984). *Journal of Gerontological Nursing, 10*(9).

Ravish, T. (October 1985). Prevent social isolation before it starts. *Journal of Gerontological Nursing, 11*(10), 10–13.

Reisberg, B. (1981). *A guide to Alzheimer's disease for families, spouses and friends.* New York: The Free Press.

Roach, M. (1983). Another name for madness. *The New York Times.* Reprinted by ADRDA.

Schmall, V., & Cleland, M. (1985). *Helping memory impaired elders. A guide for caregivers.* Corrallio, OR: Oregon State University Extension Service.

Senility: Myth or madness. Age Page. (1980). Bethesda, MD: National Institute on Aging, U.S. Department of Health and Human Services.

Senility reconsidered. Treatment possibilities for mental impairment in the elderly. (July 18, 1980). *Journal of the American Medical Association, 244*(3), 259–263.

Sincox, R. B., & Stacy-Cohen, P. (1986). *Adapting the adult day care environment for the demented older adult.* Springfield, IL: The Illinois Department on Aging.

The sixth sense. Understanding sensory changes and aging. (1985). Washington, DC: The National Council on Aging, Inc.

Springer, D., & Brubaker, T. H. (1984). *Family caregivers and dependent elderly. Minimizing stress and maximizing independence.* Beverly Hills, CA: Sage Publications.

Thornton, S. M., & Fraser, V. (1982). *Understanding "senility"—a layperson's guide.* Buffalo, NY: Potentials Development for Health and Aging Services, Inc.

Trockman, G. (September 1978). Caring for the confused or delirious patient. *American Journal of Nursing*, 1495–1499.

Update on Alzheimer's (Special issue). (Winter 1984). *Generations: Journal of the Western Gerontological Society, 9*(2), 1–72.

Wagnild, G., & Manning, R. (December 1985). Convey respect during bathing procedures (patient well-being depends on it). *Journal of Gerontological Nursing, 11*(12), 6–10.

Williams, L. (February 1986). Alzheimer's: The need for caring. *Journal of Gerontological Nursing, 12*(2), 21–27.

Wolanin, M. O., & Phillips, L. (1981). *Confusion. Prevention and care.* St. Louis: C. V. Mosby.

Zarit, S. H. (April 1984). Interventions for families of dementia patients. *Alzheimer's Disease Handbook.* Volume I. U.S. Department of Health and Human Services, Administration on Aging.

RESOURCES—DAILY LIVING SKILLS

HIP
Help for Incontinent People
P.O. Box 544
Union, S.C. 29379
803-579-7900

The Simon Foundation
Box 815
Wilmette, Il. 60091
800-23-SIMON

References—Enhancing Communications

Aging and vision: Making the most of impaired vision. (1985). New York: American Foundation for the Blind.

Alzheimer's disease. A description of the illness for the family and friends of patients with this disorder. Washington, DC: National Institute on Aging.

Bell, M. F., & Bell, C. C. (1985). *Aging and senile dementia: What every Pennsylvanian needs to know about Alzheimer's disease and other types of senile dementia.* Harrisburg, PA: Pennsylvania Department of Aging.

Bozian, M., & Clark, H. (March 1980). Counteracting sensory changes in the aging. *American Journal of Nursing, 80*(3), 473–476.

Campos, R. G. (February 1984). Does reality orientation work? *Journal of Gerontological Nursing, 10*(2), 53–61.

Caring: A family guide to managing the Alzheimer's patient at home. (1985). New York: The New York City Alzheimer's Resource Center.

Cohen, D., & Eisdorfer, C. (1986). *The loss of self: A family resource for the care of Alzheimer's disease and related disorders.* New York: W. W. Norton and Company.

Deichman, E. S., & Kirchhofer, M. V. (1985). *Working with the elderly—a training manual and teaching guide.* Potential Development for Health and Aging Services, Inc. Buffalo, NY.

Dolinsky, E. (September 1984). Infantilization of the elderly: An area for nursing research. *Journal of Gerontological Nursing, 10*(9), 12–19.

Ebersole, P., & Hess, P. (1981). Toward healthy aging—human needs and nursing response. St. Louis, MO: C. V. Mosby Company.

Fisk, A. A. (April 1983). Alzheimer's disease: A five article symposium. Management of Alzheimer's disease. *Post Graduate Medicine, 73*(4), 237–250.

Gray, M., & McKenzie, H. (1980). *Take care of your elderly relative.* London: Allen and Unwin and Beaconsfield.

Guide to caring for the mentally impaired elderly. (1985). Washington, DC: American Association of Homes for the Aging.

Gwyther, L. P. (1986). *Care of Alzheimer's patients: A manual for nursing home staff.* American Health Care Association and Alzheimer's Disease and Related Disorders Foundation.

Harris, C., & Ivory, P. (December 1976). An outcome evaluation of reality orientation therapy with geriatric patients in a state mental hospital. *The Gerontologist, 16*(6).

Henderson, J. N., & Pfeiffer, E. (1984). *Mental health and aging: A curriculum guide for nursing home caregivers.* Tampa, FL: Suncoast Gerontology Center, University of South Florida.

Hooker, S. (1976). *Caring for elderly people—understanding and practical help.* London: Routledge and Kegan Paul.

Horne, J. (1985). *Caregiving—Helping an aging loved one.* Washington, DC: American Association of Retired Persons.

Huss, A. J. (January 1977). Touch with care or a caring touch: 1976 Eleanor Clarke Slagle lecture. *The American Journal of Occupational Therapy, 31*(1), 11–18.

Keane, E. E. (Ed.) (June 1980). *Coping with senility: A guidebook.* COBS Society, Inc. of Pennsylvania.

Letcher, P., Patterson, L., & Scarbrongle, D. (December 1974). Reality orientation: A historical study of patient progress. *Hospital and Community Psychiatry, 25*(12), 801–803.

Mace, N. L., & Rabins, P. (1981). *The 36-hour day: A family guide to caring for persons with Alzheimer's disease, related dementing illnesses, and memory loss in later life.* Baltimore, MD: The Johns Hopkins University Press.

Marston, K. *Communication . . . or "I want to tell you what I don't want to say."* Buffalo, NY: Roswell Park Memorial Institute, New York State Department of Health.

McDowell, F. H., & Lincoln, E. M. (Ed.) (1980). *Managing the person with intellectual loss at home.* White Plains, NY: Burke Rehabilitation Center.

Nowakowski, L. (September 1985). Accent capabilities in disorientation. *Journal of Gerontological Nursing, 11*(9), 15–20.

Pajk, M. (February 1984). Alzheimer's disease. Inpatient care. *American Journal of Nursing,* 216–224.

Panella, J., Jr., & McDowell, F. H. (1983). *Day care for dementia: A manual of instruction for developing a program.* White Plains, NY: The Burke Rehabilitation Center Auxiliary.

Powell, L. S., & Courtice, K. (1983). *Alzheimer's disease: A guide for families.* Massachusetts: Addison-Wesley Publishing Company.

Ravish, T. (October 1985). Prevent social isolation before it starts. *Journal of Gerontological Nursing, 11*(10), 10–13.

Schmall, V., & Cleland, M. (1985). *Helping memory impaired elders. A guide for caregivers.* Corrallio, OR: Oregon State University Extension Service.

Sensory changes of aging. (1982). Pittsburgh, PA: Visiting Nurse Association of Allegheny County.

Service coordination for the blind and visually impaired elderly. (1986). Pittsburgh, PA: Vintage, Inc. and Pittsburgh Blind Association for the Pennsylvania Department of Aging.

Sincox, R. B., & Stacy-Cohen, P. (1986). *Adapting the adult day care environment for the demented older adult.* Springfield, IL: The Illinois Department on Aging.

The sixth sense. Understanding sensory changes and aging. (1985). Washington, DC: The National Council on Aging, Inc.

Thornton, S. M., & Fraser, V. (1982). *Understanding "senility"—a layperson's guide.* Buffalo, NY: Potentials Development for Health and Aging Services, Inc.

Trockman, G. (September 1978). Caring for the confused or delirious patient. *American Journal of Nursing,* 1495–1499.

Update on Alzheimer's (Special issue). (Winter 1984). *Generations: Journal of the Western Gerontological Society,* 9(2).

Witte, K. (January/February 1987). Discourse and dialogue: Prolonging adult conversation in the Alzheimer patient. *The American Journal of Alzheimer's Care,* 2(1), 30–40.

Wolanin, M. O., & Phillips, L. (1981). *Confusion. Prevention and care.* St. Louis, MO: C. V. Mosby Co.

Zachow, K. (August 1984). Helen, can you hear me? *Journal of Gerontological Nursing,* 10(8), 18–22.

Zarit, S. H. (April 1984). Interventions for families of dementia patients. *Alzheimer's Disease Handbook.* Volume I. U.S. Department of Health and Human Services, Administration on Aging.

RESOURCES—COMMUNICATION

Sensory Changes

American Association of Retired Persons
Free Loan Audiovisual Programs
Program Scheduling Office
Program Resources Department
AARP/Department AW
1909 K Street, N.W.
Washington, DC 20049
(202) 872-4700

National Council on Aging
600 Maryland Avenue, S.W.
West Wing 100
Washington, DC 20024
(202) 479-1200

- *"The Sixth Sense."* A training program to sensitize people to sensory changes.

Vision Aids

Talking Books
National Library Service for the Blind and Physically Handicapped
Library of Congress
Washington, DC 20542

- Lends recorded tapes and equipment free

American Foundation for the Blind
Consumer Products Department
15 West 16th Street
New York, NY 10011
(212)620-2000

- Catalog of low vision aids

References—Managing Problems

Alzheimer's disease: A personal care management system and trainer's guide. (1984). Rockville, MD: Alzheimer's Care Management System.

Alzheimer's disease. A description of the illness for the family and friends of patients with this disorder. Washington, DC: National Institute on Aging.

Alzheimer's disease. An information paper. (January 1984). U.S. House of Representatives, Select Committee on Aging, 98th Congress.

Alzheimer's disease. A scientific guide for health practitioners. Bethesda, MD: National Institute of Health.

Alzheimer's disease and related disorders. (Fall 1982—Special Issue). *Generations: Journal of the Western Gerontological Society, 7*(1), 1–72.

Bell, M. F., & Bell, C. C. (1985). *Aging and senile dementia: What every Pennsylvanian needs to know about Alzheimer's disease and other types of senile dementia.* Harrisburg, PA: Pennsylvania Department of Aging.

Brice, G., & Novak, C. (October 7, 1983). *Managing geriatric residents with special problems.* Seminar held at St. John's Lutheran Home, Mars, PA.

Brown, D. S. (1984). *Handle with care: a question of Alzheimer's disease.* New York: Prometheus Books.

Burnside, I. M. (January 17, 1979). *Wandering behavior.* Speech presented at Rocky Mountain Gerontology Center, University of Utah, Salt Lake City.

Burnside, I. M. (1984). *Working with the elderly: Group processes and techniques.* Monterey, CA: Wadsworth, Inc.

Caring: A family guide to managing the Alzheimer's patient at home. (1985). New York: The New York City Alzheimer's Resource Center.

Cohen, D., & Eisdorfer, C. (1986). *The loss of self: A family resource for the care of Alzheimer's disease and related disorders.* New York: W. W. Norton and Company.

Dietsche, L., & Pollman, J. (February 1982). Alzheimer's disease: Advances in clinical nursing. *Journal of Gerontological Nursing, 8*(2), 97–100.

Dobrof, R. (Ed.) Social work and Alzheimer's disease: Practical issues with victims and their families. *Journal of Gerontological Social Work, 9*(2), 5–126.

Dolinsky, E. (September 1984). Infantilization of the elderly: An area for nursing research. *Journal of Gerontological Nursing, 10*(9), 12–19.

Ebersole, P., & Hess, P. (1981). Toward healthy aging—human needs and nursing response. St. Louis, MO: C. V. Mosby Company.

Fisk, A. A. (April 1983). Alzheimer's disease: A five article symposium. Management of Alzheimer's disease. *Post Graduate Medicine, 73*(4), 237–250.

Gray, M., & McKenzie, H. (1980). *Take care of your elderly relative.* London: Allen and Unwin and Beaconsfield.

Guide to caring for the mentally impaired elderly. (1985). Washington, DC: American Association of Homes for the Aging.

Gwyther, L. P. (1986). *Care of Alzheimer's patients: A manual for nursing home staff.* American Health Care Association and Alzheimer's Disease and Related Disorders Foundation.

Hemshorn, A. (January 1985). They call it Alzheimer's disease. *Journal of Gerontological Nursing, 11*(1), 36–38.

Henderson, J. N., & Pfeiffer, E. (1984). *Mental health and aging: A curriculum guide for nursing home caregivers.* Tampa, FL: Suncoast Gerontology Center, University of South Florida.

Heston, L. L., & White, J. A. (1983). *Dementia: A practical guide to Alzheimer's disease and related illnesses.* New York: W. H. Freeman and Company.

Hooker, S. (1976). *Caring for elderly people—understanding and practical help.* London: Routledge and Kegan Paul.

Horne, J. (1985). *Caregiving—Helping an aging loved one.* Washington, DC: American Association of Retired Persons.

Jacobs, B. (1981). *Working with the at-risk older person: A resource manual.* Washington, DC: The National Council on the Aging, Inc.

Keane, E. E. (Ed.) (June 1980). *Coping with senility: A guidebook.* COBS Society, Inc. of Pennsylvania.

Lindeman, D. A. (1984). *Alzheimer's disease handbook.* Aging Health Policy Center, University of California, San Francisco: U.S. Department of Health and Human Services, Office of Human Development Services, Administration on Aging, Volume I.

Losing a million minds: Confronting the tragedy of Alzheimer's disease and other dementias. (1987). Washington, DC: Congress of the United States, Office of Technology Assessment.

Mace, N. L. (January 1984). Facets of dementia: Catastrophic reactions. *Journal of Gerontological Nursing, 10*(2), 28.

Mace, N. L., & Rabins, P. (1981). *The 36-hour day: A family guide to caring for persons with Alzheimer's disease, related dementing illnesses, and memory loss in later life.* Baltimore, MD: The Johns Hopkins University Press.

McDowell, F. H., & Lincoln, E. M. (Ed.) (1980). *Managing the person with intellectual loss at home.* White Plains, NY: Burke Rehabilitation Center.

Minaker, K. L. (March 31, 1987). *Diagnostic approach to patients with senile dementia Alzheimer type and related disorders.* Pittsburgh, PA: West Penn Hospital and Vintage, Inc. Second Annual Forum on Geriatric Care.

Nowakowski, L. (September 1985). Accent capabilities in disorientation. *Journal of Gerontological Nursing, 11*(9), 15–20.

Pajk, M. (February 1984). Alzheimer's disease. Inpatient care. *American Journal of Nursing,* 216–224.

Powell, L. S., & Courtice, K. (1983). *Alzheimer's disease: A guide for families.* Massachusetts: Addison-Wesley Publishing Company.

Rabins, P., Mace, N., & Lucas, M. J. (July 16, 1982). The impact of dementia on the family. *Journal of the American Medical Association, 248,* 92–94.

Schmall, V., & Cleland, M. (1985). *Helping memory impaired elders. A guide for caregivers.* Corrallio, OR: Oregon State University Extension Service.

Senility reconsidered. Treatment possibilities for mental impairment in the elderly. (July 18, 1980). *Journal of the American Medical Association, 244*(3), 259–263.

Springer, D., & Brubaker, T. H. (1984). *Family caregivers and dependent elderly. Minimizing stress and maximizing independence.* Beverly Hills, CA: Sage Publications.

Thornton, S. M., & Fraser, V. (1982). *Understanding "senility"—a layperson's guide.* Buffalo, NY: Potentials Development for Health and Aging Services, Inc.

Trockman, G. (September 1978). Caring for the confused or delirious patient. *American Journal of Nursing,* 1495–1499.

Update on Alzheimer's (Special issue). (Winter 1984). *Generations: Journal of the Western Gerontological Society, 9*(2).

Williams, L. (February 1986). Alzheimer's: The need for caring. *Journal of Gerontological Nursing, 12*(2), 21–27.

Wolanin, M. O., & Phillips, L. (1981). *Confusion. Prevention and care.* St. Louis, MO: C. V. Mosby Co.

Zarit, S. H. (April 1984). Interventions for families of dementia patients. *Alzheimer's Disease Handbook.* Volume I. U.S. Department of Health and Human Services, Administration on Aging.

Zarit, S. H., Orr, N., & Zarit, J. (1983). *Working with families of dementia victims: A treatment manual.* Volume IV. Department of Health and Human Services, Office of Human Development, Administration on Aging.

References—Caregiving

Adult Children and Aging Parents. A Resource for Ministry with Older People. Atlanta, GA: The Presbyterian Office on Aging.

Bosshardt, J. P., Gibson, D., Snyder, M., & Petty, D. (1979). *Family Survival Handbook. A guide to the financial, legal and social problems of brain damaged adults.* San Francisco, CA: Family Survival Project for Brain Damaged Adults, Inc.

Caranasos, G., Fennell, E., Belles, D., & Krischer, J. (April 1985). Caregivers of the Demented Elderly. *Journal of the Florida Medical Association, 72*(4), 266–270.

Chenoweth, B., & Spencer, B. (June 1986). Dementia: The Experience of Family Caregivers. *The Gerontologist, 26*(3), 267–272.

Cohen, D., & Eisdorfer, C. (1986). *The Loss of Self: A Family Resource for the Care of Alzheimer's Disease and Related Disorders.* New York: W. W. Norton.

Dehardt, D. Psychological Impact of Alzheimer's Disease on the Family. Reprint distributed by the Alzheimer's Disease Related Disorders Association (ADRDA). *ADRDA Orange Co. Chapter Newsletter.*

Fitting, M., Rabins, P., Lucas, M. J., & Eastham, J. (June 1986). Caregivers for Dementia Patients: A Comparison of Husbands and Wives. *The Gerontologist, 26*(3), 248–252.

George, L. K. (Spring 1987). Adult Child Caregivers: Caught in the Sandwich of Competing Demands. *ADRDA Newsletter, 7*(1).

George, L. K., & Gwyther, L. (June 1986). Caregiver Well-Being: A Multi-dimensional Examination of Family Caregivers of Demented Adults. *The Gerontologist, 26*(3), 253–259.

Gray, M., & McKenzie, H. (1980). *Take Care of Your Elderly Relative.* Boston: Allen and Unwin and Beaconsfield.

Hirst, S. P., & Metcalf, B. (April 1986). Learning Needs of Caregivers. *Journal of Gerontological Nursing, 12*(4), 72–77.

Horne, J. (1985). *Caregiving: Helping an Aging Loved One.* Washington, DC: American Association of Retired Persons.

LeRoux, C. (1986). *Coping and Caring: Living with Alzheimer's Disease.* Washington, DC: American Association of Retired Persons and Chicago, IL: Alzheimer's Disease and Related Disorders Association.

Lund, D. A., Feinhauer, L. L., & Miller, J. (November 1985). Living Together: Grandparents and Children Tell Their Problems. *Journal of Gerontological Nursing, 11*(11), 29–33.

McCann, J. T. (Summer 1986). Family Oriented Interventions in Alzheimer's Care. *The American Journal of Alzheimer's Care and Related Disorders,* 16–21.

McGreehan, D., & Warburton, S. (June 1978). How to Help Families Cope with Caring for Elderly Members. *Geriatrics,* (33), 99–103.

Miles Away and Still Caring: A Guide for Long Distance Caregivers. (1986). Washington, DC: American Association of Retired Persons.

Montgomery, R. (Ed.) (1984). *Family Seminars for Caregiving—Helping Families Help.* Technical Assistance Manual. Seattle, WA: Pacific N.W. Long Term Care Center, University of Washington.

Morscheck, P. (Fall 1984). Introduction: An Overview of Alzheimer's Disease and Long Term Care. *Pride Institute Journal of Long Term Care, 3*(4), 4–10.

Olsen, J. K. (March 1980). Helping Families Cope. *Journal of Gerontological Nursing, 6*(3), 152–154.

Otten, J., & Shelley, F. (1977). *When Your Parents Grow Old. Information and Resources to Help the Adult Son or Daughter Cope with the Problems of Aging Parents.* New York: The New American Library, Inc.

Rabins, P. V., Mace, N., & Lucas, M. J. (July 18, 1982). The Impact of Dementia on the Family. *Journal of the American Medical Association, 248,* 92–94.

Reever, K. E. (1984). *Self-Help Groups for Caregivers Coping with Alzheimer's Disease: The ACMA Model.* The Pride Institute Journal of Long Term Home Health Care, (3)4, 23–30.

Richards, M. (Summer 1986). Family Support Groups. *Generations, 10*(4), 68–69.

Riessman, F. (December 1983). What Makes an Effective Self-Help Group. *Self-Help Reporter, 6*(4), 1–3.

Schmall, V., & Isbell, L. (July 1984). *Aging Parents: Helping When Health Fails.* A Pacific Northwest Extension Publication.

Silverstone, B., & Hyman, H. K. (1976). *You and Your Aging Parent: The*

Modern Family's Guide to Emotional, Physical and Financial Problems. New York: Pantheon Books.

Springer, D., & Brubaker, T. (1984). *Family Caregivers and Dependent Elderly: Minimizing Stress and Maximizing Independence.* Beverly Hills, CA: Sage Publications.

Warshauer, J. (Spring 1983). Helpful Hints On When to Place in A Nursing Home. *ADRDA Newsletter, 3*(1).

Warshauer, J. (Summer 1983). Helpful Hints on Coping Following Placement of a Loved One. *ADRDA Newsletter, 3*(2).

Warshauer, J., Aronson, M. & Shaw, S. (Fall 1983). Helpful Hints: On the Costs of Caring. *ADRDA Newsletter, 2*(3).

Weaver, D. A. (Fall 1982). Tapping Strength: A Support Group for Children and Grandchildren. *Generations*, 45.

Wentzel, M. L. (1979). *The Emotional Effect of Parental Institutionalization Upon the Elderly.* North Texas State University Center for Studies in Aging.

Your Aging Relatives—How You and Your Family Can Help Them. (1980). Fort Washington, PA: McNeil Pharmaceutical.

Zarit, S., Todd, P., and Zarit, J. (June 1986). Subjective Burden of Husbands and Wives as Caregivers: A Longitudinal Study. *The Gerontologist, 26*(3), 260–266.

RESOURCES FOR CAREGIVING

Choosing a Nursing Home for the Person with Intellectual Loss. (1980). White Plains, NY: The Burke Rehabilitation Center.

FAMILY CAREGIVERS OF THE AGING. Membership group of the National Council on Aging, Dept. 5087. Washington, D.C.

Family Home Caring Guides, The National Council on the Aging, Inc., 600 Maryland Avenue, SW, West Wing 100, Washington, DC 20024. Eight booklets of practical information for caregivers.

Guthrie, D. *Grandpa Doesn't Know It's Me.* New York: Human Sciences Press, Inc. in cooperation with ADRDA.

A Handbook about Care in the Home. Information on Home Health Services. (1987). Washington, DC: American Association of Retired Persons.

How to Hire Helpers: A Guide for Elders and Their Families. Church Council of Greater Seattle, Task Force on Aging, 4759 15th NE, Seattle, WA 98105.

Montgomery, J. (February 11, 1985). Making the Decision Everybody Hates: Choosing a Nursing Home for Ill Parent. *The Wall Street Journal.*

A Path for Caregivers (1987) American Association of Retired Persons. Washington, D.C.

Richards, M., Hooyman, N., Hansen, M., Brandts, W., Smith-DiJulio, K., & Dahm, L. (1985). *Choosing a Nursing Home: A Guidebook for Families.* Seattle, WA: University of Washington Press.

The Right Place at the Right Time. A Guide to Long Term Care Choices. (1985). American Association of Retired Persons.

Where to Turn for Help for Older Persons. A Guide for Action on Behalf of an Older Person. Washington, DC: U.S. Department of Health and Human Services, Administration on Aging.

White, D., & Neal, M. (1981). *A Guidebook for the Family and Friends of Older Adults.* Portland, OR: Institute on Aging, Portland State University.

References—Activities

Carter, M. J., Van Andel, G., & Robb, G. (1985). *Therapeutic recreation: A practical approach.* St. Louis, MO: Times Mirror/Mosby College Publishing.

Cornish, P. M. (1975). *Activities for the frail aged.* Buffalo, NY: Potentials Development for Health and Aging Services, Inc.

Griffith, H. K. *Areas of need: The profile evaluation program.* Colorado Springs, CO.

Gwyther, L. P. (1985). *Care of Alzheimer's patients: A manual for nursing home staff.* American Health Care Association and Alzheimer's Disease and Related Disorders Association.

Hamill, C. M., & Oliver, R. (1980). *Therapeutic activities for the handicapped elderly.* Rockville, MD: Aspen Publications.

Hastings, L. E. (1981). *Complete handbook of activities and recreational programs for nursing homes.* Englewood Cliffs, NJ: Prentice-Hall.

Hirst, S. P., & Metcalf, B. J. (February 1984). Promoting self-esteem. *Journal of Gerontological Nursing,* 10(2), 72–77.

James, R. H. (Fall 1986). Activities for AD: "Celebrating the temporary." *ADRDA Newsletter,* 6(3), 6–10.

Judd, M. W. (1971). *Why bother—he's old and confused.* Winnipeg, Manitoba, Canada: Winnipeg Municipal Hospital.

Levy, L. L. (January 1986). A practical guide to the care of the Alzheimer's victim: The cognitive disability perspective. *Topics in Geriatric Rehabilitation,* 1(2).

Mace, N. L., & Rabins, P. V. (1984). *A survey of day care for the demented adult in the United States.* National Council on Aging.

Parent, C. J., & Whall, A. (September 1984). Are physical activity, self-expression and depression related? *Journal of Gerontological Nursing,* 10(9), 8–11.

Project Life. Leisure is for everyone's mind. (1985). Columbia, MO: University of Missouri, Department of Recreation and Park Administration.

Salamon, M. J., & Nichol, A. (November–December 1982). R_x for recreation: Part of the doctor's role. *Aging.* DHHS Publication #82-20949, Nos. 333–334, 18–22.

Shivers, J. S., & Fait, H. F. (1985). *Special recreational services. Therapeutic and adapted.* Philadelphia, PA: Lea and Febiger.

Zgola, J. M. (1987). *Doing things: A guide to programming activities for persons with Alzheimer's disease and related disorders.* Baltimore, MD: The Johns Hopkins University Press.

RESOURCES—ACTIVITIES

Activities, Adaption and Aging
The Haworth Press
12 West 32nd Street
New York, NY 10001
Journal of activities management for professional and non-professional
activity personnel

Activity Director's Guide
Eymann Publications, Inc.
Box 3577
Reno, NV 89505
A monthly newsletter full of recreational programming ideas

Nissenboim, S., & Vromon, C. (1988) *Interactions by Design. The Positive Interactions Program for Victims of Alzheimer's Disease and Related Disorders.* St. Louis, MO: Geri-Active Consultants.

Potentials Development for Health and Aging Services, Inc.
775 Main Street
Buffalo, NY 14203
(716)842-2658
Resource materials for a variety of activity programs

Sharing the caring. (1988). Sharing the caring programming in successful adult day care centers. Kansas City, MO: D. L. Webb & Associates.

References—Group Work

Bresler, E. (January–February 1981). The Use of Poetry Therapy with Older People. *Aging, (315–316)*, 23–27.

Burnside, I. (1976). *Nursing and the Aged.* New York: McGraw-Hill.

Burnside, I. (1984). *Working with the Elderly. Group Processes and Techniques.* Monterey, CA: Wadsworth, Inc.

Feil, N. (1982). *Validation: The Feil Method.* Buffalo, NY: Potentials Development for Health and Aging Services.

Jacobs, B. (1981). *Working with the At-Risk Older Person: A Resource Manual.* Washington, DC: The National Council on the Aging, Inc.

Senior Center Humanities Program. Manual for Leading Humanities Discussion Groups. (1981). Washington, DC: National Council on the Aging, Inc.

Witte, K. (January–February 1981). Discourse and Dialogue: Prolonging Adult Conversation in the Alzheimer Patient. *The American Journal of Alzheimer Care, 2*(1), 30–39.

RESOURCES—GROUP WORK

American Association of Retired Persons
Institute of Lifetime Learning
1909 K Street, N.W.
Washington, DC 20049
(202)728-4666

Bi-Folkal Productions, Inc.
911 Williamson Street
Madison, WI 53703
(608) 251–2818

Multi-media and multi-sensory group program materials for rent or purchase. Group programming guides are also available.

Ideals Publishing Corporation
P.O. Box 2100
Milwaukee, WI 53201

Eight issues per year filled with stories and poems of interest to older adults, including such topics as Friendship, Old-Fashioned, Hometowns and Summertime.

Merrill, T. (1974). *Discussion topics for oldsters in nursing homes.* Springfield, IL: Charles Thomas.

Schlenger, G. L. (1988). *Come and Sit By Me. Discussion Programs for Activity Specialists.*

References—Remotivation Therapy

Bennett, R. (1980). *Aging, isolation and resocialization.* New York: Van Nostrand Reinhold.

Deichman, E. S., & Kane, C. P. (1973). *Activity leaders training manual.* Erie, PA: Lake Area Health Education Center.

Dennis, H. (1984). Remotivation Therapy. *Working with the elderly: Group process and techniques.* Monterey, CA: Wadsoworth.

Ebersole, P., & Hess, P. (1981). *Toward healthy aging. Human needs and nursing response.* St. Louis, MO: C. V. Mosby.

Merrill, T. (1967). *Activities for the aged and infirm: A handbook for the untrained worker.* Springfield, IL: Charles C Thomas.

Health Careers Education, Training and Consultation Service. *Remotivation Technique.* (1978). White Plains, NY: The Burke Rehabilitation Center.

Stracke, D. Climates in Remotivation in Therapeutic Recreation. *Therapeutic Recreation Journal,* 9–34.

ADDITIONAL RESOURCES

National Remotivation Therapy Organization, Inc.
National Headquarters
P.O. Box 1096
West Brentwood, NY 11717

References—Reminiscence

Baker, H. C., Kotkin, A., & Yocum, M. (1976). *Family folklore interviewing guide and questionnaire.* Folklife Program, Smithsonian Institution. Washington, DC: U.S. Government Printing Office.

Baker, N. J. (July 1985). Reminiscing in group therapy for self-worth. *Journal of Gerontological Nursing, 11*(7), 21–24.

Burnside, I. (1984). *Working with the elderly: Group process and techniques.* Monterey, CA: Wadsworth Health Sciences Division.

Butler, R. N. (1963). The life review: An interpretation of reminiscence in the aged. *Psychiatry, 26,* 65–76.

Cook, J. (1984). Reminiscing: How it can help confused nursing home residents. *Social Casework, 65*(2).

Ebersole, P. (1976). Reminiscing. *American Journal of Nursing, 76*(8), 1304–1305.

Fiedler, A. J. (1981). *Memory sharing: Group programs for the older adult.* Buffalo, NY: Potentials Development for Health and Aging Services, Inc.

Fry, P. S. (Spring 1983). Structured and unstructured reminiscence training and depression among the elderly. *Clinical Gerontologist, 1*(3), 15–37.

Hammer, M. L. (February 1984). Insight, reminiscence, denial, projection. Coping mechanisms of the aged. *Journal of Gerontological Nursing, 10*(2), 66–81.

Henderson, J. N., & Pfeiffer, E. (1984). *Mental health and aging: A curriculum guide for nursing home caregivers.* Tampa, FL: Suncoast Gerontology Center, University of South Florida.

Huber, K., & Miller, P. (1984). Reminiscence with the elderly—do it! *Geriatric Nursing, 5*(2).

Hughston, G. A., & Merriam, S. B. (1982). Reminiscence: A nonformal technique for improving cognitive functioning in the aged. *International Journal of Aging and Human Development, 15*(2).

Kaminsky, M. (guest editor). (1984). The uses of reminiscence: New ways of working with older adults. *Journal of Gerontological Social Work, (7)*1–2, 4–203.

Lesser, J., Lazarus, L. W., Frankel, R., & Havasy, S. (June 1981). Reminiscence group therapy with psychotic geriatric patients. *The Gerontologist, 21*(3), 291–296.

Lewis, M., & Butler, R. (1974). Life review therapy. Putting memories to work in individual and group psychotherapy. *Geriatrics, 22*(11), 165–173.

Matteson, M. A., & Munsat, E. (1982). Group reminiscing therapy with elderly clients. *Issues in Mental Health Nursing, 4*(3).

Merriam, S. B. (1985). Reminiscence and life review: The potential for educational intervention. *Introduction to Educational Gerontology*, 49–65.

Montgomery, R. (Ed.) (1984). *Family seminars for caregiving—helping families help.* Technical Assistance Manual. Pacific N.W. Long Term Care Center and Institute on Aging, University of Washington, Seattle, Washington. Washington, DC: U.S. Department of Health and Human Services, Office of Human Development Services, Administration on Aging.

Perschbacher, R. (1984). An application of reminiscence in an activity setting. *Gerontologist, 24*(4), 343–345.

Quigley, P. (1981). *Those were the days: Life review therapy for elderly residents in long term care facilities.* Buffalo, NY: Potentials Development for Health and Aging Services, Inc.

Romaniuk, M., Ph.D. (Spring 1983). The application of reminiscing to the clinical interview. *Clinical Gerontologist, 1*(3), 39–43.

Wolf, M. A. (Spring 1985). The meaning of education in late life. An exploration of life review. *Gerontology and Geriatrics Education, 5*(3), 51–59.

Wysocki, M. (1983). Life review for the elderly. *Nursing, 13*(2).

RESOURCES—REMINISCENCE

Case, P. A. (1977). *How to Write your Autobiography.* Woodbridge Press.

Dylong, J. (1979). *Living History 1925–1950. Family Experiences of Times Remembered.* Chicago: Loyola University Press.

Hartley, W. G. (1976). *Preparing a personal history.* Salt Lake City: Primer Publications.

Jenkins, S. (1978). *Past, Present—Recording Life Stories of Older People.* Washington, DC: St. Alban's Parish.

Schlesinger, A. M., Jr. (1983). *The Almanac of American History.* Bison Books.

Wiebe, K. F. (1979). *Good Times with Old Times—How to Write Your Memoirs.* Scottdale, PA: Herald Press.

Williams, N. (1967). *Chronology of the modern world.* New York: McKay Co.

Zeitlin, S., Katkin, A., & Cutting, H. (1982). *A celebration of American family folklife.* New York: Pantheon.

References—Sensory Stimulation

Dickey, H. (1980). *Reality and the Senses. Activities for Sensory Stimulation.* Buffalo, NY: Potentials Development for Health and Aging Services, Inc.

Gwinnup, P. B. (1985). *Fragrance Projects for Sensory Stimulation.* Buffalo, NY: Potentials Development for Health and Aging Services.

Judd, M. (1983). *Keep in Touch.* Winnipeg, Manitoba, Canada: Winnipeg Municipal Hospital.

Judd, M. W. (1979). *Why Bother? He's Old and Confused.* Winnipeg, Manitoba, Canada: Winnipeg Municipal Hospital.

References—Music

DePeters, J., Gordon, L., & Wertman, A. (1981). *The Magic of Music: Three Programs for Older Adults*. Buffalo, NY: Potentials Development for Health and Aging Services, Inc.

Dickey, H. (1980). *Reality and the Senses*. Buffalo, NY: Potentials Development for Health and Aging Services.

Hennessey, M. J. (1976). Music and Group Work with the Aged. Chapter 21 in *Nursing and the Aged*. McGraw Hill.

Kartman, L. L. (June 1984). Music Hath Charms . . . *Journal of Gerontological Nursing, 10*(6), 20–24.

McCullough, E. (December 1983). Music Programs for Older Adults. *Collage, 2*(3), 2.

Music: Reaching the Confused and Withdrawn Through Music. (November–December 1982.) *Aging*, (333–334), 8–11.

Sing Out: All Time and Old Time Favorites for Senior Citizens. (1985.) Ontario government Minister without portfolio (Senior Citizens Affairs).

RESOURCES—MUSIC

Geiger, J. (1979). *Adventures in Movement*. AIM for the Handicapped, Inc., Dayton, OH.

American Association for Music Therapy
66 Morris Ave.
Springfield, NJ 07081
201-379-1100

Bitcon, C. (1976). *Alike and Different*. Orff Lincoln Music Co., Anaheim, CA, Santa Ana, CA, Rosha Press.

Douglas, D. (1981). *Accent on Rhythm*. LaRoux Enterprises, Salem, OR

Favorite Hymns (in large print)
Sight Saving Division
Lutheran Braille Workers, Inc.
495 9th Avenue
San Francisco, CA 94118

Heritage Songster. (1980). William C. Brown Co., Dubuque, IA. Compiled by L. Dallin.

Increasing Awareness and Sensitivity through World Music. (1972). *Music Educators' Journal, 59*(2)

Karras, B., (Ed.) (1987). *"You Bring Out the Music in Me" Music in Nursing Homes*. New York: The Haworth Press.

References—Exercise and Physical Activity

Basic exercises for people over sixty. (1976). Washington, DC: National Association for Human Development.

Corbin, D. E., & Corbin, J. M. (1983). *Reach for it. A handbook of exercise and dance activities for older adults.* Dubuque, IA: Eddie Bowers.

Etten, M. J., Hall, D., & Traynor, C. (1983). *Wealth of health. An exercise program for older adults.* Tampa, FL: University of South Florida Suncoast Gerontology Center.

Frankel, L. J., & Richard, B. B. (1977). *Be alive as long as you live.* Charleston, WV: Preventicare Publications.

Harris, R., & Frankel, L. J. *Guide to fitness after fifty.* New York, NY: Plenum Press.

Hastings, L. E. (1981). *Complete handbook of activities and recreational programs for nursing homes.* Englewood Cliffs, NJ: Prentice-Hall, Inc.

Moderate exercises for people over sixty. (1976). Washington, DC: National Association for Human Development.

National Association for Human Development. *Exercise—Activity for people over sixty.* (1977). Washington, DC: National Association for Human Development.

Paillard, M., & Nowak, K. (July 1985). Use exercise to help older adults. *Journal of Gerontological Nursing, 11*(7), 36–39.

Paradini, A. (April–May 1984). Exercise, vitality and aging. *Aging.* 344, 19–29.

Physical fitness and mental health. (1984). Rockville, MD: U.S. Department of

Health and Human Services. Public Health Service. Alcohol, Drug Abuse and Mental Health Administration. DHHS Publication No. (ADM)84-1364.

Skeist, R. J., R.N. (1980). *To your good health*. Chicago, IL: Chicago Review Press.

RESOURCES—EXERCISE AND PHYSICAL FITNESS

BODY RECALL
Berea College
Berea, KY 40404
(606)986-4363

Workshops, training and written materials on fitness for seniors

Fallcreek, S., & Metter, M. (Eds.) (1983). *A healthy old age: A sourcebook for health promotion with older adults*. New York, NY: Haworth Press.

Franks, P., Lee, P., & Fullarton, J. (1983). *Lifetime fitness and exercise for older people*. San Francisco, CA: Aging Health Policy Center, University of California.

Healthwise, Inc.
P.O. Box 1989
Boise, ID 83701
(208)345-1161

Health promotion and fitness programs for older adults

National Association for Human Development
1620 Eye Street, NW
Washington, DC 20006

Booklets, training manuals, audio-visual aides and other materials on exercise and physical fitness

National Resource Center
Health Promotion & Aging
American Association of Retired Persons
1909 K Street NW
Washington, DC 20049
202-872-4700

Thomas, G. S., Lee, P., Franks, P. and Paffenbarger, J. R. (1981). *Exercise and health: The evidence and implications*. Cambridge, MA: Oelgeschlager, Gunn and Hain.

Resources—Games

Agel, J. (1985). *Beyond trivia*. New York: Simon and Schuster.

Bartlett, J. (1980). *Bartlett's familiar quotations*. Boston, MA: Little, Brown & Co.

Coffin, T. P., & Cohen, H. (1978). *The parade of heroes: Legendary figures in American lore*. New York: Anchor Press/Doubleday.

Darnell, Virginia (1986). *This and That "Trivia For Seniors"* Sullivan, IL: Golden Horizon.

Delzs, C. (1958). *A treasury of American superstitions*. New York: Philosophical Library.

Hastings, L. E. (1981). *Complete handbook of activities and recreational programs for nursing homes*. Englewood Cliffs, NJ: Prentice-Hall, Inc.

Kane, J. N. (1976). *Famous first facts and records*. New York: Ace Books.

Lacey, J. M. (1981). *The Games Older People Play*. P.O. Box 146, Hanover, NH 03755.

Leisure is for everyone's mind. A programming book of mental stimulation activities. Griegs; S. (1985). Columbia, MO: Project Life, Department of Recreation and Park Administration, University of Missouri-Columbia.

Merrill, T. (1979). *Activities for the aged and infirm. A handbook for the untrained worker*. Springfield, IL: Charles C Thomas, Publisher.

Musselman, V. W. (1967). *Learning about nature through games*. Harrisburg, PA: Stockpole Books.

Ragan, D. (1976). *Who's who in Hollywood 1900–1976*. New York: Arlington House Publishers.

Who's who in America. (1984). Marquis' Who's Who. Chicago, IL.

Zimmerman, W. (1984). *A Book Of Questions To Keep Thoughts and Feelings* New York: Guarionex Press.

Games for the memory impaired older adult. These games are designed to stimulate memory, encourage communication and be fun.

Eldergames
11710 Hunters Lane
Rockville, MD 20852
(301)881-8433

Elder Triva, Peel'n Fold and Memory Joggers

Generations, Inc.
P.O. Box 41069
St. Louis, MO 63141

Generations—The Game

Medical and Activities Sales
P.O. Box 4068
Omaha, NE 68104
402-571-7625

Large Print Games and Game Books

Senex Enterprises, Inc.
1506 Holly Bank Circle
Dunwoody, GA 30338

Three Score and Ten

Other

Lauri, Inc.
Puzzle Books
P.O. Box F
Phillips-Avon, ME 04966
(207)639-2000

World Wide Games
Colchester, CT 06415
1-800-243-9232

Potentials Development for Health and Aging Services, Inc.
775 Main Street
Buffalo, NY 14203
(716)842-2658

Foam puzzles with colorful, adult themes

Resources—Arts and Crafts

Creative Crafts International
16 Plains Road, P.O. Box 819
Essex, CT 06426
(203)767-2101

Dover Publications, Inc.
180 Varick Street
New York, NY 10014
Dover Pictorial Archive Series
(212) 255-3755

Illustrations from nature to copy from or color

Flaghouse
Supplies and equipment
150 N. McQuesten Parkway
Mt. Vernon, NY 10550
(914) 699-1900
800-221-5185

Kurtz Brothers
School supplies and equipment
47th and Reed Streets
Clearfield, PA
(814)765-6561

Craft/art supplies, games, puzzles, wall decorations, rhythm band instruments, signs

Triarco Arts and Crafts, Inc.
14650 28th Avenue N.
Plymouth, MN 55441
1-800-328-3360

National Artcraft Company
23456 Mercentile Road
Beachwood, OH 44122
(216)292-4944

S & S Arts and Crafts
Colchester, CT 06415
(203)537-3451

U.S. Toy Company, Inc.
Wholesale Fund Raising Carnival Catalog
1227 E. 119th Street
Grandview, MO 64030
(816)761-5900
1-800-255-6124

References—Horticulture

Bardach, J. L. (1975). *Some principles of horticulture therapy with the physically disabled.* National Council for Therapy & Rehabilitation through Horticulture (NCTRH) Gaithersburg, MD.

Brownlee, J. Guidelines for the therapeutic recreation consultant in nursing homes, convalescent hospitals, and mental facilities for the aged. *Therapeutic Recreation Journal, IV*(3).

Burlingame, A. W., & Waston, D. P. *Therapy through horticulture.* New York: Macmillan Company.

Chaplin, M. (1978). *Gardening for the physically handicapped and elderly.* London: Batsford Press. (Available from David and Charles, Inc., P.O. Box 57, N. Pomfret, VT 05053).

A comprehensive view of horticulture and the aging. (April 1981). *Horttherapy, 1*(2). National Council for Therapy & Rehabilitation through Horticulture (NCTRH) Gaithersburg, MD.

Disabled Living Foundation. (1979). *Gardening for the Disabled.* London: Author.

Duda, E. J., & Olszowy, D. R. (1977). *Horticultural therapy handbook.* Storrs, CT: University of Connecticut, Bartlett Arboretum.

Fox, S. (1976, 1977). *Drying, preserving and utilizing plant materials; Indoor horticultural activities for nursing homes;* and *Horticulture for the visually impaired.* Clemson, SC: Clemson University Horticulture Department.

Gardening for handicapped and elderly persons. National Library Service for the Blind and Physically Handicapped. Washington, DC: The Library of Congress.

Houseman, D. H. (1986). Developing links between horticultural therapy and aging. NCTRH. *Journal of Therapeutic Horticulture, 1*.

Jones, B. W., & Brander, B. (1978). *Harvest of hope: Gardening for the handicapped*. Washington, DC: U.S. Science and Education Administration Extension Service.

Krell, D., & Brandt, L. (1977). *Gardening in containers*. Menlo Park, CA: Lane Publishing, Co.

Mendelson, S. (1986). *Places for the elderly to grow/impact on thoughts and design*. Muncie, IN: Ball State University.

Miller, D. B. (1975). Suggested methodologies for auditing activity programs in long term care facilities. *Therapeutic Recreation Journal, IX*(3).

Moore, B. (1987). *Growing with gardening—a horticultural training manual*. Chapel Hill, NC: University of North Carolina at Chapel Hill.

Muhich, M. (1978). *Willard and Spackman's Occupational Therapy*. Philadelphia, PA: Hopkins and Smith.

Rothert, E., & Daubert, J. (1981). *Horticulture therapy for senior centers/nursing homes/retirement living*. Glencoe, IL: Chicago Horticultural Society.

Successful senior citizen gardens. Burlington, VT: National Gardening Association.

Tyson, M. M. (1987). *Memories of grandma's backyard. Designing the outdoor environment: Horticulture therapy in long term care facilities*. Milwaukee, WI.

Union Carbide. (1985). *A guide to gardening for people with special needs*. Research Triangle Park, NC: Union Carbide Agricultural Products Company, Inc.

RESOURCES—HORTICULTURE

National Council for Therapy and Rehabilitation through Horticulture
9220 Wightman Road, Suite 300
Gaithersburg, MD 20879

National Gardening Association
180 Flynn Avenue
Burlington, VT 05401

Cooperative Extension Services at state land grant university and county agents

Audio-Visual Materials—Horticulture

National Council for Therapy and Rehabilitation through Horticulture
• *Growing-Growing*—A montage of experiences related to plants and their growth.

- *Ordinary Work*—An Israeli film documenting the use of horticultural therapy in Israel.
- *From These Seeds*—Horticultural therapy in an urban setting.
- *NCTRH Tape Presentation*—A broad overview of horticultural therapy.

National Gardening Association
- *Old Friends in the Garden*—The benefits of gardening, highlighting successful gardening projects for the elderly.

University of Michigan Media Center
400 Fourth Avenue, Ann Arbor, MI 48103-4816
- *Ruth Stout's Garden*

Tools for Horticultural Activities

W. Atlee Burpee Company
300 Park Avenue
Warminister, PA 18974
(215) 674-4900

Smith and Hawken
25 Carte Madera
Mill Valley, CA 94941
(415) 383-4415

David Kay
4509 Taylor Lane
Cleveland, OH 44128
(614)891-2030

Gardener's Supply
128 Intervale Road
Burlington, VT 05401
(802) 863-1700

Tools and Techniques for Easier Gardening
The National Association for Gardening
180 Flynn Avenue
Burlington, VT 05401

References—Children and the Elderly

Children Today. Special Intergenerational Theme Issue. U.S. Department of Health and Human Services, *14*(5).

Ideas for Intergenerational Programming. *Caring:* Alternatives for the Aged. Atlantic City, NJ.

Jacobs, B., Lindsley, P., and Feil, M. (February 1976). *A Guide to Intergenerational Programming*. National Institute of Senior Centers, National Council on the Aging.

McDuffie, W., & Whiteman, J. (March 31, 1987). *Day Care and Intergenerational Activities and Alzheimer's Clients = Fun*. Chicago, IL: National Council on Aging Conference.

McMahon, M. A. (1987). The Value of Intergenerational Relationships. *Journal of Gerontological Nursing, 13*(4), 25–29.

Peterson, C. F. (October 1986). Across the Age Boundaries. *Journal of Gerontological Nursing, 12*(10), 12–16.

Pennsylvania Department of Aging. *Reaching Across the Years: Selected Intergenerational Programs in Pennsylvania*. Harrisburg, PA: Author.

Struntz, K. A., & Reville, S. (1985). *Growing Together: An Intergenerational Sourcebook*. American Association of Retired Persons and the Elvirita Lewis Foundation.

Tice, C. (May–June 1982). Creating Caring Communities. Linking the Generations. *Aging*, (327–328), 20–23.

The Beverly Foundation. (1984). *A Time and Place for Sharing: A Practical Guide for Developing Intergenerational Programs.* (1984) South Pasadena, CA: Author.

Yuknavage, P. (May–June 1982). Intergenerational Issues. *Aging,* (327–328), 15–19. U.S. Department of Health and Human Services, Administration on Aging.

RESOURCES—CHILDREN AND THE ELDERLY

National Center on Aging and Community Education. University of Central Arkansas. Conway, Arkansas 72032.

Aging in the 80's and *Bridging the Gap.* Video presentations on intergenerational programs. Curriculum on aging for preschoolers.

Generations United. National Council on the Aging. Washington, D.C. A national coalition on intergenerational issue and programs.

Intergenerational Clearinghouse Newsletter, RSVP of Dane County, Inc. 540 W. Olin Ave., Madison, WI 53715.

Generations Together. Preschool Curriculum on Aging Guide (1988). University of Pittsburgh, University Center for Social and Urban Research, 811 William Pitt Union Building, Pittsburgh, PA 15260.

References—Elders and Pets

Aging. (September–October 1982). Special issue on pets for the elderly. U.S. Department of Health and Human Services, (331–332).

Arkow, P. *How to start a pet therapy program* and *Pet therapy: A study of the use of companion animals in selected therapies.* Colorado Springs, CO: The Humane Society of the Pike's Peak Region.

Carson, S., & Carson, E. *Pet Animals as Nonverbal Communication Mediators in Psychotherapy in Institutional Settings.* Columbus, OH: The Ohio State University.

Cusack, O., & Smith, E. (1984). Pets and the Elderly: The Therapeutic Bond. *Activities, Adaption and Aging, 4*(2–3). The Haworth Press.

Frank, S. J. (January 1984). The Touch of Love. *The Journal of Gerontological Nursing, 10*(2), 28–35.

Friends for the Elderly. (Summer 1983). *Carnation Research Digest, 19*(2).

Humeston, B. (August 1983). How Pets Help People Cope. *Better Homes and Gardens.*

Kelly, J. A. (February 1984). Love Comes in All Shapes and Sizes. *Good Housekeeping.*

Lund, D. A., Johnson, R., Baraki, H., & Dimond, M. (June 1984). Can Pets Help the Bereaved? *Journal of Gerontological Nursing, 10*(6), 8–12.

McLeod, C. *Animals in the Nursing Home: Guide for Activity Directors.* Colorado Springs, CO.

Rovner, J. (November 26, 1981). Self-Help: Happiness Is A Warm Kitten. *The Washington Post.*

Schmall, V., & Pratt, C. (Summer 1986). Special Friends: Elders and Pets. *Generations, 10*(4).

RESOURCES—ELDERS AND PETS

These organizations provide information and resources on pet therapy programs and research on the relationships between people and pets.

The Delta Society
Century Building
Suite 303
321 Burnett Avenue S.
Renton, WA 98055-2569
(206)226-7357

The Humane Society of the U.S.
2100 L Street, N.W.
Washington, DC 20037
(202)452-1100

The Latham Foundation
Latham Plaza Building
Clement and Schiller Streets
Alameda, CA 94501
(415)521-0920

References—Miscellaneous Activities

Byre, Sister Mary. (April 1985). A zest for life. *Journal of Gerontological Nursing, 11*(4), 30–33.

Darnell, V. (1986). *This and That "Trivia For Seniors."* Sullivan, IL: Golden Horizon.

Hastings, L. E. (1981). *Complete Handbook of Activities and Recreational Programs for Nursing Homes.* Englewood Cliffs, NJ: Prentice-Hall, Inc.

Morycz, R. K. (1980). Formative perspectives on life review and pastoral counseling for the elderly. *Studies in Formative Spirituality, Spirituality and Aging, 1*(3).

Report of the Technical Committee on Creating an Age Integrated Society: Implications for Spiritual Well-Being. The 1981 White House Conference on Aging.

RESOURCES

American Association of Retired Persons
The Institute of Lifetime Learning
American Association of Retired Persons
1909 K Street NW
Washington, DC 20049

Minicourse study booklets on the Bible and religions of the world and discussion leaders' guides.

Klim, M. K. (1985). *Bible studies for senior citizens.* Buffalo, NY: Potentials Development for Health and Aging Services.

Modern Talking Picture Service
5000 Park Street N.
St. Petersburg, FL 33709
(813)541-5763

Film rentals available. Pay return postage only.

Appendix A: Organizations that Service the Elderly

Administration on Aging
Department of Health and Human
  Services
200 Independence Avenue, SW
Washington, DC
Information: (202)245-2205
Dissemination of Materials:
  (202)245-0641

ADRDA, Inc.
Alzheimer's Association
National Office
70 E. Lake Street
Chicago, IL 60601
(800)621-0379

Alzheimer Society of Canada
1320 Young St.
Suite 302
Toronto, Canada
Canada M4T 1X2
(416)925-3552

**American Academy of Opthal-
mology**
655 Beach Street
P.O. Box 7424
San Francisco, CA 94120
(415)561-8500

**American Association of Homes for
the Aging**
1129 20th Street, NW
Suite 400
Washington, DC 20036
(202)296-5960

**American Association of Retired
Persons (AARP)**
1909 K Street, NW
Washington, DC 20049
(202)872-4700

* Free-loan audiovisual programs
* Fulfillment section—to obtain copies of free AARP materials
* AARP Books
  Scott Foresman and Co.
  1865 Miner Street
  Des Plaines, IL 60016
* Institute of Lifetime Learning—minicourse study booklets and discussion guide

American Foundation for the Blind
15 West 16th Street
New York, NY 10011
(212)620-2000

American Geriatrics Society
770 Lexington Ave.
Suite 400
New York, NY 10019
(212)308-1414

American Health Care Association
1201 L St., NW
Washington, DC 20005
(202)842-4444

**American Occupational Therapy
Association, Inc.**
1383 Piccard Drive, P.O. Box 1725
Rockville, MD 20850
(301)948-9626

**American Physical Therapy
  Association**
1111 N. Fairfax Street
Alexandria, VA 22314
(703)684-2782

American Society on Aging
833 Market Street
Suite 512
San Francisco, CA 94103
(415)543-2617

**American Speech-Language-
  Hearing Association**
10801 Rockville Pike
Rockville, MD 20852
(301)897-5700

Centre for the Study of Aging
706 Madison Avenue
Albany, NY 12208
(518)465-6927

Consumer Information Center
U.S. Office of Consumer Affairs
Pueblo, CO 81009
(719)948-3334

**Family Survival Project for Brain
  Damaged Adults**
425 Bush St., Suite 500
San Francisco, CA 94108
(415)434-3388 or (800)445-8106

National Association for the Deaf
814 Thayer Avenue
Silver Spring, MD 20910
(301)587-1788

**National Association for Home
  Care**
519 C Street, NE
Stanton Park
Washington, DC 20002
(202)547-7424

**National Association of Area Agen-
  cies on Aging**
600 Maryland Avenue, SW
Suite 208
Washington, DC 20024
(202)484-7520

**National Association of the State
  Units on Aging**
2033 K Street, NW
Suite 304
Washington, DC 20006
(202)785-0707

National Council on Aging
600 Maryland Avenue, SW
West Wing 100
Washington, DC 20024
(202)479-1200

* National Centre for Health Promotion and Aging
* Family Caregivers Program
* National Institute on Adult Day Care

National Geriatrics Society
212 W. Wisconsin Avenue
Milwaukee, WI 53203
(414)272-4130

**Foundation for Hospice & Home-
  care**
519 C Street, NE
Washington, DC 20002
(202)547-6586

National Institute of Health
9000 Rockville Pike
Bethesda, MD 20892
(301)496-4000

* National Institute on Aging
  Building 31, Room 5C-36

**National Institute on Aging In-
  formation Center**
2209 Distribution Circle
Silver Spring, MD 20903
(301)495-3455

* Alzheimer's Disease Technical Specialist and information available

**National Institute of Neurological
  and Communicative Disorders
  and Stroke**
Office of Scientific and Health Reports
Building 31, Room 8A-06
National Institutes of Health
Bethesda, MD 20892
(301)496-5751

**National Recreation and Park
  Association**
3101 Park Centre Drive
Alexandria, VA 22302
(703)820-4940

**National Remotivation Therapy
  Organization, Inc.**
National Headquarters
P.O. Box 1096
West Brentwood, NY 11717

**Self-Help for Hard of Hearing
  People**
7800 Wisconsin Avenue
Bethesda, MD 20814
(301)657-2248

U.S. Government Printing Office
Superintendent of Documents
Washington, DC 20402
(202)783-3238

Appendix B: Administration on Aging Long Term Care Gerontology Centers

The Administration on Aging is funding eleven long term care gerontology centers in major universities around the country as training and research centers in geriatric/gerontological education. The centers have undertaken a number of activities to build a knowledge base about Alzheimer's Disease and developing support systems for caregivers. The Long Term Care Gerontology Centers (LTCGC) are:

Southeastern New England LTCGC
Brown University
Providence, RI

Center for Geriatrics and Gerontology/LTCGC
Columbia University
New York, NY

Mid-Atlantic LTCGC
Temple University
Philadelphia, PA

Suncoast Gerontology Center LTCGC
University of S. Florida
Tampa, FL

Milwaukee LTCGC
Medical College of Wisconsin
Milwaukee, WI

Southwest LTCGC
University of Texas
Dallas, TX

University of Kansas LTCGC
Kansas City, KS

Intermountain West LTCGC
University of Utah
Salt Lake City, UT

UCLA/USC LTCGC
University of California, Los An-
  geles
Los Angeles, CA

University of Arizona LTCGC
Tucson, AZ

Pacific Northwest LTCGC
University of Washington
Seattle, WA

Appendix C: State Agencies on Aging

Contact the State Agency on Aging in your state. They will provide you with the telephone number of the Area Agency on Aging in your community. Call that agency to get the help you need.

State Agency	Telephone Number
Alabama Commission on Aging	(205)261-5743
Older Alaskans Commission	(907)465-3250
American Samoa Territorial Administration on Aging	(684)633-1252
Arizona Office on Aging and Adult Administration	(602)542-4446
Arkansas Department of Human Services	(501)371-2441
California Department of Aging	(916)322-5290
Colorado Aging and Adult Services Division	(303)866-3851
Connecticut Department on Aging	(203)566-3238
Delaware Division on Aging	(302)421-6791
District of Columbia Office of Aging	(202)724-5626
Florida Aging and Adult Services	(904)488-8922
Georgia Office of Aging	(404)894-5333
Guam Public Health and Social Services	(671)734-2942
Hawaii Executive Office on Aging	(808)548-2593
Idaho Office on Aging	(208)334-3833
Illinois Department on Aging	(217)785-3356
Indiana Department on Aging and Community Services	(317)232-7006

Iowa Commission on Aging	(515)281-5187
Kansas Department on Aging	(913)296-4986
Kentucky Division for Aging Services	(502)564-6930
Louisiana Governor's Office of Elderly Affairs	(504)925-1700
Maine Bureau of Elderly	(207)289-2561
Maryland Office on Aging	(301)225-1100
Massachusetts Department of Elder Affairs	(617)727-7750
Michigan Office of Services to the Aging	(517)373-8230
Minnesota Board on Aging	(612)296-2707
Mississippi Council on Aging	(601)949-2070
Missouri Division of Aging	(314)751-3082
Montana Community Services Division	(406)444-3865
Nebraska Department on Aging	(402)471-2307
Nevada Division for Aging Services	(702)885-4210
New Hampshire State Council on Aging	(603)271-2751
New Jersey Division on Aging	(609)292-4833
New Mexico State Agency on Aging	(505)827-7640
New York State Office for the Aging	(518)474-5731
North Carolina Division of Aging	(919)733-3983
North Dakota Aging Services	(701)224-2577
Northern Mariana Islands Department of Community and Cultural Affairs	(670)234-6011
Ohio Commission on Aging	(614)466-5500
Oklahoma Services for the Aging	(405)521-2281
Oregon Senior Services Division	(503)378-4728
Pennsylvania Department of Aging	(717)783-1550
Puerto Rico Gericulture Commission	(809)722-8686
Rhode Island Department of Elderly Affairs	(401)277-2858
South Carolina Commission on Aging	(803)735-0210
South Dakota Office of Adult Services and Aging	(605)773-3656
Tennessee Commission on Aging	(615)741-2056
Texas Department on Aging	(512)444-2727
Trust Territory of the Pacific Islands Office of Elderly Affairs	(670)322-9328
Utah Division of Aging and Adult Services	(801)533-6422
Vermont Office on Aging	(802)241-2400
Virgin Islands Commission on Aging	(809)774-5884
Virginia Department for the Aging	(804)225-2271
Washington Bureau of Aging and Adult Services	(206)586-3786
West Virginia Commission on Aging	(304)348-3317
Wisconsin Office on Aging	(608)266-2536
Wyoming Commission on Aging	(307)777-7986

Appendix D: Aids for Daily Living

Abbey Medical Catalog Sales
2370 Grand Ave.
Long Beach, CA 90815
(213)538-5551
1-800-421-5126
1-800-262-1294 CA

**Comfortably Yours—Aids for
Easier Living**
61 West Hunter Avenue
Maywood, NJ 07607
(201)368-0400
(includes clothing)

**Directory of Living Aids for the
Disabled (1982)**
Veterans Administration
For sale from the Superintendent
of Documents
U.S. Government Printing Office
Washington, DC 20402
(202)783-3238

The Gadget Book
American Association of Retired
    Persons
AARP/Scott Foresman and Com-
    pany
1865 Miner Street
Des Plaines, IL 60016
(312)729-3000

Independent Living Aids
27 East Mall
Plainview, NY 11803
(800)537-2118

Maxi Aids
86-30 102nd Street
Richmond Hill, NY 11418
(718)846-4799
Aids and appliances for the blind,
    visually impaired, physically dis-
    abled, hearing impaired and
    senior citizens with special needs

**Products for People with Vision
    Problems**
Consumer Products
American Foundation for the Blind
15 West 16th Street
New York, NY 10011
(201)862-8838

Sears Home Health Catalog
Sears Roebuck and Co.
Sears Tower
Chicago, IL 60684
(800)366-3000

WanderGuard, Inc.
P.O. Box 80238
Lincoln, NE 68501
800-824-2996
(402)475-4002 in Nebraska
Alarm system for wanderers

Appendix E: Guides for Developing Caregiver Support Groups

Alzheimer Support Groups: Leadership Training Guide.
Alzheimer Society of Canada, Toronto, Ontario, Canada

As Parents Grow Older. A manual for program replication.
The Institute of Gerontology
University of Michigan
Ann Arbor, MI.

Bressler, D. *Hand in Hand: Learning from and Caring for Older Parents.* A
   community-based educational and support program for adult caregivers.
   American Association of Retired Persons, Washington, DC.

Family Caregiver's Program
The National Council on Aging
600 Maryland Avenue, SW
West Wing 100
Washington, DC 20024
(202)479-1200

A central resource on programs for families who are caring for frail and
   dependent elders.

Guides for Caregiver Support Groups.
The National Council on the Aging
Washington, DC

Hayes, C. *Manual for the Development, Implementation and Operation of Family Support Groups for the Relatives of the Functionally Disabled Elderly.* Center on Aging, Catholic University of America, Washington, DC.

In Support of Caregivers: A Guidebook for Planning and Conducting Educational Workshops for Caregivers of the Elderly.
University of Wisconsin-Madison
Madison, WI

Instructional Manual for Parent Caring Program
The College of St. Scholastica
Duluth, MN

Lidoff, L., & Beaver, L. (1983). *Caregiver Support Groups. Guidelines for Practice Based on Federally Funded Demonstrations.* The National Council on the Aging, Washington, DC.

Lidoff, L. & Harris, P. (1985). *Idea Book on Caregiver Support Groups.* Summary of findings of a national survey and directory of responding groups. National Council on the Aging, Inc., Washington, DC.

Media Assistance to Caregivers
Brookdale Center on Aging of Hunter College
New York, NY
Series of videotapes dealing with the issues of caregiving

Middleton, L. (1984). *Alzheimer's Family Support Groups: A Manual for Group Facilitators.* Suncoast Gerontology Center, Tampa, FL.

Mobilizing Networks of Mutual Support: How to Develop Alzheimer's Support Groups
Duke Family Support Program
Duke University Medical Center
Durham, NC

Montgomery, R. (Ed.) (1984). *Helping Families Help: Family Seminars for Caregivers.* University of Washington Press, Seattle, WA.

Pierskalla, C. S. & Heald, J. (1982). *Help for families of the aging:* A small group seminar. Swarthmore, PA: National Support Center for Families of the Aging.

Practical Help: Caring for an Elderly Person in the Community: An Informal Caregiver's Curriculum. (1982). Volumes I and II New York State Office for the Aging. Albany, NY.

Rzetelny, H., & Mellor, J. *Support Groups for Caregivers of the Aged: A Training Manual for Facilitators* (1982). New York: Community Service Society.

Self-Care and Self-Help Groups for the Elderly: A Directory. 1984.
National Institute on Aging
U.S. Department of Health and Human Services
U.S. Government Printing Office
Washington, DC 20402

Something for the Families: Family Support Group Leaders' Guide
University of Wisconsin-Madison
Madison, WI

State and Area Agency Instructional Guide for Alzheimer's Disease Family Support Groups (1984)
University of California
San Francisco, CA

Support Groups for Caregivers of the Aged: A Training Manual for Facilitators
Community Service Society
New York, NY

Supports for Family Caregivers of the Elderly: Highlights of a National Symposium
National Council on the Aging, Inc.
Washington, DC

Zarit, S. H., Orr, N. K., & Zarit, J. M. (1983). *Working with Families of Dementia Victims: A Treatment Manual.* Los Angeles, CA: Andrus Gerontology Center, University of Southern California.

Appendix F: Guide to Community Services

ADULT DAY CARE

Adult Day Care services are provided during the day in a community setting. The services provided may include recreational activities, meals, health care, educational programs, counseling and rehabilitation services. Adult day care centers are for older persons who need assistance because of a physical or mental impairment. Adult day care services can be used regularly or part-time to provide respite to family members. Adult day care provides the frail elderly with an opportunity to socialize with their peers.

AREA AGENCY ON AGING (AAA)

A private or public non-profit agency responsible for planning and coordinating services for the elderly. The AAA can best serve as the focal point for accessing community services. Contact the state agency on aging in your state to find the AAA that serves your community.

BOARD AND CARE HOMES

A board and care home provides room, meals and personal assistance to residents. The services, quality and cost vary considerably. The basic rent generally includes meals, utilities, housekeeping and laundry. Most board and care homes are privately operated.

CAREGIVER SUPPORT GROUPS

Mutual help groups that provide information and emotional support to the caregivers of older persons. Support groups may be sponsored by community agencies, churches and self-help organizations. They may focus on special needs such as Alzheimer's disease. Contact the ADRDA or the AAA to locate a support group in your area.

FRIENDLY VISITOR PROGRAM

This service provides a companion to visit the older adult on a regular basis. The companion's visit is usually scheduled for a pre-determined regular time, usually once or twice a week.

HOME-DELIVERED MEALS (MEALS ON WHEELS)

An agency or organization that provides home-delivered meals to elderly or disabled persons who are unable to cook for themselves. A hot, nutritious meal is provided at least once a day, five days a week.

HOME HEALTH CARE

Home health care is a range of supportive services provided in the home for people who require assistance in meeting their health care needs. Services include skilled nursing, physical therapy, occupational therapy and speech therapy and personal care assistance (assistance with bathing, dressing, toileting, medications).

HOMEMAKING AND CHORE SERVICES

Assistance with light housekeeping, laundry, shopping, errands, meal preparation and home maintenance.

HOSPICE

Hospice is a program of physical, emotional and spiritual support to terminally ill persons and their families. Hospice care emphasizes the relief of pain and a warm, caring environment to make life as full and meaningful as possible until death. Hospice services are usually provided in the individual's own home but it may also be provided in a special hospice setting.

NURSING HOMES (EXTENDED CARE FACILITIES)

Nursing homes provide care to persons who are chronically ill or recuperating from an illness and need regular nursing care and other health services. Services include meals, social activities, rehabilitation programs, personal care assistance and nursing care. There are three levels of nursing home care:

Skilled Nursing Care—provides physician coverage and 24-hour nursing care for a person who has serious health care needs but does not require hospital care.

Intermediate Care—provides room and board and regular—but not round-the-clock—nursing care.

Custodial Care—provides meals and sheltered living for individuals who need supervision but only require minimal medical attention.

RESPITE CARE

Respite care service provides short-term relief for caregivers who attend an older person at home. Respite may range from short-term care provided for a few hours to an extended vacation of several weeks. It may include nursing care, homemaker services and/or meals, depending on the provider. Respite may be provided in the home, the community, or within institutions.

SENIOR CENTER

A group program offering a variety of social, recreational, nutritional, educational and health services for older adults.

TRANSPORTATION

Transportation programs provide transportation to and from medical facilities, grocery shopping, senior centers, adult day care centers and other community facilities. Some communities provide door-to-door transportation. Escort services may also be available.

Appendix G: Audiovisual Resources

Alzheimer's Disease and Related Disorders Association
70 E. Lake Street
Chicago, IL 60601-5997
(312)853-3060
1-800-621-0379
• Caring
• Living with Grace
• Someone I Once Knew
• Whispering Hope

Institute of Gerontology, University of Michigan
300 N. Ingalls
Ann Arbor, MI 48109-2007
(313)764-3493
• Responding to Difficult Behaviors
• Wesley Hall: A Special Life
• Encouraging Self Care
• Designing a Physical Environment for the Memory Impaired Elderly

The MacNeil-Lehrer Report
WNET/THIRTEEN
356 W. 58th Street
New York, NY 10019
(212)560-3045
• Living with Alzheimer's—The MacNeil-Lehrer Report

McNeil Pharmaceutical
McNeilab, Inc.
Welsh and McKean Road
Spring House, PA 19477
(215)628-5000
* A Time for Caring: Understanding and Managing Disruptive Behavior in the Elderly Patient

National Audio Visual Center
8700 Edgeworth Drive
Capital Heights, MD 20743
(301)763-1896
* December Spring (illustrates the application of reality orientation)

Oregon State University Extension Service
161 Milam Hall
Corvallis, OR 97331-5106
(503)754-3211
* When Dependency Increases—A series of Multi-Media Programs for Caregivers

Pennsylvania Department of Aging
231 State Street
Barto Building
Harrisburg, PA 17101-1195
1-800-367-5115 (PA residents)
(717)783-7247
* Alzheimer's Disease Support for Family Caregivers
* Alzheimer's Disease—Training for Health and Social Service Practitioners
* Adapting to the environment
* Community resources
* Understanding and coping with Alzheimer's disease
* Legal and financial planning

Sandoz Pharmaceuticals
Medical Film Department
East Hanover, NJ 07936
* Symptoms of senility
* Dementia in the middle and later years
* Behavioral problems in the elderly
* Organic brain syndrome

Suncoast Gerontology Center, University of S. Florida Medical Center
Box 50
12901 North 30th Street
Tampa, FL 33612
* Understanding and Coping with Dementia

University of Southern California
Gerontology Center
Los Angeles, CA 90089-0191
* Alzheimer's Disease and Related Disorders. An Annotated Bibliography of Audiovisual Media

Appendix H: Journals and Newsletters

Advice for Adults with Aging Parents or a Dependent Spouse
Helpful Publications, Inc.
P.O. Box 339
Glenside, PA 19038
1-800-445-8811
(215)247-5473 (PA)

ADRDA Newsletter
The Alzheimer's Association
70 E. Lake Street
Chicago, IL 60601-5997
1-800-621-0379

Agelink
Newsletter on adult development and aging
University of Pittsburgh
1617 Cathedral of Learning
Pittsburgh, PA 15260
(412)624-3790

Aging Network News Newsletter
Omni Reports, Limited
P.O. Box 34031
Bethesda, MD 20817
(301)231-3678

**The American Journal of Alzheim-
er's Care and Research**
Prime National Publishing Corporation
470 Boston Road
Weston, MA 02193

Caregiving Tips
Series of articles on caring for aged
Family Caregivers Program
The National Council on the Aging,
Inc.
600 Maryland Avenue, S.W.
West Wing 100
Washington, DC 20024
(202)479-1200

Care-Line
Andrus Gerontology Center
University of Southern California
Los Angeles, CA 90089-0191
(213)743-6829

**The Elvirita Lewis Foundation Elder
Press Newsletter**
Suite 144, Airport Park Plaza
255 N. El Cielo Road
Palm Springs, CA 92262

Geriatric Care
Monthly newsletter for caregivers of
the aged
Box 3577
Reno, NV 89505
(702)826-0795

**Monthly Mini-Lessons in Care of the
Aging**
Eymann Publications, Inc.
1490 Huntingdon Circle
Box 3577
Reno, NV 89505

**Parents Care Resources to Assist
Family Caregivers**
Bi-monthly newsletter
Parent Care
Gerontology Center
316 Strong Hall
University of Kansas
Lawrence, KS 66045

Productive Aging News
Monthly newsletter
Center for Productive Aging
13-30 Annenberg Blvd.
The Mt. Sinai Medical Center
New York, NY 10029

Respite Report
Dementia Care & Respite Services
    Program
The Bowman Gray School of Medi-
    cine of Wake Forest University
300 South Hawthorne Rd
Winston Salem, NC 27103

Glossary of Terms

Acalculia Inability to do simple arithmetic calculations.

Ageism Prejudice and discrimination of the elderly based on age.

Agnosia Loss of the ability to recognize sensory stimuli; failure to recognize people or things.

Agraphia Inability to write intelligible words.

Alexia Inability to read.

Alzheimer's disease A chronic, progressive disorder that is the major cause of degenerative dementia in the U.S. It was first described in 1906 by German neurologist Alois Alzheimer.

Aphasia Loss or impairment of the ability to use or understand language.

Apraxia Impairment of the ability to perform purposeful, coordinated movements such as walking or dressing. The individual remains physically capable of performing the movements, but he is unable because of brain damage.

Catastrophic reaction Excessive anxiety displayed in situations that confuse and frighten or when the individual cannot communicate or perform a task. The individual dramatically overreacts to a situation.

Cognitive abilities The functions of memory, intelligence, learning ability, calculation, problem solving, judgment, comprehension, recognition, orientation, and attention. Impairment of these functions is a central feature of dementia.

DAT   Dementia of the Alzheimer's type.

Delirium   A temporary mental state characterized by confusion and decreased awareness of surroundings. It develops rapidly but can usually be treated (successfully). It may be caused by fever, alcohol or drug intoxication, head injury or some other medical disorder.

Delusion   A false fixed idea. The idea is maintained despite logical argument and evidence to the contrary.

Dementia   The severe impairment of mental function and global cognitive abilities for a prolonged period of time in an alert individual.

Disorientation   Confused as to time, place, person, and situations.

Dysphasia   Impairment of speech, lack of coordination and failure to arrange words in the proper order.

Dyspraxia   Partial loss of ability to perform coordinated tasks.

Echolalia   The persistent repetition of meaningless words, phrases, and movements.

Expressive aphasia   Difficulty producing speech, writing, or gestures.

Hallucinations   Sensory perceptions with no external source. These are unique to the individual and are not experienced by other people.

Hyperorality   Extremely strong tendency to touch and examine all objects with the mouth.

Hyperventilation   Overbreathing associated with anxiety and marked by reduction of blood carbon dioxide, subjective complaints of light-headedness, faintness, tingling of the extremities, palpitations and respiratory distress.

Illusions   Perceptual distortions; the misunderstanding of information leading to an incorrect or distorted perception of reality.

Incontinence   Lacking voluntary control over the bladder or bowel.

Intellectual Impairment   A diminished capacity to think or understand

Mirror Sign   Inability to recognize self in a mirror.

Multiinfarct Dementia (MID)   Dementia caused by brain damage resulting from multiple cerebral infarcts.

Organic Brain Syndrome (OBS)   Any mental disorder resulting from, or associated with, organic changes in brain tissue.

Paraphrasia   Speech defect characterized by the disorderly arrangement of spoken words.

Perseveration   Continuous repetition of a word, phrase or movement.

Presbycusis The most common type of hearing loss in the elderly. Results in a gradual decline in the ability to hear high pitched sounds or to distinguish consonants.

Presbyopia A gradual decline in the ability to focus on close objects or to see small print.

Primary degenerative dementia A degenerative brain disease causing dementia of insidious onset and a gradually progressive course.

Pseudo dementia A false confusion or lack of response caused by depression or some other reversible mental condition.

Receptive aphasia Inability to understand language.

SDAT Senile dementia of the Alzheimer's type.

Senescence Aging. The normal process of growing old.

Senility An outdated and incorrect term commonly used to describe serious forgetfulness and confusion in the elderly.

Sundowner's syndrome Confusion, restlessness, disorientation, and behavior problems that occur more frequently in the late afternoon or evening.

Vascular dementia Dementia resulting from brain damage caused by cerebral infarction or other diseases of disorder due to the blood vessels.

Index

Index